VISUAL
MEETINGS
Let's try it.
Someone left magic markers.

VISUAL MEETINGS

HOW GRAPHICS, STICKY NOTES & IDEA MAPPING CAN TRANSFORM GROUP PRODUCTIVITY

IMAGINE

Visions

Actions

Values

Results

ENGAGE

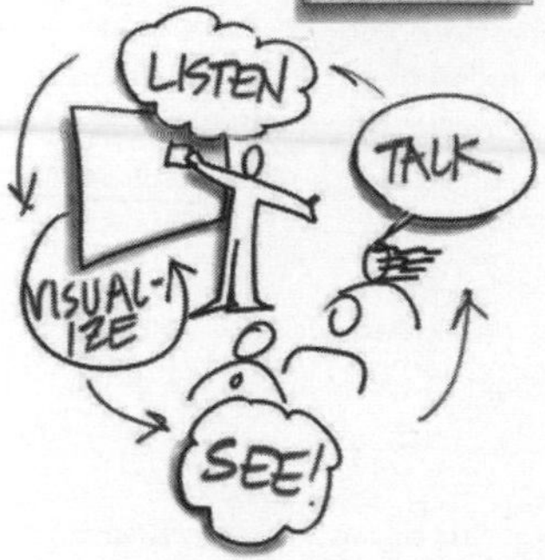

ENACT

THINK

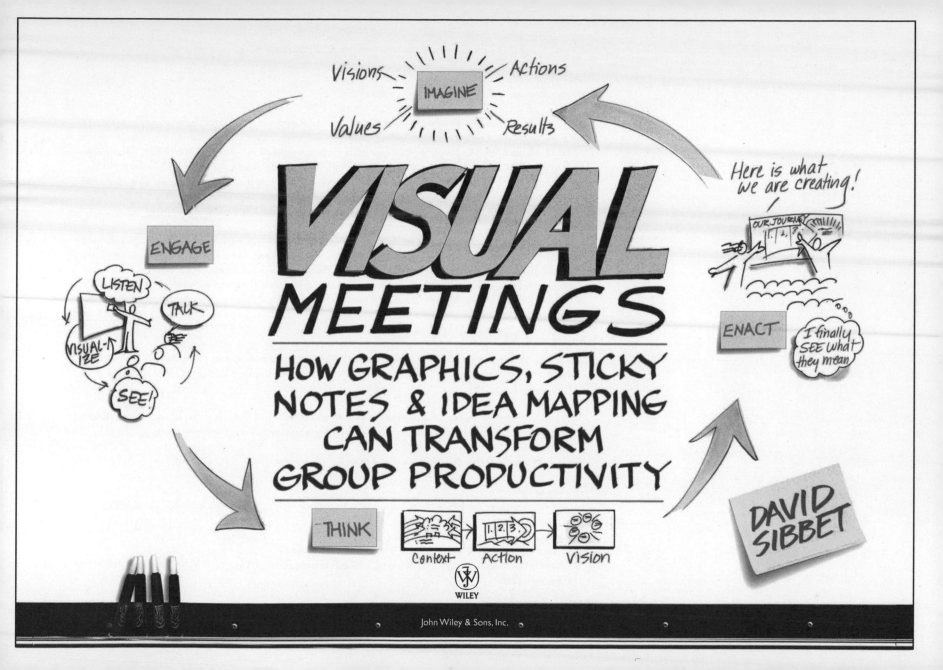

DAVID SIBBET

WILEY

John Wiley & Sons, Inc.

Published by John Wiley & Sons, Inc., Hoboken, New Jersey.
Published simultaneously in Canada.

For general information on our other products and services or for technical support, please contact our Customer Care Department within the United States at (800) 762–2974, outside the United States at (317) 572–3993 or fax (317) 572–4002.

Wiley also publishes its books in a variety of electronic formats. Some content that appears in print may not be available in electronic books. For more information about Wiley products, visit our website at www.wiley.com.

Library of Congress Cataloging-in-Publication Data:

Sibbet, David.
Visual meetings : how graphics, sticky notes, and idea mapping can transform group productivity / David Sibbet.
p. cm.
Includes bibliographical references and index.
ISBN 978–0–470–60178–5 (pbk); ISBN 978 0–470–90104–5 (ebk)
1. Teams in the workplace. 2. Business meetings. 3. Visual communication. I. Title.
HD66.S564 2010
658.4'56—dc22

2010014480
Printed in the United states of America.
10 9

For my children and grandchildren, the sons and daughters of our Grove team, all the young people my poet wife Susan teaches, and all the other young people who will be taking civilization on the next part of its journey.

Contents

Visions
Actions
IMAGINE
Values
Results

ENGAGE
LISTEN
TALK
VISUAL-IZE
SEE!

III: Graphics for Visual Thinking

IV: Graphics for Enacting Plans

V: Seeing It All Come Together

IS THIS IT?
YES, I SEE WHAT HE MEANS!
POWERS OF VISUAL MEETINGS
BIG PICTURE THINK
PRO-DUCT
PARTICIPATION

Introduction
The Power of Visual Meetings

Do you wish you had a better way to run all the meetings you have? Do you wish you could not only be very productive but also have fun in the process? Is your organization putting pressure on people to be more innovative? These are some of the challenges people who run meetings are facing in the work world. These are some of the needs that gave rise to the practice of visual meetings, and to my desire to share the result of 38 years of running really great meetings all over the world.

But it's not the only reason I chose to write this book. I'm very concerned about people seeming to be more polarized and disconnected, with civil discourse degrading in democracies and conflict and authoritarianism rising as tempting alternatives. I'm also concerned about pressures at work and in the classroom. Responding to the complexity and scale of changes in the economy and the environment is starting to outstrip our capabilities. Running our organization lean, with slim or no travel budgets, and less and less time for real dialogue and engagement is challenging the quality of communications. I think that what I am calling visual meetings is a direct response, as you will see as we go along.

WHAT'S THE POINT?
HE'LL EXPLAIN

What Is Visual Language & What Are Visual Meetings?

Before going further it's important for you to understand what I mean by visual meetings. For 35 years I've been participating in a creative upwelling in ways of communicating coming from Silicon Valley and the wider San Francisco Bay Area in California, now spreading worldwide. We visual practitioners have been inspired by how architects and designers work, and now with social media by how natural systems organize. Those of us supporting all these developments in organizations have been busy inventing new ways for people to work together. We know people can get a lot more accomplished when collaborating and working together than by themselves. Better tools and methods, while not sufficient without intention and motivation, do provide hopeful ways of facing rising levels of dynamism and change. I share a lot of these with you over the course of the chapters in this book. You'll find a lot of them are very simple and powerful.

We visual practitioners have been inspired by how architects and designers work, and now with social media by how natural systems organize.

SO I CAN THROW LINES AROUND!
HE MEANS ON PAPER, SILLY

Can We Support Being Smarter as Groups?

Alan Briskin, a key leader in the Fetzer Institute's Collective Wisdom Initiative and author of a book by that title, argued that what undermines our ability to work together and be open to our differences is finding that we are no longer able to handle the complexity of what we are facing. In the face of confusion, people at work, and people in meetings, retreat into simplistic explanations and intolerant positions of non-listening.

Showing how visual language and visual listening can be a hopeful response to these kinds of problems is a key motivation for writing this book. As we will see, visualization is a powerful way to resolve confusions in groups that arise from inadequate or conflicting mental models. This is crucial when those models involve our ideas of how work gets done, how teams cooperate, how to make decisions, how to organize, and how to learn. A huge amount of time in meetings is spent working out these differences.

As you will hopefully come to appreciate, much of our understanding of systems and how things work together is represented by imagery, story, and metaphor animated by our experience. Upgrading our ways of thinking will require becoming conscious of all the ways we represent how we think about the world to ourselves and to others. Visual meetings have unusually productive properties in this regard in both providing a safe way to become conscious of our metaphors, and providing creative ways to cocreate new ones.

Power Tools for Effective Meetings

While for many people meetings are a necessary pain, and often have a deserved bad reputation, running effective meetings is possible—and not just effective meetings, but meetings that break through to extraordinary results. There are some very accessible and very powerful tools available. Sharing those having to do with visualization is a primary goal of this book.

Natural Ability to Communicate Visually The most powerful of these tools is your natural ability to draw. Believe it or not, this capability is built right into your body. The kind of drawing I'm talking about is the kind we do when we gesture—simple, expressive movements. Can you even think about talking without making gestures? This is so natural people even gesture when they are on the phone! In fact gestures and painting pictures in the air develops in children before being articulate with spoken language. In this book you'll learn how easy it is to translate this natural way of communicating to paper, and perhaps to tablet computers. All you need to do is learn a few tricks about holding markers and throwing lines around. And now that digital media is so supple with visual material, there is literally no barrier to returning to this tested and effective way of communicating.

LET'S CREATE THIS ONE OURSELVES!

Sticky Notes and Other Interactive Media The second set of power tools is interactive media. This is symbolized in the title of this book by "sticky notes," those inventions of 3M now available from many suppliers in a huge range of colors, shapes, and sizes. Sticky notes are cousins of image cards, mind mapping software, and other kinds of media you can move around like little blocks. Working with little chunks of information that can be combined and recombined is what movie and video designers do with little sketches—creating storyboards of possibility. Well, it's possible to work this way across a wide range of meetings with lots of other purposes than design. Humans love to interact, and letting people get their hands right on information is a direct path to high engagement.

Idea Mapping I'm calling a third set of tools "idea mapping." By that I mean using visual metaphors embedded in graphic templates and worksheets that allow groups to think visually. Inventors have always fiddled around with diagrams and drawings in their journals, and engineers and designers work on whiteboards and drawing tablets. But you don't have to be an engineer or designer to benefit from the power of idea mapping. It's a flexible approach that goes all the way from working on blank paper to well-structured graphic templates and software that help groups visualize what they are thinking and planning.

YOU CAN COUNT ON
THESE FROM THE START.
1. PARTICIPATION
2. BIG PICTURE THINKING
3. GROUP MEMORY

The Powers of Visual Meetings

My confidence in this way of working is rooted in three phenomena that I have experienced since the first time that I picked up magic markers and began facilitating groups visually.

1. **Participation:** Engagement explodes in meetings when people are listened to and acknowledged by having what they say recorded in an interactive, graphic way.
2. **Big Picture Thinking:** Groups get much smarter when they can think in big picture formats that allow for comparison, pattern finding, and idea mapping.
3. **Group Memory:** Creating memorable media greatly increases group memory and followthrough — a key to group productivity.

Since these are some of the reasons visualization has long roots in design communities, you may wonder why there is a visualization revolution going on now in business. I think there are several reasons. One is rooted in the tools themselves.

For the last few decades a *lot* of energy has been absorbed learning to use new computing tools that for quite a while were very clumsy with visual material. Now they aren't! A set of breakthroughs began when desktop and personal computers made graphic production easy. Design tools—draw programs, paint programs, layout software, graphics on spreadsheets, and presentation software—became available for all kinds of workers, not just designers.

Laser printers then gave all these tools high quality output and now many of these produce color. Digital cameras made it possible to capture and share hand drawn charts and visual material electronically. Wonderfully flexible tablets and even touch screen walls now allow for hands-on interaction with imagery. I think the iPad is the speartip of the visualization revolution on the tools side.

Responding to Drivers of Change

A second reason for the acceleration of interest in visual meetings is the rising need and in many cases demands for more interesting and productive meetings. I made a list of the drivers of change I encounter with my clients. Look at the list to the right on this page and check off the ones that you are experiencing.

In writing this book I assumed that a lot of people are facing these pressures and are not professional facilitators, but need to run effective meetings nonetheless. You might be a team leader or first-line manager wanting well-run staff and project meetings. Or you might be an HR generalist or trainer responsible for people development. I imagined salespeople who are under pressure to sell solutions and create lasting relationships and have many small and larger meetings in connection with the sales process. I was thinking of functional managers who are responsible for budgets, alignment, and quality. I was also thinking about those in government and nonprofit organizations who are working to respond to social needs and community concerns. I also believe teachers would be able to use the approaches I describe.

If you think about how much time and effort gets tied up in meetings you will begin to appreciate how much value can come from running them more effectively. If you can tap everyone's innovation and creativity at the same time I guarantee you will be perceived as a real winner in your organization.

The Power of Visual Language

Learning effective tools and applying them to visual meetings is one thread that runs through this book. The other involves visual language, and the impact it has on your own brain when you begin to think and work this way. All during the last 38 years I and a growing network of visual practitioners have been exploring the "wetware" side of visual language—meaning how it works with cognition and thinking, in the brains of participants in meetings, and in our lives as practitioners. We've used large paper and magic

DRIVERS OF CHANGE

- ❏ Everyone is having to work leaner and quicker.
- ❏ Many teams and organizations have to work across function, geography, and cultural boundaries and can't meet face-to-face.
- ❏ There is a *lot* more information and it is harder to get people to make sense out of it.
- ❏ Pressure to get results makes alignment and followthrough from meetings critically important.
- ❏ Many problems are systems level challenges, that require groups be able to think big picture, over longer periods of time.
- ❏ Rapid change requires everyone to upgrade their mental models of how things work on a frequent basis.
- ❏ Attracting and retaining good workers is increasingly a core challenge, especially as boomers retire.
- ❏ Increasing complexity and speed of events accelerates impatience and resistance to accepting differences and change.

Visual Meetings are for:

Team leaders
HR generalists
Line managers
Salespeople
Consultants
Teachers
Trainers
Volunteers
Club leaders
Professionals
&
Anyone else who likes to be creative with groups

markers for most of this exploration, waiting for the technical and research communities to catch on. Well, they finally have. Researchers on learning and cognitive intelligence now know humans process information very differently, and that visual thinking is a large part of what we do. It seems our brains are massively evolved to process visual information—some claim up to 80% of our brain cells are involved.

Bob Horn, a good friend and tracker of this phenomenon, wrote a book in the 1990s called *Visual Language*. In it he describes visual language as a "tight integration of text and graphics." This is a relatively recent development, he observes. Historically, text handled words and illustrations handled pictures. But information graphics, maps, and the kind of murals we visual practitioners are creating are of a different order. Increasingly, this integration is showing up in multimedia work on the Internet, in games, and modern advertising and signage. Visual language is directly tackling the issues of synergy and integration of what we know across text and graphics. And this takes thinking to a whole new level.

Visualization Addresses Important Issues

There are certain properties of working with images and graphic metaphor that, in my experience, directly address a number of important issues involving our awareness and thinking:

- Visual recording in a meeting immediately acknowledges that someone was heard and *how* they were heard in ways that verbal communication alone does not.
- Working visually is deeply integrative—it combines both visual (right brain) and verbal (left brain) ways of operating with interaction and physical movement.
- Graphic displays can contain contradictory information on the same sheet of paper, softening the either/or thinking that our spoken language reinforces.
- Working with graphic metaphors allows people to talk directly about how they are making sense of things.

- Working with visual imagery taps people's imaginal realms, making the stuff of hopes and dreams, intentions, and visions more accessible.
- Arranging information on journal pages or wall displays addresses not only the individual words and symbols, but also their overall interconnection and organization.
- Translating from spoken word to visual representation forces everyone to become conscious of the patterns in both.

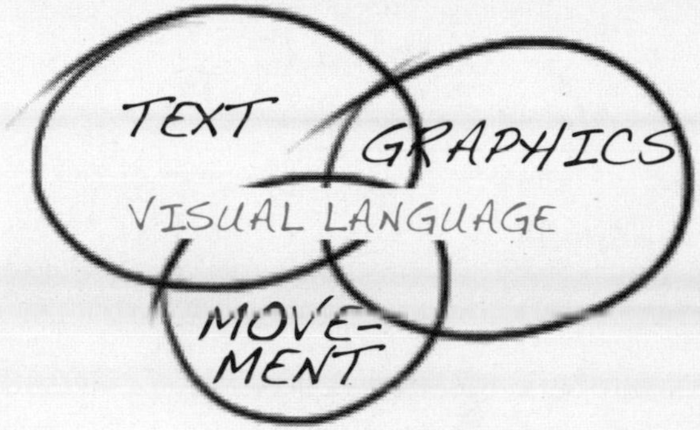

With the rising amount of visual media that all of us consume now, and the extent to which our screen, book, magazine, and movie interactions are mediated by visuals, it is surprising one would even have to make the argument that visual meetings are more effective. But as much media as we consume, we are just at the start of understanding how to use it interactively, like we do spoken language. I hope this book raises your awareness of how much opportunity there is in this new development.

Visual language is emerging as any other language does by people creating it and speaking it... it is being born of people's need, worldwide, to deal with complex ideas that are difficult to express in text alone.

Bob Horn
Visual Language

Organization of Visual Meetings

The spark for this book came from an editor at Wiley & Sons, Richard Narramore, who sought me out and wondered if I could do a book on visual thinking for groups. He felt that Dan Roam's *Back of the Napkin* does a marvelous job of arguing for using simple visuals for problem solving and strategy. Nancy Duarte's *Slideology* illustrates all the ways we can use presentation software in effective ways. But where was a book for teams and meetings? Richard knew that I and my company, The Grove Consultants International, have been pioneering graphic facilitation and visual thinking for groups since the mid-1970s. In fact, we've been central in creating a field of practice for this work. Many of our trainees and colleagues have created businesses conducting visual meetings.

Over the years I've written many books for professional practitioners on this subject. Richard wanted to know if I was willing to share this way of working with a much wider audience. I welcomed the invitation,

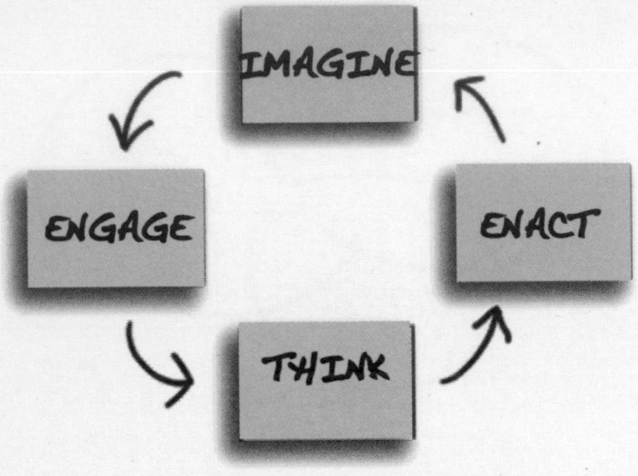

GROUP LEARNING PROCESS

This model will be explained in more detail in Chapter One. It reflects a deeply embedded pattern of how a person or group learns about what they need to do together.

for, now more than ever, I think the world of work needs innovation and renewal to cope with the enormity of challenges we all face.

Part I—Just Imagine!

This book presents the core ideas and practices involved in Visual Meetings following a progression that mirrors how people actually work in the process of moving from ideas to action. It's reflected in the little diagram on the cover of the book—the progression of IMAGINING, ENGAGING, THINKING, and ENACTING. The sections of this book match this progression, each one summing up with a section on how to pull it all together.

To get full value from this book it will help to begin with your own imagination and an overview of what you could accomplish if you began to run visual meetings. I will argue that a person's point of view—or, in popular language, where we are coming from—colors everything one learns and perceives. Learning begins with the spark of intention. *Part I—Just Imagine: Power Tools in the Visualization Revolution*, will help you imagine what you might do. It begins with a story of how Apple and others have used visualization in meetings. It will also bring together my and The Grove's experience in teaching people to access their inborn ability to draw the simple drawings used to support visual listening.

If you are convinced by my argument that everybody already knows graphic language, much of the rest of the book will be like having a basket of presents to open. Interestingly, many people confuse graphics with realistic drawing, and decide early that they can't draw well and aren't going to using drawing for communication. But graphics for visual meetings are a completely different kind of thing, and rely on simple images that anyone can produce with a few tips. We've trained thousands and know this for sure. I'll show you some easy ways to get started with your own note taking and with small groups.

Part II—Engaging Groups Visually

Once you can imagine visual meetings being possible, you and your groups' next step will be to immerse yourself in the subject. Engagement is all about participation. With a book this will mean doing some of the exercises suggested in the little side boxes with colored bars on top. With groups it means learning to invite participation all the way along. I don't believe that people are open, receptive brains like some basketball hoop we can throw your well-designed communications through. People are full of their own ideas and interests, and reluctant to change. Thus the art of engaging begins with listening and establishing a connection and rapport. The way interactive visualizing does this is truly remarkable. Understanding this is the focus of *Part II—Building Rapport and Engaging Groups: Why Visual Listening Is so Compelling (and Easy!)*. In this section we look closely at interactive note taking and media you can use right away, such as sticky notes. I also share how wonderful this way of working is in building rapport during a sales situation.

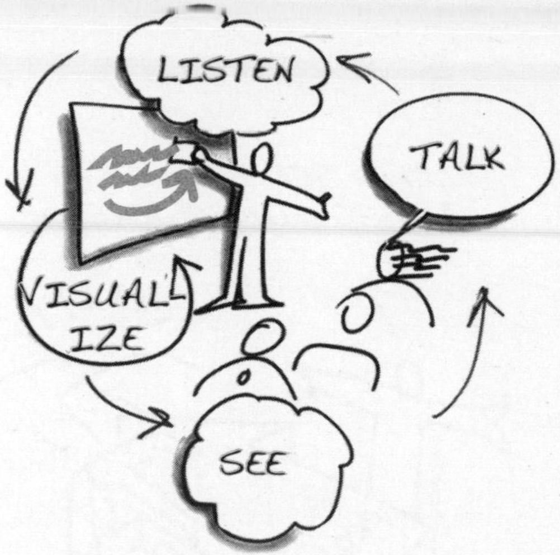

Interactive visualizing is truly remarkable in the way it engages people who see their ideas drawn out as they speak.

Part III—Graphics for Visual Thinking

With full engagement, you and your groups will want to get to work making sense of things and finding relevant patterns of understanding in all the information you generate. Part III is titled *Graphics for Visual Thinking: Mapping Ideas and Finding Key Patterns*. It describes where working visually can support real breakthroughs in insight and understanding. I make the case that to think about anything that has a lot of parts that connect with each other you have to visualize in some form to understand the larger pattern. This is called "systems thinking" in some quarters. Peter Senge argues that this is the fifth discipline of a real learning organization, and named his book on learning organizations after this skill (*The Fifth Discipline*). Planning, mind mapping, design, and training all benefit from groups understanding big pictures. I show you how you can get those effects without having to be a professional facilitator. There are some tools involved, but they are readily available. You'll also discover that the real power in this step of any process is having your groups cocreate their own understanding of things. The act of mapping and diagramming is itself a kind of thinking, and the quality of the visuals is not nearly as important as going through the construction process. These practices also reflect new research showing that people are much more apt to accept and implement ideas that come from within their group than ones imposed from the outside—even by experts.

LET'S GET IN THIS AND GO SOMEWHERE
PROJECT
I'LL MAKE A SPACE!

Part IV—Graphics for Enacting Plans

The move from ideas to action is critical if you are going to get results from meetings. *Part IV— Graphics for Enacting Plans: Visuals for Teams, Projects, and Getting Results* will show you how to use visual meetings to launch teams, make decisions, track and guide progress on projects, and lead change processes. There are many easily learnable tools that make a big difference in all the regular work that you have to do. We've found that the act of creating roadmaps, Grove Storymaps®, prototypes, and other visualizations showing who will do what, when, actually allows groups to rehearse actions. Visualizing and sharing action plans becomes a step in the critical process of moving from thinking to action.

Part V—Seeing It All Come Together

The final section, called *Seeing it All Come Together: Tools for the Seriously Hooked*, directly addresses the well-worn paths to competency for a visual practitioner. I share some of my current visions about where all this is headed in the context of digital media and the Internet. The book concludes with a review of the resources mentioned in the text that are available if you want to learn more. This includes an annotated guide to some of the websites that are loaded with additional information and ideas.

My Hope and Dream

I have had so much fun and success running visual meetings over the years, that it is my hope and dream that people can reclaim some of this natural and universally appreciated way of communicating. I've been struck over the years how fascinated people are with hand drawn imagery, even very simple drawings. And this fascination seems to cross age differences and cultures.

Some cultures have visual thinking embedded in their core language. The characters that are used in Chinese, Japanese, Korean, and many other Asian languages began as little pictures created so that people could talk across the barriers of different spoken dialects. In some ways The Grove and its network of visual practitioners have been recreating a modern kind of kanji for organizational work. But unlike kanji, graphic language of the sort described in this book is an intentional integration of text and image. In today's world, words and images coexist in the same visual frameworks whether they are graphics, sticky note displays, or idea maps. This is a development very much supported and amplified by the multimedia communication we are all learning to appreciate.

My dream is that you, in reading this book, will be able to look past gee-whiz technologies to the simple, powerful methods that humans with simple tools can use to work visually. For many, it is a truly eye-opening experience to realize that creativity and productivity are not polar choices, but partners in a new and playful way of working. It is also a very hopeful experience to see people learn to cooperate across differences because they have learned to listen to each other, cooperatively explore their meaningful metaphors, and come to images of success that operate at a new level of integration and complexity.

If you have ever felt a twinge of remorse at having to give up all that creative expression you experienced as a young child, you will be delighted to discover that not only is it reclaimable, but also it can help you access some of the most powerful meeting methods available.

Acknowledgments

This book would not have been possible without the amazing support I receive from my life partner and poet/teacher, Susan, and the team at The Grove Consultants International. Thanks to my assistant Megan Hinchliffe for running interference since I wrote this while working; to designers Bobby Pardini and Tiffany Forner for deeply influencing my aesthetic over the years; to my consulting colleagues Laurie Durnell and Tomi Nagai-Rothe, both seasoned visual practitioners, for championing accessibility and best practices; to our customer support team Noel Snow and Andrew Underwood for customer feedback about what works; to Eddie Palmer for his insights into technology; to Donna Lafayette for knowing what works in trainings; and to Thom Sibbet for partnering with me all these years to create a real publishing and tools business.

I wouldn't even be in this business were it not for being mentored by Michael Doyle, cofounder of Interaction Associates, or inspired by Geoff Ball and Fred Lakin, two cocreators of Group Graphics® in the 1970s who saw the visualization revolution coming. During the early days of developing a lot of these methods two early colleagues who affirmed the transferability of these approaches were Jennifer Hammond Landau and Howell Thomas. In those early days we also had an Image Exchange group that voraciously scouted all the visualization strategies growing up on the West Coast. It included David Reardon, Lanier Graham, Carol Sanford, Geoff Ball, Sandra Florstedt, Sherrin Bennett, and Ed Beyeler. A special thanks to Geoff and Sandra for co-teaching the first public Group Graphics Workshop with me in 1980, and to Sandra for introducing me to the Organization Development Network, and to Lanier, for fueling my interest in visual journaling

As the work of The Grove expanded in the '80s and '90s , so did our consulting team. Suzanne

Otter, Joan McIntosh, Diana Arsenian, Christina Merkley, Deirdre Crowley, and Kayla Kirsch all worked closely with me for years and have gone on to establish thriving professional visual practices of their own, many continuing to work with us as associates. They were an especially talented group who taught me a great deal. I'm very grateful to my strategic consulting colleagues: Ed Claassen for encouraging us to develop Graphic Guides for those who don't draw well, Rob Eskridge for teaching me strategic planning, and David Cawood, Mary O'Hara Devereaux, and Meryem Le Saget for cross cultural applications. I'm also grateful to The Grove's associates for providing a real community of practice at close quarters, particularly Tom Benthin, Steven Wright, Bill Bancroft, Konrad Knell, Maketa Wilborn, Cheryl Nigro, Sue Nenneman, Karen Stratvert, Eliska Meyers, Teri Kent, Emily Shepard, Scott Wheeler, and Sunni Brown. A special thanks to Kara Nichols, The Grove's recent marketing director, for helping me more actively embrace The Grove's thought leadership in this field.

A great deal of what I know about the results that visual meetings can achieve comes from my clients, who more often than not became cocreative colleagues. The experiences of creating Apple University in 1980s, working on the Groupware Users Project with the Institute for the Future in the late 1980s and 1990s; leading an internal consulting team at National Semiconductor in the early 1990s, teaching Mars associates worldwide how to graphically facilitate, and working with Hewlett Packard in the 1990s were all especially formative and deserve mention.

Ranny Riley, Jim Kouzes, and I were the external consultants when John Scully took over Apple and began to help its rambunctious culture learn business. We and Dorothy Largay and Sue Cook, the internal HR managers we worked with most closely, cocreated the Apple Leadership Experience and experimented with all kinds of visualization methods in the process. It was here I met my close friend and colleague Lenny Lind, founder of CoVision, who later shared office space with us at The Grove and introduced us all to what multimedia photography, video production, and decision support software could do. Jim Ewing was another member of our team who has remained a close friend. He created many wonderful visual tools for working with leadership assessment and strategy. Later Christina Hooper and Jim Sporer at the Apple Advanted Technology Labs introduced me to multimedia thinking and geo-data mapping.

Kevin Wheeler, head of National University, sponsored the first 24-foot-long Storymaps for National's Vision and Leading Change program. This led to four years of work with over 16 divisions—all using visual planning to manage their successful turnaround. David Kirjasoff, Kathy Ureda, and Sharadon Smith became adept at visual planning and collaborated on applications to reengineering, goal alignment, training, and process improvement. NSC sponsored the initial facilitator training manuals that eventually became *Graphic Facilitation*.

I thank Patricia Moore for bringing me in to teach Graphic Facilitation at HP in 1985. Later, Vivian Wright became an adept internal practioner. Srinivas Sukumar, head of strategy for HP Labs, and Barbara Waugh, HR director for the Labs, collaborated on some of the breakthrough applications of visual meetings for high tech innovation that led to serious work with large graphic templates.

At Mars I worked closely with Joan Scarrott and Eileen Matthews in formulating their global facilitation training. They both became certified trainers and huge contributors to expanding the best practices for visual meetings. A second wave of trainers in Ingrid Uden and Katherine Woods became certified and eventually formed Meeting Magic, a London-based consulting firm devoted to visual meetings that are closely partnered with The Grove.

All during the 1990s The Grove and The Institute for the Future in Palo Alto were strategic partners in mapping out the terrain and implications of group-oriented technology on organizations. We used visual-meeting techniques throughout the project so successfully that they became a trademark of the Institute. I owe special recognition to Bob Johansen, Paul Saffo, Stephanie Schacter, Robert Mittman, Mary O'Hara Devereaux, and Andrea Saveri, my close colleagues in the early years of the project when we were creating our key ideas about groupware.

For the past 15 years a growing network called the International Forum of Visual Practitioners has been a community of practice to which I owe a great deal for inspiration regarding the enormous range of applications visualization can have for meetings. There are far too many close friends and colleagues to mention them all, but Leslie Salmon Zhu, Susan Kelly, and Lynn Kearny, founders of the network, do deserve mention. Gordon Rudow and Emily Shepard showed what was possible with this medium at Bonfire, a communications consulting group inspired by visualization work. Christine Valenza has contributed a great deal to documenting the growth of this field. Lynn Carruthers brought graphic recording to the Global Business Network's scenario planning. There are dozens of other fine graphic facilitators who are taking the field to its next level as I write. I especially appreciate Ulric Rudebeck, Jonas Kjestrand, and Roy Bartilson, for collaborating on bringing strategic visioning to Sweden in the 1990s and Vagn Strangaard and Ole Qvist Sorenson for partnering in bringing these tools to Denmark. I thank Gabriella Melano for keeping the opportunities in Latin America in our minds and Arinya Talerngsri of APM Group for bringing us to Thailand. Tamio Nakano and his Hakuhodo Original Workshop group in Japan convinced me how powerful visual meetings can become in that culture.

In formulating the core ideas behind the Group Graphics® Keyboard I owe an inestimable amount of gratitude to my teacher Arthur M. Young, and The Institute for the Study of Con-

ABOUT THIS BOOK

This book is a testimony to the evolution of graphic production tools. I've always worked with available tools to demonstrate what is possible for anyone with commitment and interest to do. Since the first Mac SE I've dreamed about completely fluid text-graphic authoring. It happened with this book

I wrote *Visual Meetings* on my MacBook Pro linked to a Wacom Cintiq tablet, so I could both draw and write at will, integrating text and graphics. I then networked those files to my new iMac loaded with Adobe InDesign and laid out the pages to see what they would look like. I could then run back to rewrite, redraw, and tweak to my heart's content—all in real time. Thanks to Wiley for being flexible and letting me both design and write the book. The text is set in Garamond Premier Pro Light Display—11 on 14 points. The side boxes are in Gill Sans Light—9 on 12 points. The chapter titles and subheads are set in Markerfelt Thin. We chose a 7 x 10 inch landscape layout to allow for the panoramic spreads that occasionally illustrate the big ideas of the book. Most all the drawings are mine. The rest are included by permission.

Thanks to Sunni Brown, my former assistant and now with Brightspot Consulting, for modeling the eager learner. She was and is.

sciousness' study group on the Theory of Process. I participated seriously for over six years in the late 1970s with Jack Saloma, Frank Barr, Jack Engstrom, Chris Payne, Michael Buchele, and Joan Schliecher. They helped deepen my understanding of this theory and its applications.

In regard to the larger field of visual thinking my inspirations have been my good friend and colleague Bob Horn, founder of Information Mapping and tracker of simulation and visual thinking methods since the 1960s. His consultation on this book has been very helpful. Jim Channon, a designer turned communicator extraordinaire for the U.S. Army, broke me out of two-dimensional visual thinking with his 3D Advanced Visual Language. Stewart Silverstone, creator of the Graphic News Network, provided invaluable guidance in the world of information design. More recently Tom Wujec, Autodesk Fellow, and David Gray, founder of XPlane, have been very influential colleagues in demonstrating how visual thinking is revolutionizing business.

In the past years I have immersed myself in both virtual meetings and deep dialogue work—both of which have magnified the value of visual meetings in my mind. I would like to thank the New Media Cosortium for orienting me to Second Life, where the Grove now has an island, and to a circle of consulting friends who have been unwavering champions of my writing this book. Thank you Pele Rouge, Firehawk Hulin, Diego Navaro, Gary Merrill, Michelle Paradis, Cheryl DeSantis, Amy Lenzo, Peter Garn, Susan Christy, Barbara Waugh, and Brian Dowd.

A final note of gratitude to my editor Richard Narramore, without whom there would be no book with John Wiley & Sons. His vision of making this work accessible to anyone who runs meetings has been my inspiration.

I: Just Imagine

What if Meetings Were Really Fun AND Productive?

I: Just Imagine

This section provides a high-level overview of visual meetings, so that you can imagine all the different ways they can work for you, and how you can start successfully. Themes begun here reappear in later chapters that begin to explain some of the ways you can build on these fundamentals.

Chapter 1: Visualization Is Worth 80 IQ Points Stories of inventing visual strategies at Apple Computer for agenda management, histories, visions, dialogue support; why point of view is so important; overview of the learning cycle and how visuals support each step; International Forum of Visual Practitioners as a mirror of what is possible.

Chapter 2: Everybody Knows Graphic Language Graphics as an outgrowth of gestural communication; how to begin playing around with graphics; exercises to unlock your ability to draw; how to hang paper; basic shapes and pictographs; thinking about basic formats.

Chapter 3: Four Easy Ways to Get Started Visualizing for your personal note taking and thinking; working with flip charts and napkins in informal situations; using simple graphic templates; getting others to do the drawing.

1. Visualization Is Worth 80 IQ Points

Tapping Energy, Intelligence, & Creativity

Let's start understanding visual meetings by imagining what is possible when you use active visualization with groups, through the lens of a real story about one of the more creative companies in our times —Apple. I was part of a team that designed and led the Leadership Experience, a flagship program of the fledgling Apple University, in 1985. Inspired by the graphical nature of Apple's products, we applied many strategies you can easily repeat.

The Apple Leadership Expeditions

One warm afternoon in the summer of that year, some 35 young leaders from what was then called Apple Computer piled off buses at Pajaro Dunes, a conference and condo site on the coast of California south of Silicon Valley. "The Journey is the Reward," read their T-shirts. Guides were dressed in mountain gear. Inside the rustic main building at Pajaro participants found a basically empty room, two huge piles of furniture draped with white nylon parachutes to look a bit like mountains, and a wall of nine screens. Everyone was invited to sit on the floor and wait in the semidarkness. Their weeklong Leadership Expedition was about to begin. IBM's PC business was exploding. Apple was entering the fray with the first really graphic computers and they needed their middle managers to take risks and act like leaders. We were focused on having them visualize this possibility, and worked to have the whole meeting communicate this intention.

The nine screens suddenly flashed into life as chest-rocking Dolby sound carried the booming voice of Jim Whittaker, first American to climb K2 (the second tallest mountain in the world) and leader of the first team to include women. "This is the story of our historic climb," he began over the pulsing sound, now carrying music themes that would transport us to another world high above Nepal. For 15 minutes the multimedia show focused on the theme of the week—that leadership was an expedition, a team event, and required initiative and daring and creativity.

WELCOME TO THE
APPLE LEADERSHIP
EXPEDITION

Our design team had worked for weeks with Dorothy Largay and the internal Apple HR team getting ready for this event. We knew, given the creativity, drive, and youth of Apple, that this gathering needed to be unique, and challenge them to the limits of their abilities. It all hinged on a premise, that their perspective on life at work needed to shift from delivering well on orders and requests to getting out front and leading into the unknowns of a new market. We had to shift their internal mental models—their point of view.

Renaming the Leadership Experience the Leadership Expedition and starting with the expedition story of K2 was just the beginning. We reinforced this "frame" with a physical and visual environment that painted a picture of possibility all through the week. We appreciated that theater has long employed imagery and visualization of this sort to move people into new frames of mind. It was in this spirit that after the opening show we said, "Under the parachutes is furniture. Your first task is to create your own base camp right here in the meeting room."

Group Graphics

I was on the Apple team because I had been building a new company around a very different, visual way of facilitating meetings called "Group Graphics®." It was a way of working interactively with visual communication inspired by the way architects and designers work in design sessions, but applied to ordinary meetings. Since 1972 when I first began working this way, I had immersed myself in the power of visualization to transform thinking and group process. I experimented with every possible way interactive imagery could be used by groups in the playful, flexible way that spoken language works.

I couldn't have been more thrilled than to be asked to work on the Apple project by Ranny Riley, the lead consultant. I was the one who led the creation of the visual environment. I also graphically facilitated the design team, the open, interactive sessions with participants, and helped keep everyone oriented with graphic agendas, simple frames of reference for our sessions, and some key visioning activities that would be key anchor points for participants. Let's continue the story with special attention to these elements.

Graphical User Interfaces for Meetings

I was animated by the idea of building a "graphical user interface" for the workshop that was as accessible and compelling as the one Apple was developing for the computer. The things we ended up doing functioned like the frames on a work of visual art. They pointed the viewer toward appropriate ways to understand what was going on, but didn't fill in the picture. In some cases these frames were metaphors and in others actual graphic templates and frameworks. As much as possible we wanted the participants to do physical and graphical things themselves to anchor the ideas in real experiences.

By having the group itself create its own base camp we got engagement early. (Part II in this book expands on this kind of idea with other suggestions.) As soon as "camp" was set up, and everyone had a chance to eat some dinner, Ranny came forward to orient them to the week, using a giant graphic agenda I had created on the wall of the meeting room. It involved using simple masking tape to create a mountain range, with little posters for our different days and events illustrating different camps along the climb. These all led to the summit, where we spelled out the overarching goal of the expedition—to create a leadership culture capable of "Getting Extraordinary Things Done at Apple." The graphics on the big agenda matched the graphic agenda handout.

The opening orientation was only the beginning of what we created to sustain the visual support of the Leadership Expedition. Some of the other visual features built in included:

GRAPHIC AGENDAS

At the Apple Leadership Experience we created a huge agenda right on the wall using masking tape and small posters for each day that looked like a mountain climb.

PEAK & VALLEY DRAWINGS

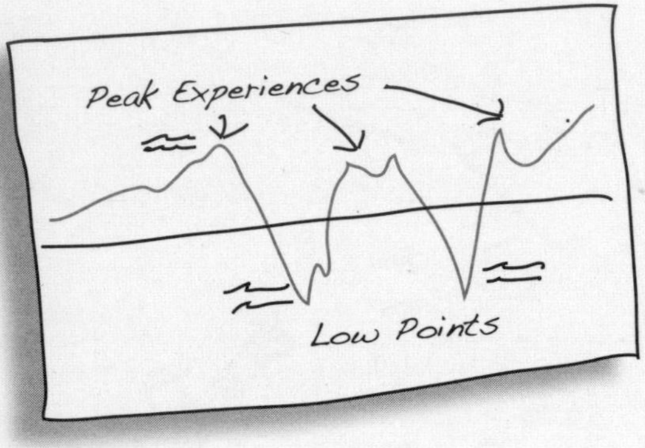

1. Begin by drawing a line across a piece of paper, and marking off the years.
2. Using your intuition, begin when you started work and draw the ups and downs in your career.
3. Go back and label the peaks and valleys.
4. Share this with a partner and discuss your insights.

- Visualizing career histories
- Graphic recording of discussions
- Quick sessions on how to draw on flip charts
- Preparation of visions for each participant's team back home
- Presentation and critique of team visions
- Creation of a slide show of the event as a concluding experience

None of these strategies required particular skill in drawing, but all engaged the participants in using imagery in ways that appropriately focused their attention. How is it that simple imagery and metaphors have such an impact? Let's zoom in and see how this works.

Peak and Valley Drawings

On day two of the Apple Leadership Expedition we invited all the participants to take a different point of view on their own careers. We asked them to use a simple graphic format called a "peak and valley diagram" as each one mapped out his or her career. The exercise involved drawing a line across a piece of paper, and then intuitively making a horizon line that represented the ups and downs in his or her life, and labeling the peaks and valleys. (See the steps-at-a-glance practice on this page.) It didn't take any graphic talent at all. We asked people to share these drawings as they told the stories of their careers in pairs. I still remember Jean Louis Gassee, the debonair Frenchman who headed Apple's marketing function, sitting on the front porch of the Pajaro Dune building next to Debbie Coleman, the brilliant, T-shirt-wearing, in-your-face CFO of Apple, and sharing their drawings. In spite of what looked like polar personal styles, the experience left them as allies during much of the rest of their tenure.

We conducted this graphic history exercise in all the eight subsequent Leadership Expeditions I helped facilitate, and the dozens more run by the Apple team that we trained to take over the process. Invariably people experienced a cascade of insights and connections. We became very used to having people discover that the down periods, or challenges, were often directly related to the up, or peak periods. And I was always fascinated by how the simple shift in perspective from a linear story to the peak and valley story is what sparked these insights. By changing the graphic framework we shifted the point of view! This is a very good example, in addition, of how visual language can resolve seeming contradictions—like seeing the ups and downs of our life as unconnected separate events. Drawing out a lifeline as a peak and valley diagram makes it very clear that life is a flow of events that are deeply interconnected. Take some time to do it yourself!

I was always fascinated by how the simple shift in perspective from a linear story to the peak and valley story is what sparked these insights.

Vision Stories

The crux of the Leadership Expedition was having all the participants create a vision for their own team that they would commit to sharing after the offsite. The process involved:

1. Listening to Dr. Martin Luther King's "I Have a Dream" speech for inspiration, and identifying the characteristics of a compelling vision.
2. Writing out their own vision for their team, by imagining it was a movie, and creating a storyboard of the main points.
3. Providing a quick training in the evening on how to draw on flip charts—simple pictographs like those that are shared in the next chapter.
4. Asking each person to deliver the vision, using flip charts for support if they wanted, to a small group that would pretend to be their team.
5. Inviting feedback from the "crossfire" team to improve the vision by sharing what was most compelling, and where it seemed to be lacking conviction.

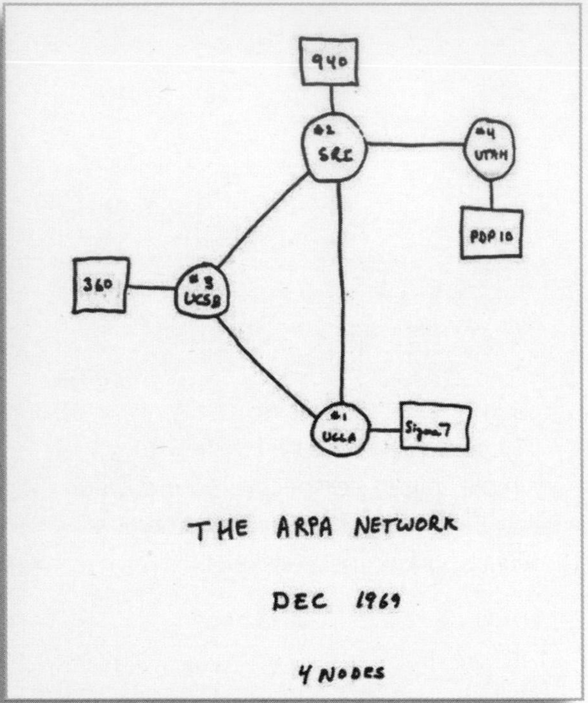

FIRST DRAWING OF THE WEB

This first drawing of the Internet is an example of diagrammatic thinking, where parts are connected in a spatial array. Even simple systems require visualization if we want to understand how they work.

6. Tape recording each of the vision presentations and having the participants leave with these.

Creating a Shared Frame of Reference

Throughout the Leadership Expedition we invited special quests that were unusually good at story telling and painting a picture of possibilities. The catalytic one was an opening presentation by Alan Kay, a pioneering thinker from Atari, Xerox, and now Apple who conceptualized the first laptop personal computer, the DynaBook. Alan was a living example of the kind of leader we hoped the Apple participants might aspire to be. His views on the power of imagery and visual thinking in human performance were in fact directly shaping Apple's future in his role as an Apple Fellow. As a trained molecular biologist, accomplished musician, and serious inventor his range and creativity were exceptional. He had everyone's attention. We also knew that in this event (as in this book) everyone needed to have some sense of possibility and purpose for all the experiences we had arranged to really yield any result.

"We haven't come close to the kind of systems we are going to build," Alan began right off. He described the modern computer as an amplifier, working directly through kits of tools and indirectly through agents and networks. (This was way before social networking.) "It's an architecture where the illusion of the viewer can be directly manipulated."

We Live in a Hallucination

"We all live inside a hallucination of our own devising," Alan claimed. He explained that we project what we know onto what we are observing. It is a "dream that is constantly being recreated." Because of this, he concluded, "Point of view is worth 80 IQ points." By that he meant that the way you view something (and he meant literally "see") directly impacts how much information and insight you obtain, and how smart you can be, to a very large extent—symbolized by the 80 IQ points. I'm pretty sure Alan was using the 80 IQ points as a symbol for intelligence and not trying to assert that IQ tests are a true measure of all the different kinds of intelligence we now know are possible. But is it true that visualization makes you smarter, and potentially can make groups smarter? My experience and study says yes.

Our Point of View and Task Orientation Guide Visual Thinking

Colin Ware's work at the Data Vizualization Research Lab at the University of New Hampshire reinforces Kay's premise. Ware and his colleagues have developed an "eye tracker" that fits over the head and allows the research team to see precisely how subjects are detecting patterns in a complex field of information. They present an array of dozens of dots representing Fortune 500 companies. The task is to find which are connected with board of director members serving on both boards. Clicking on a dot reveals the names of the board members. In a more advanced task the participant is asked who in the transportation sector is best connected to those in the finance sector.

Point of view is worth 80 IQ Points.

Alan Kay

What Ware and his team discovered was that everyone went through a common process guided by the task they were given (that very much follows the process of this book).

1. They started by imagining the problem to solve, the task, and getting that clear.
2. They made visual queries to explore the pattern.
3. They stored chunks of information.
4. They then found patterns in the links.

They discovered that people could only hold 2 or 3 chunks of information in visual memory at a time, so they had to query and search a lot. (This is why having actual working displays is so helpful in visual thinking.) Subjects were generally moving about three eye movements per second. Success in pattern finding was the result of connecting their top down task orientation with the bottom up stimulus from the visual searching around.

Ware is convinced that our task orientation literally drives the way we look at things. In this process we scale up through the layers of our cortex, searching for the patterns that connect. The first level of pattern finding is recognition of the basic visual material as vertical, horizontal, diagonal lines, or dots. A second level is seeing contours and lines, looking for boundaries and similarities. We look at both line and form. We then assess whether those patterns relate to our task focus and maybe at higher levels begin to make value judgements about value and such.

Our task orientation (read point of view) literally drives the way we look at things. In many ways we see what we are looking for.

Ware's research reinforces my experiences in meetings. In many ways we see what we are looking for. People begin with the purpose and outcomes, either explicitly or in their own imagination, then move to exploration and making probes to figure things out. In the visual space this involves scanning. As we store different chunks of information and cluster them we begin to see patterns, and when we find patterns we can then move to actions.

Visualization Makes Groups Smarter

The importance of perspective and point of view applies to groups and meetings. If participants share a common purpose they work more effectively. If groups are able to see different patterns in their thinking they get smarter. If they can remember the ideas they come up with they get more productive.

The little visual model on the front of this book illustrates the process by which groups move from imagining what is possible to taking action. Some would call this a cycle of learning. It is also, as Ware's research shows, a pattern of how we think visually. Each step involves visualization. Let's look at them one by one to appreciate what is possible at each step.

Meetings Start in Our Imagination

The first step in any learning process in a group is having some spark of purpose. This is an event that happens in the imagination. When people join a meeting they are always trying to imagine what it is supposed to be about. This process starts before the meeting, and is supported by e-mails and other communications. It is the part of the process where people are crafting a personal story about the potential of the gathering, and probably imagining how much they want to invest. What we imagine our task to be frames our perceptions.

It really helps to provide a way for people to have this conversation with themselves, and appropriate imagery invites this. It provides a visual space into which everyone can project the purpose of a meeting—especially in these busy times. If people are confused or can't imagine much that is productive going on it is much harder to have a productive meeting.

Imagining purpose happens in the privacy of your imagination. There you are pretty free to imagine almost anything, using pictures, words, feelings, or combinations. Our brains are like miniature holodecks, capable of very rich representations. They are limited by our life experiences and exposures, but the fact that we can recombine memories and create new patterns that are wholly imaginary doesn't make this much of a limitation.

In my experience, visualizing meeting purposes and objectives is one of the most helpful things you can do to make a meeting work. And getting people involved early in talking about

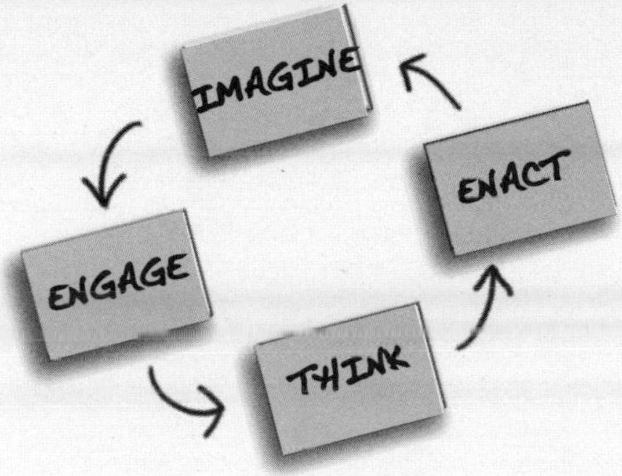

LEARNING CYCLE

Groups and individuals move through a predictable cycle of learning when working on new ideas. It begins in the imagination with intention and task focus, moves to exploration and engagement, then thinking and pattern finding, and finally decisions to move to action and application These steps integrate the intuition, feeling, thinking, and sensing parts of our perception.

expectations and hoped-for outcomes is even more effective. Because people are free to imagine whatever they want and often do, this investment is the first step in focusing group intelligence. You can't control thinking, but can guide it. That is why connecting with your own experiences of visual meetings, and using real stories and pictures as catalysts for your imagination, is so important. If you think back to the Apple story, the room setup, graphic agenda, and other visuals all provided a frame for people's imaginations.

I remember one of my colleagues telling me how she would prepare for a meeting by creating a very abstract pattern with chalks while thinking about the purpose of the gathering she was leading. She would then share this with people at the very start of the meeting, and ask everyone to share what they saw in the picture. Amazing things would come up right from the beginning.

Another colleague and I began a meeting with some generals in the U.S. Army by scattering a variety of interesting photographs around on the floor and asking everyone to pick one that appealed, for whatever reason. Then the meeting began with us standing in a circle and introducing ourselves and sharing what we associated with the image. Again the meeting came alive immediately as people shared things about themselves that couldn't possibly have been anticipated. Our imagination and in fact our consciousness is at some level a great mystery, and often connected with many more things that we are aware of. Simple imagery can pull this out.

Then We Engage and Explore

The tangible part of meetings starts when people actually engage with each other, and whatever it is they are gathering to work on. This involves playing around and exploring new information and ideas. In fact no one can make connections and see patterns until he or she has some chunks of information to work with!

VISUALIZING THE PURPOSE OF MEETINGS

It's amazing how important simple visualizations can be to support people in understanding the purpose of a meeting. Here are some examples of the types of things you might do.

1. Put a poster with a catchy title and simple graphic out in the hall so people start getting excited about the meeting even before they come into the room.
2. Have people sign in graphically on a large sheet of paper and indicate what they consider to be a hot issue or a pressing question related to the meeting.
3. Illustrate the name of your meeting in a big banner and have it be a presence during the meeting. Ideally the name would point toward the purpose of the event.
4. Graphically illustrate your agenda and keep it posted, so everyone can support staying on schedule.
5. Create a graphic scoreboard of the results you are hoping to achieve the following year and have it posted up high in the room all during your planning meeting.

This is why so many meetings begin with presentations and overviews to bring everyone up to a similar level of familiarity with the topic. But people's minds are not passive. To think creatively and productively everyone needs to be engaged with more than information. By this I mean paying attention, feeling excited, and actually participating in sharing information, observations, and whatever else is needed. Movement and direct involvement are all part of this stage.

John Dewey, one of America's most challenging education theorists, believed that discovery-based education would yield the most learning. I spent eight years designing and leading discovery-based learning programs for young leaders in public affairs, and came to believe the same thing.

You can count on having participation and engagement shoot up in a meeting as soon as you begin to let people talk and express themselves, and demonstrate that you are actually listening by writing and drawing what people are saying on large sheets of paper. This kind of graphic note taking is becoming widespread because it so predictably has this effect. I am convinced that it is not the quality of the drawing or writing that has the power, but the experience of being listened to. I suspect people are far more starved for acknowledgment than they let on. If you grasp this idea you will have connected with one of the most important ideas in this book.

My first book on this subject was titled *I See What You Mean! A Workbook Guide to Group Graphics.* This common phrase expresses the feeling that people associate with making sense of things visually—of connecting, engaging, and getting involved. It's the most important result you can achieve in the early stages of a group or team.

You can count of having a sense of participation and engagement shoot up in a meeting as soon as you begin listening to the people, especially if you write out and draw what people are saying.

Blah blah blah blah
blah blah blah
blah blah blah
SLIDE
42
I CAN'T THINK
ANY MORE!!

A Lot of Thinking Is Visual Pattern Finding

THINK

When people feel like they have enough information to work with they begin focusing on finding key patterns relating to whatever purpose they came in with. Some might call this the analysis or sense-making stage. Thinking is a process of finding connections that explain things, solving problems, revealing a design, or setting the criteria for decisions. How many meetings have you been in when people say during a round of expectation gathering, "let's think out of the box." The boxes in our minds are the ruts we get in from looking at information the same way all the time. You will discover as you begin to work with visual meetings, that display making, mapping, diagramming, and graphic recording all shift what we can see and can't see in different ways. Without these tools groups are very handicapped in thinking about anything that is very complex.

There is a simple experiment you can do to appreciate how much visual patterns affect how well we can think. On the following page I describe a bean experiment that you can try yourself. It involves seeing how many beans you can count given a very short period to look at a plate full of them. Most people can't be accurate beyond 6 to 7 beans unless they are organized in visual patterns. It should convince you that organizing information on displays is a necessary and powerful tool for thinking about anything more complex than 2 to 3 points.

I am convinced from my own experience that it is impossible to do what is called "systems thinking" without visualization. Chapter 10 explores this in depth. For now think about it in a common sense sort of way. When you want to understand anything you can't experience all in one moment, say how a restaurant actually works, or how to improve your business, or solving a marketing problem, then you need to be able to connect different pieces of information experienced at different times. If you want to think about how things connect and are related you will have to make some kind of display. It may be completely between your ears, in your imagination, but if you want to share it and have a whole group share the same idea, you will end up making some kind of visual display.

This idea seems so obvious to me now I sometimes have trouble understanding why people think that listening to presentation after presentation is a skillful way to learn. I would much rather engage people in cocreating a display where they find their own patterns in the information. That kind of learning sticks. That is what visual thinking is all about. This is why teachers work through ideas step by step on blackboards!

Taking Vision to Action

The bottom line for most meetings is having them contribute to making progress and getting results! Visualization becomes important at this step as a guide to seeing how actions play out over time. Roadmaps, game plans, dashboards, progress maps, and cases are all examples of visualization that reflect action over time, and help us think about implementation. I think enacting

through visualization is tapping the power of simulation—I was always fascinated by how the simple shift in perspective from a linear story to the peak and valley story is what sparked these insights "conceptual prototyping." The tools and techniques for this kind of visualizing are also not about drawing ability, but about the process of creating the maps and diagrams. At the point a group is ready to swing into action, if they participate in designing action plans, the chances of having team ownership and followthrough are many times greater than if they are handed assignments. Chapters 15 through 20 will share the visual tools for decision making, project management, action planning, and other forms of enactment.

BEAN COUNTING EXPERIMENT

Conduct a simple experiment with a plate of beans to see how the human brain handles complexity.

1. Put four or five beans at random on the plate and hold it high so a partner can't see how many are on the plate.

2. Then lower it and raise it quickly, giving your partner only a glance at the plate. At 4 to 5 beans everyone will immediately know how many beans.

3. Now put 8 or 9 on the plate and you will see some variation. Some will say 7. Some will say 8, and so on. Our brains cannot process more than about 6 or 7 bits of information at a time.

4. Now organize the beans in clusters, say, of four each. You can put 16 or 20 on the plate and your partner will know at a glance. This characteristic of our visual perception is behind the practice of keeping outlines and categories to 5 to 7 at each level).

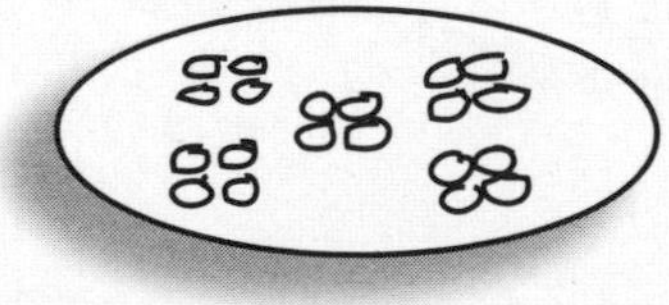

VISUAL TOOLS FOR TRACKING PROGRESS

- ❑ Task lists
- ❑ Process Diagrams
- ❑ Graphic Gameplans
- ❑ Roadmaps
- ❑ Journey Charts
- ❑ Dashboards
- ❑ Graphic KPIs (Key Performance Indicators)

When you work with visuals the charts provide a way of tracking progress. I remember an engineer from Bechtel Corporation who was in one of our graphic facilitation workshops and had the experience of making a simple graphic action plan for a project, much like the one illustrated on this page. He got so excited he went back to his company, and every week would photocopy his little drawing and use a highlighter to show which parts had been accomplished. The drawing was very simple and unpolished, and for that reason actually stood out from all the other communications. It worked like one of those graphic thermometers in a fund-raising campaign!

The most important thing in enactment is having people remember what they agreed to do, and be able to refer back to documents that trigger that memory. When I first learned to record graphically for groups, I was interested that Interaction Associates called the flip chart displays "group memories." They asserted, and I concur from experience, that when a group sees its work recorded, their trust in its validity increases, and groups will use those charts as their collective memory. Since remembering what we commit to do in meetings is so critical in implementation, I think any investment in improving retention is a direct link to greater productivity.

Doug Englebart, another one of the legendary pioneers of modern computing (inventing the mouse, windows, and hypertext), had a study group at Stanford Research Institute in the 1970s looking at how to enhance human intellect. One of Englebart's team, Geoff Ball, wrote a little unpublished paper on *Explicit Group Memory.* He reported that of all the ideas he and other members of the project were exploring, the use of a common working display made the most difference. They believed that shared computer displays would be the power tools of the future. I took display to mean any kind of visual display, and understood through Geoff's paper why chalkboards are probably the last tool a teacher would ever give up.

Fast Forward

The summer of 2008 a group of people met in a building that over-looked Chicago's Millennium Park. This was the 15th annual meeting of the International Forum of Visual Practitioners. These are people who make their living visualizing—literally writing and drawing on the wall. Some were recorders who create visual illustrations of meetings and presentations. Others were graphic facilitators, leading strategy and innovation sessions from the front of the room with graphic templates, whiteboards, and interactive visual media. Some were traditional designers and illustrators who were jumping professions and going "real time," using their skills for listening and creating. Some were teachers using graphics interactively in their classroom. Others were coaches and consultants just getting involved.

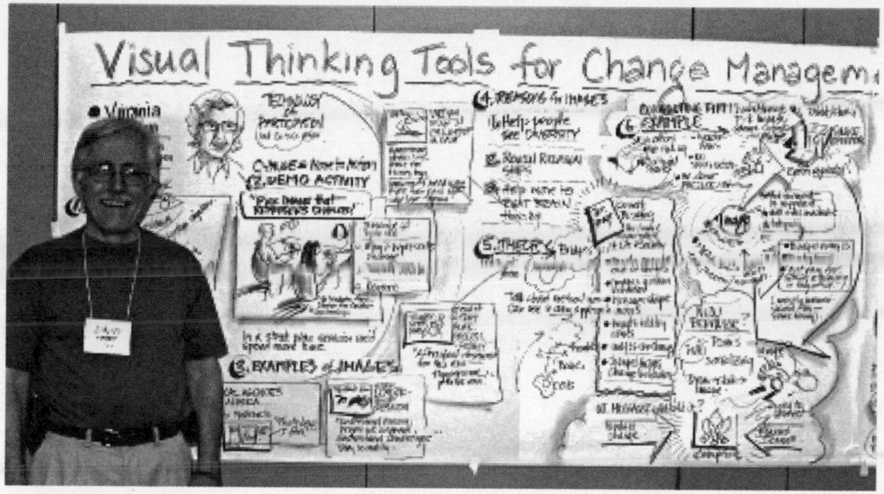

RECORDING AT the INTERNATIONAL VISUAL PRACTITIONERS FORUM

Graphic recording involves taking visual notes while people talk. The picture shows my work capturing a talk on Change Management by Virginia Hamilton.

As a pioneer in this way of working, I attended and supported a session on using Visual Thinking for Change Management. My and other sessions offered a symbolic map of what is going on now in this movement many years after those days at Apple. I include these stories here because I hope you will see that this way of working has an enormous range, at least as broad and varied as music, the mother of performing arts. The very simple things you can do right away have a lot of impact, and visual language can expand to symphonic levels with some practice.

- Several sessions explored the use of photographic images and evocative illustrations to support group dialogue. One session reviewed the Center for Creative Leadership's Visual Explorer kit.

- Ole Qvist Sorenson from Denmark uses Bigger Pictures to support sustainability planning in companies and cross sector meetings all over Europe. He recruited a special group of

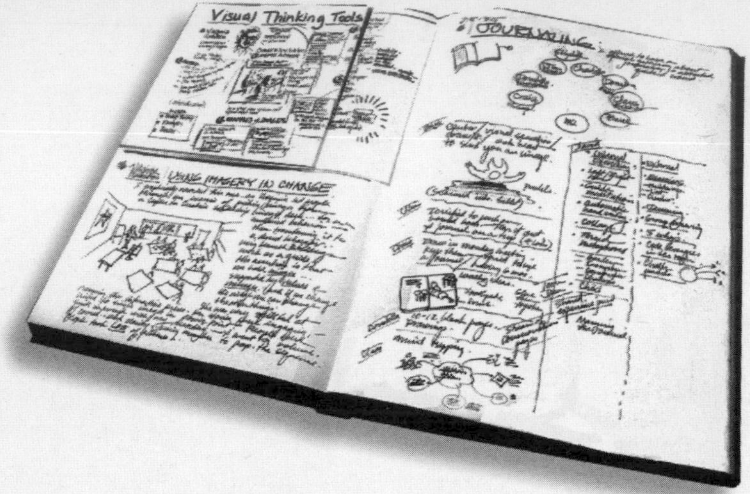

PERSONAL NOTES

I took these during our journal workshop at the International Forum of Visual Practitioners.

visual practioners to participate in visualizing the Copenhagen environmental summit in the fall of 2009.

- Virginia Hamilton, leader of the California Workforce Development Institute, shared how she uses imagery to explore shadow problems and conflict in public sector groups trying to set policy. (My recording of her session is on page 17.)
- John Ward led a workshop on kinesthetic modeling, using clay and model making to think through planning and other problems.
- Regina Rowland, Tomi Nagai-Rothe, and Julie Geisike led a session on visualization for cross-cultural work.
- Several people brought and demonstrated tablet computers they were using for visualizing in virtual meetings.
- I led another session on journaling, reviewing a range of visualization and writing strategies for reflecting on one's own journey.

THE POWERS OF VISUAL MEETINGS

1. Sparking imagination
2. Engaging people actively
3. Thinking BIG PICTURE
4. Supporting group memory and productivity

If you haven't heard of visual meetings, graphic facilitation, graphic recording, sketch notes, visual recording, imagineering, storyboarding, visual listening, group graphics, graphic templates, mind mapping, idea mapping, real-time design, or group graphics, don't despair. Revolutions take time to gather momentum, spreading along for years and then exploding into sight.

You are catching up at just the right time. Let's go to the next chapter, which is all about how you can reclaim your ability to draw in the simple ways that allow you to use visuals for listening and idea mapping.

2. Everybody Knows Graphic Language

It's Gesture with a Pen

Get ready for a potentially exciting experience. Having it hinges on your revisiting your early childhood years and decisions you made about whether you could draw. Over the years I've asked people in workshops how many people consider themselves good at drawing. Usually only 20% or less raise their hands. When I ask the others how many stopped drawing in the second grade I get more than half. If you are one of those who hasn't drawn much, or believes you can't, I'll bet you aren't thinking about the kind of graphics this book is about, but about whether or not your horse looked like a horse. If this chapter does its work it will get you to reconsider your decision, and know what you can do to reclaim your ability to be graphic.

noun
Graph•ic
1: written, drawn or engraved 2: marked by or capable of clear and lively description or striking imaginative power 3: of or relating to the pictorial arts… syn GRAPHIC, VIVID, PICTURESQUE, PICTORIAL means giving a clear visual impression in words. GRAPHIC stresses the evoking of a clear, lifelike picture.

Roget's Thesaurus

The kind of graphics used for meetings are rooted in gesture and simple, universal icons and not in making drawings that look like photographs. If I asked you if you felt comfortable gesturing, I'll bet you would raise your hand. If you had a pen in it and you were near a wall it might look like a straight line!

Gesture Is One of Our First Languages

My first book on this subject was *Graphic Facilitation: Transforming Group Process with the Power of Visual Listening*. I wrote the following for people wanting to become professional graphic recorders and facilitators:

> Babies and parents use gesture to communicate long before words are understood. Pointing, waving, grabbing, holding, reaching out, and even dancing start in our earliest years. Faces themselves are a graphic statement. Frowning, smiling, showing surprise, disinterest, concern, full attention—all of these states show up in our faces, and babies learn to recognize each of them. The ways people express emotion is universal. Smiles communicate! Gestural language carries over into our whole lives. Although some cultures and people are more talkative with their hands and bodies than others, everyone communicates through the visual symbolism of gesture. Recall a time you visited a country where people spoke a language you didn't know. You probably focused a great deal on facial expression and body language.

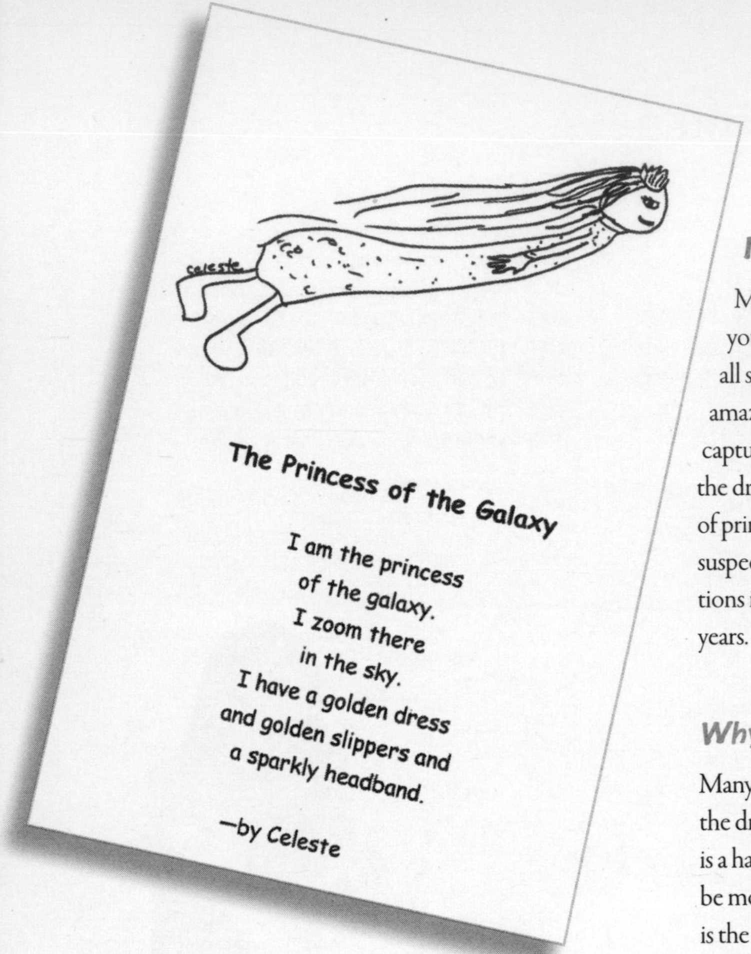
celeste
The Princess of the Galaxy
I am the princess
of the galaxy.
I zoom there
in the sky.
I have a golden dress
and golden slippers and
a sparkly headband.
—by Celeste

A third grade San Francisco student created this in a session sponsored by California Poets in the Schools.

Most Kids Love to Draw

My wife is a poetry teacher in the San Francisco schools, and works with children K-12. She loves the younger grades, and works with many children who don't yet know how to write very well. But they all seem to know how to draw. For years I've watched her make books out of the kids' poetry, and been amazed at the graphic power of their drawings and the poems they write about them. This one by Celeste captures the magic children feel when they can express themselves. But sometime in the 3rd or 4th grade the drawings begin to change. The boys start drawing little vehicles and machines. The girls' drawings of princesses start having tight curls. Somehow it becomes important to draw realistically or not at all. I suspect that fluency in graphic language isn't on anyone's tests so it gets ignored.. There are of course exceptions in a growing number of schools that understand the important of creativity expression in the early years. But this is not the norm.

Why Cartoonists Draw Like Second Graders

Many cartoonists go out of their way to make their drawings look innocent and unpolished, often like the drawings I see on the light table with my wife's books. Most cognitive scientists agree that the cortex is a hard-wired, pattern recognizing organ. It would be logical to assume, then, that people's brains would be most activated *not* with clearly recognizable drawings, but ones that are slightly ambiguous! I think this is the reason that most realistic clip art is so boring. We recognize it too quickly. The little drawings and cartoons I'm using in this book are much more stimulating because they require participation in the act of figuring out what they mean.

Bob Horn, who I mentioned earlier, came to one of my first workshops in 1980 and completely accepted the premise that simple little drawings are more engaging. He isn't particularly good at drawing realistically, but he is fearless about drawing in his simple, whimsical way and his journals from his trips are wonderful! He knows that the act of drawing is a form of seeing, and a type of observation that greatly amplifies the drawer's ability to remember and understand things. He also knows if he has the guts to draw his little figures with flair, he'll have his audience's full attention.

Discover the Fun of Playing Around

Adults naturally learn new things just like children, by fooling around first and then figuring out what's going on from the results. That is what trial and error is all about. It's a state that inventors and innovators embrace and cultivate. It's the process described in this book of imagining, engaging, thinking, and then enacting.

If you are somewhat inhibited by your school experiences, play around with kids a bit to remember what it's like to have free expression. A fun exercise with drawing is "Add a Line." Ask a child to draw something, anything, and after he or she does, it's your turn. You add a line, any kind. Then she adds a line. Then you add one. It gets wild fast. It's a great experiment in letting go of preconceptions.

Practice in a Blank Sketchbook

The practical way to begin reclaiming your ability to draw is to get a blank sketchbook at an art store, the kind without lines. The blank pages invite experimentation and play. If you get some pencils, pens, and colors that allow for easy drawing, it becomes even more fun. In your own book no one is looking, so it's a perfect place to begin. Make mistakes. Play around. In fact, working through the exercises illustrated in this chapter would be a good way to begin.

A very natural way to start working visually is take your own graphic meetings notes in meetings. On the following page are some things you can do with a blank journal to exercise your visual imagination.

ADD A LINE

Play this game with a young person.

1. Get a white sheet of paper and some markers or pens. Explain that one person draws any kind of line.
2. When that child lifts up the pen, then the other person can draw any kind of line.
3. Then the first person draws another line.
4. Keep going until you want to start again.

Great Beginning Journal Activities

- **Draw Seating Charts:** The next meeting you are in draw a picture of the tables where people are sitting as though you were looking down from the ceiling. Then use little circles and put them around the table where everyone is sitting, and write in their names as they introduce themselves. You will be amazed at how this simple activity will increase your ability to remember a meeting and people's names.

- **Practice Bullet Points:** Doodle out different kinds of bullet points. Look at the illustration on this page to see some different kinds. Make them round, square, asterisks, stars, and see how consistent you can be.

- **Play with Lines and Borders**: Hold your pen with your little finger out along the edge of the book. Then slowly pull the pen down, holding your hand rigid. This will create a line that is amazingly straight. Play with wavy lines and dotted lines. Box in different parts of your text.

- **Doodle Little People:** There are lots of ways to make little figures. Page through this book to the part that shows you how to draw them and make up some of your own.

- **Play with Cartoon Bubbles:** Cartoonists use little circles with a point to indicate talk and clouds to indicate thoughts. When you have thoughts about what you are hearing begin putting them in little clouds or in the margins so you can scan back.

- **Take Notes in Different Formats**: List things out one time, arrange in clusters and diagrams another time. Break chunks of information into groups and create borders.

The key thing is to experiment and try different layouts. This kind of playing with information will free up your expressive abilities and make it easier to have some discipline about it later. Chapter 3 has a series of more developed exercises you can play with to have a meeting with yourself about important things you need to reflect about.

All Graphics Are Made of Basic Shapes

In the 1970s when I first discovered working visually with groups, I was fascinated with understanding the basic elements. As a piano player I was aware that one of the inventions that really advanced the ability of musicians to play across different borders and cultures was the standardization of the eight-tone scale. It's not the only way to organize notes, but it was a very flexible one. With the addition of the black notes it became a keyboard of possibilities that allowed for tremendous experimentation and improvisation. I knew that visual language could have the same flexibility.

My first effort at thinking this through was influenced by the fact I was studying different ways of thinking about process, and one way was to ask "what are the simplest and most fundamental elements" and work toward the most complex. Well, the simplest thing to do visually was to just rest the pen on paper and make a dot. The next most simple thing was to move the pen and make a line, then to change directions on the line and make a shape, like a triangle. Formalizing the shapes into neat squares and rectangles seemed the next hardest. I could then combine the square and triangle and make what I called a hollow arrow. With some practice I could make this arrow spiral, and finally get around to the circle. Now, the circle wasn't the hardest to draw, but seemed the most comprehensive. These seven basic shapes became my building blocks for diagramming and illustrating. I could create any kind of picture out of these elements.

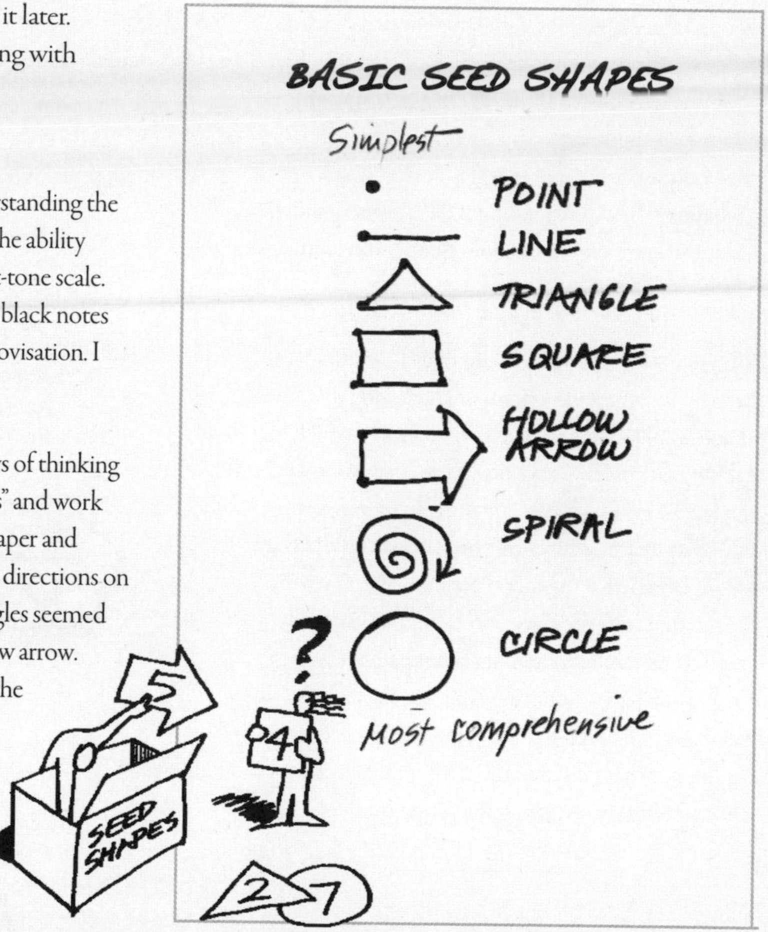

I was delighted to discover an art teacher named Mona Brooks who was teaching children to draw the same way. She wasn't so concerned about the process of drawing, but had grouped the shapes into "families." She had children identify the "point" families, the "cloud" families, the "angles," the "boxes," and the "lines." She found that if she asked children to draw pictures of just one or two of these they would learn to see the basic shapes in whatever they were looking at. Within very short periods of time they could draw quite proficiently.

Your Body Knows Graphic Language

I began teaching people how to draw by getting them up to large sheets of paper and having them feel what it was like to make these basic shapes, which for teaching ultimately broke down into six movements or what we now call "basic strokes." In trainings we demonstrate physically how this is done and then have people experience making these movements on the paper, often with their eyes closed so they can feel how natural it is. The exercise reconnects everyone to the gestural basis of drawing. This was the exercise we shared with the Apple participants in the Leadership Experience that prepared them for making their own vision presentations during the program.

DROP LINES

1. Hold your pen lightly on the paper, touching it with your little finger.
2. When the image of a heavy rock is clear, drop the line. Flex your body to follow your hand and the pen as it drops.
3. Notice any wiggles or other movements the next time you repeat the activity and see if you can tell what you are doing other than dropping.

HORIZON LINES

1. Imagine your paper is a window looking out over the ocean or the plains.
2. Imagine the horizon line.
3. Draw a small segment of it across the paper.
4. Repeat. Do some with eyes closed. Do some with a wiggle.

COMBOS

THROW LINES

1. Put your pen on the beginning of the line you want.
2. Find the point where you want to end up.
3. Literally "throw" the line to the point without shifting your focus. Let your body follow.
4. Observe the result. Repeat and see what you are doing other than throwing straight to your target.

FRAMES

All frames are combinations of drop lines and horizon lines.

1. Drop a line on the left. Recenter. Draw a horizon line along the bottom.
2. Move to the top and repeat the horizon line.
3. Drop another line on the right.
4. Repeat at a smaller scale. All drop lines should line up with the gravity line.

TRIANGLES & HOLLOW ARROWS

Combine horizon, drop, and throw lines.

1. Draw a base line in the direction you want.
2. Drop down 90 degrees for the baseline of the triangle.
3. Throw to the point, to the base, to the shank.
4. Use muscle memory to draw a second base line parallel to the first.

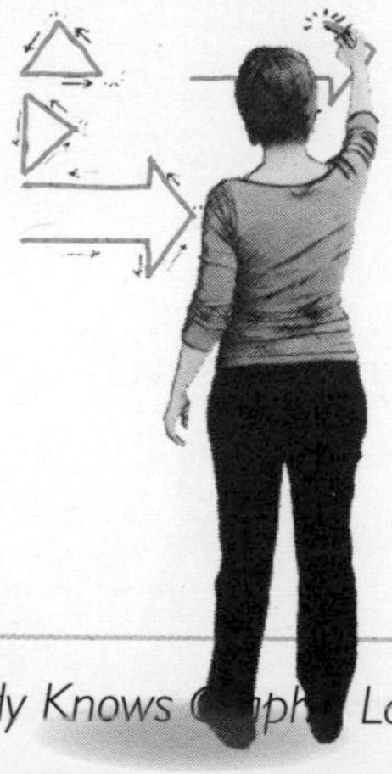

CIRCLES

Everyone's arm is a natural compass. It makes easy circles around the shoulder socket.

1. Swing your arm in a circle and feel your shoulder warming. Do it with your eyes closed.
2. Center on the chart. Unfocus your vision and "stir" a circle onto the paper, going around until you feel it warm up.
3. Repeat at a smaller scale. Repeat backward.

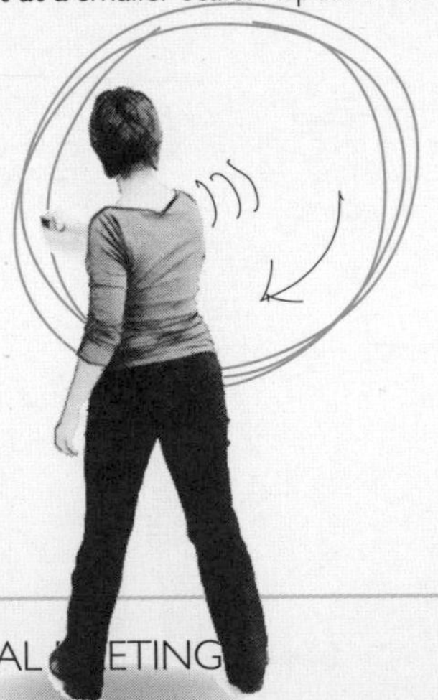

SPIRALS

Additional instructions from your imagination can be added on top of basic strokes.

1. Tune in to the stirring feeling in your shoulder by moving your arm in a circle.
2. If you start big, tell yourself "smaller" as you draw the circle and it will tighten into a spiral.
3. If you start small, tell yourself "bigger" and it will spiral out.

CURVES

1. Center yourself and imagine the curve you want by seeing it on the paper.
2. Throw the curve line.
3. Use your muscle memory to help you repeat that line.

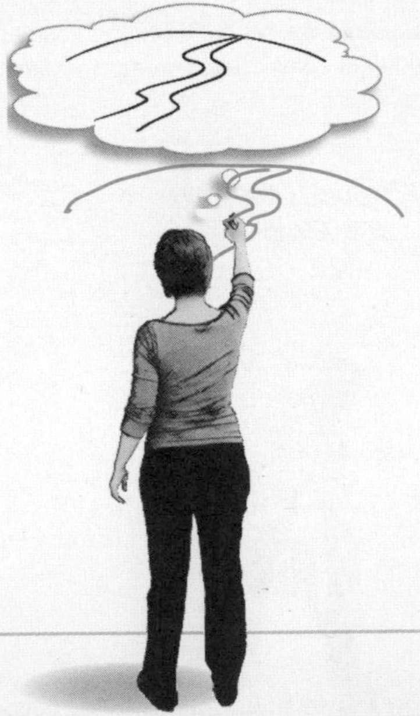

COMBO

RIBBONS & FORCE ARROWS

Use muscle memory to create parallel curved lines for ribbons and arrows with dynamic force.

1. Imagine the line you want; throw the curve.
2. Repeat immediately using muscle memory.
3. For arrows, pause to draw a triangle point, then use muscle memory to throw a line back to where you started. It will follow the same path as the original line.

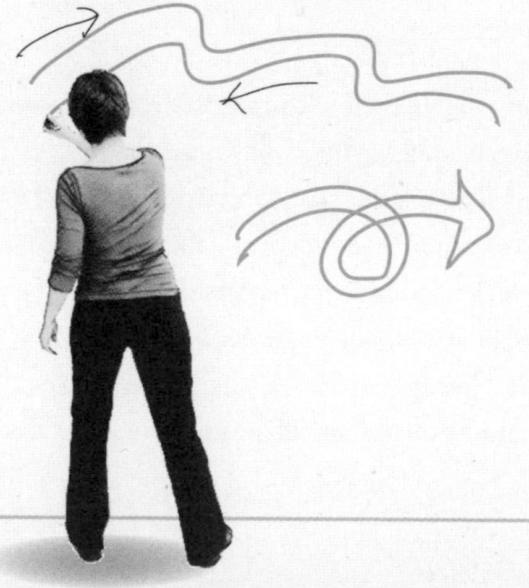

IT'S LIKE NATURE - CREATING COMPLEXITY OUT OF BUILDING BLOCKS - LITTLE ELEMENTS COOPERATING!
HEY, I CAN IMPROVISE ON TOP OF THESE BASIC STROKES!

SUPPLIES

Basic supplies for working on the wall are easy to get. Paper rolls for large plotters are available at art stores and office supply stores. Masking tape and white tape are also available at art stores. Use a box cutter for the large paper. Watercolor markers are the best so you don't mark the walls. Check the next page for more specific information.

ADVANTAGES OF LARGE PAPER

- ❑ Large paper allows you to move an entire display to a new wall and keep it posted.
- ❑ People feel immersed in their information when the scale is big.
- ❑ Large paper provides flexibility when you want groups to help organize the sticky notes.
- ❑ You can write category names and other information on the paper during discussions.
- ❑ Large paper rolls up easily if you want to keep the display.

SOURCES

- ❑ Roll ends of newsprint from newspaper companies (sometimes free)
- ❑ Butcher paper (the least expensive)
- ❑ Plotter paper (this costs a bit, but is lightweight and easy to hang up). It comes in 3-foot and 4-foot wide roles with different levels of absorbency. You want to get the lower levels of absorbency paper.

There aren't sources of recycled large paper yet that are widespread enough to be available, but the large paper itself can be recycled. If the total carbon footprint of inefficient meetings were mapped against the productivity of using large displays, I bet large paper might come out ahead.

Working with Big Paper and Larger Meetings

Working visually is much more flexible and effective if you work on large paper, not only in learning how to unlock your ability to draw, but also for working in meetings. It's a very helpful support for active recording, sticky notes processes, and idea mapping. By large paper I mean paper that is 3 to 4 feet wide and as much as 16 to 24 feet long. (If you are working on a whiteboard and digitally photographing the results, then you won't have to use paper.)

There are two logistical challenges to large paper. One is knowing where to get it and the other is knowing how to hang it up. There are several sources of long paper, shown in the sidebar box.

How to Hang Big Paper

The easiest way to explain this is visually! The drawing on the next page shows a person hanging paper and numbers the steps. After years of working this way, I've found some things that consistently work. (See the tips box for these.)

A team of people can usually figure out how to hang paper even without instructions, so you might consider making the construction of the display area for the sticky notes a group energizer project! This is a great way to get everyone engaged. The same is true for hanging up and moving big templates. After reading through this chapter tape up a piece of paper on the wall, or take a flip chart, and go through the basic strokes exercises yourself. After a couple of repeats, do them with your eyes closed to experience how much is built into your basic orientation to gravity and your environment. I think you will experience just how simple the basics are. Combining them is where it begins to feel like music, and the possibilities become endless. The rest of the book is about all the improvisations that are possible from these basics.

Getting it Straight and Flat

1. Hold a 4" piece of tape in one hand and hold the paper and tape in the other. Attach the upper-left corner, taping out at a 45-degree angle.

2. Unroll 4' of paper, holding the roll lightly against the wall. Don't pull too hard or the first tape will come off.

3. Visually line up the top of the paper parallel to the ceiling and floor: Press it against the wall with your body: Tear off a second piece of tape: Smooth out and tape.

4. Repeat the rolling out, holding, tearing, smoothing, and taping process.

5. Tape the right corner, and hold the roll against the wall. Retrieve your cutter, which you should always keep somewhere on your person.

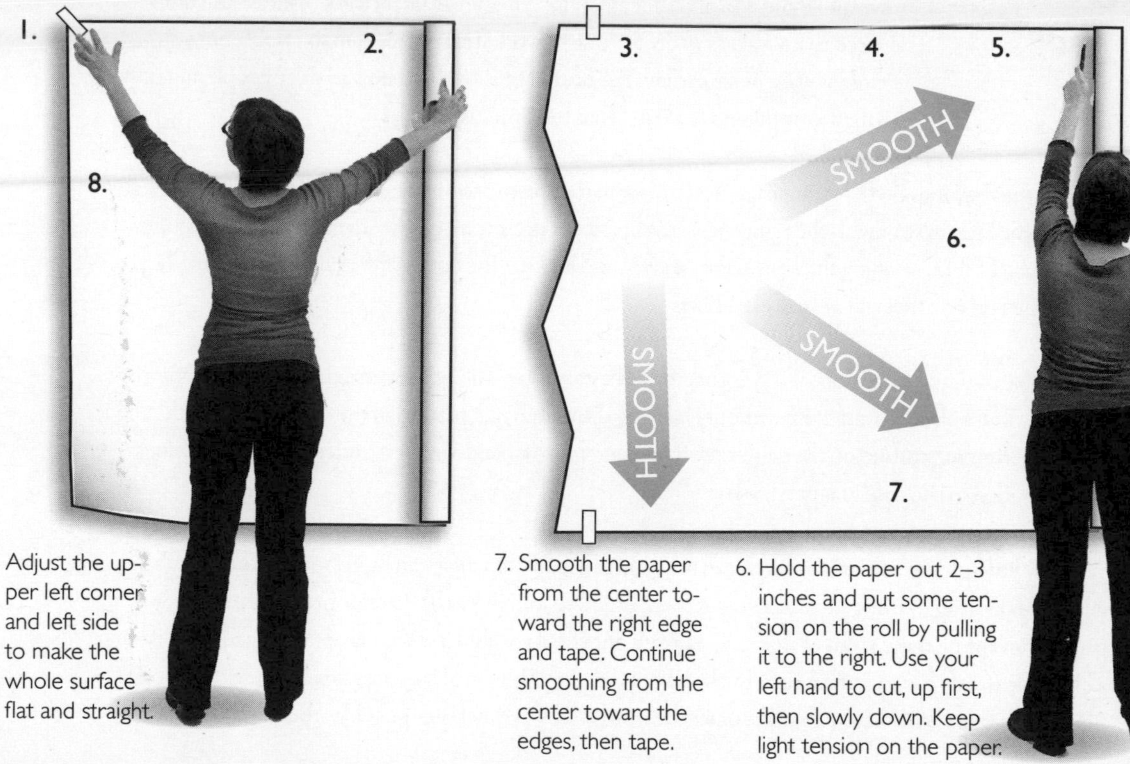

8. Adjust the upper left corner and left side to make the whole surface flat and straight.

7. Smooth the paper from the center toward the right edge and tape. Continue smoothing from the center toward the edges, then tape.

6. Hold the paper out 2–3 inches and put some tension on the roll by pulling it to the right. Use your left hand to cut, up first, then slowly down. Keep light tension on the paper.

TIPS FOR HANGING LARGE PAPER

- ❑ Focus on taping down the top first, then work around clockwise
- ❑ Make sure no air pockets are under the paper by smoothing it out
- ❑ Use a box cutter or knife to cut the paper (these can't be carried on airplanes). If you use scissors cut the paper on the floor before hanging it up.
- ❑ Use artists tape or masking tape
- ❑ Make sure you are allowed to tape on the walls. If not then make sure you have panels of some sort on easels to attach the paper.
- ❑ On fuzzy air walls in hotels or walls with anti stick coatings, tape to the moldings

This page is from *Graphic Facilitation: Transforming Group Process with the Power of Visual Listening*, (The Grove, 2006). This is an in-depth book for anyone wanting to be a professional graphic facilitator.

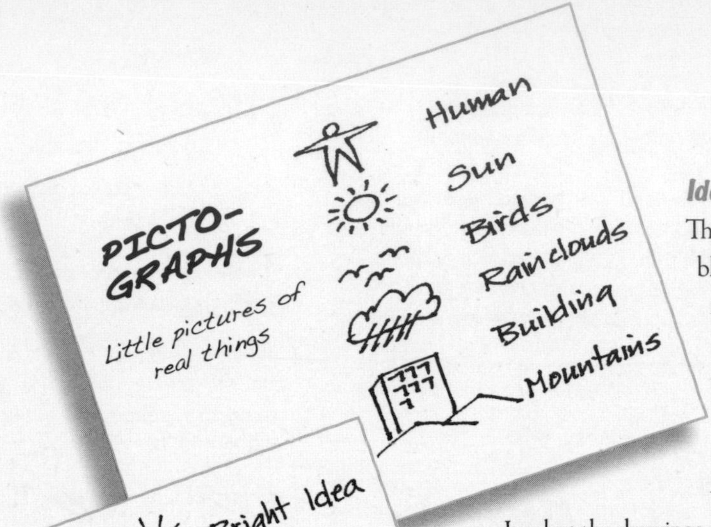

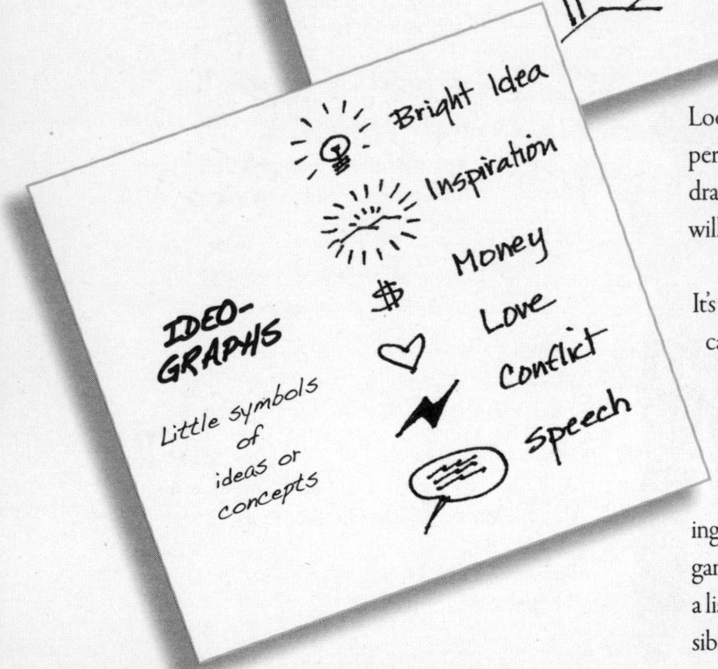

Ideographs, Pictographs, and Seed Shapes

The basic strokes and the little seed shapes I described earlier become the building blocks for making up pictures of just about anything. Some of these little pictures are meant to look like real things and are called "pictographs." Others are completely symbolic and are called "ideographs." They are little pictures of ideas. You don't need to know very many of these to work with the ideas in this book, but you might want to have a few. The next page shows you how to draw people and how to draw computers for a start. That will impress people!

Look at the drawings on the facing page. You will see at the top the sequence you would use to draw a star person. The little drawings on the right end of the first sequence show you the stroke order. Play around, drawing *lots* of these, making the arms skinny and fat, and making the bodies different sizes. Eventually you will happen on one that will be really satisfying.

It's possible to draw people lots of ways other than as a star shape. This way emerged because each point can become a place to improvise without changing the underlying pattern of the drawing. The little people running around on the pages of this book often have hands and feet and hair and other things I've added to the basic star person shape.

Any little pictograph or ideograph can function as a seed shape, if it can be elaborated without changing the underlying drawing pattern. Every year at our International Visual Practitioners Forum we play a game of inventing these kinds of shapes to increase our visual vocabulary. You can do this, too. Write down a list of the words you might have to visualize if you are running a visual meeting. Then as quickly as possible sketch out a little picture that illustrates the word. Work as quickly as possible. You might do a couple.

DRAWING STAR PEOPLE, COMPUTERS, AND BUILDINGS

Starperson
computer
Buildings
WOW, YOU GOT IT!
THIS JUST LOOKS LIKE THROWING LINES AROUND IN A GIVEN ORDER

GRAPHIC JAM

Make a list of words you would like to be able to illustrate quickly.

1. Give everyone a stack of white paper and markers.
2. Read the word and quickly draw a picture.
3. Compare the results and look at what people saw as the essential element in the concept.

4. Tuck your ideas away in your brain or journal!

Then look at the pictures and ask yourself—"What are the lines that point at the essence of this idea?" These become the foundation of the seed shape.

The Meaning of Shapes

As I played with different graphics I was fascinated with whether they had meanings that could be trusted. I knew the basic movements were universal because they flow from how we are shaped as humans. Could there be general meanings?

With spoken language meaning is a function of several things. The word's position in the sentence tells us whether it is a subject, a verb, or an object. A general definition provides some guidance as to common meanings. But under this is a deeper meaning, which is our personal experiences with a word—it's what language experts call "connotations," or in common language, the "loading" on a word. It's our personal relationship with the symbol.

George Lakoff, author and professor of cognitive science and linguistics at U.C. Berkeley, concludes after a career studying artificial intelligence and cognitive theory, that meaning is anchored in our early experiences, not in the rules of grammar. These and the more socialized definitions are layered over the top of our experienced meanings. If you look at basic shapes with these assumptions, and think about what it feels like to make the movements, a pattern of meaning begins to emerge that is deeper than the symbolic meanings assigned by culture. It is a meaning embedded in what it feels like to make that movement.

The Experience of Drawing Provides a Clue to Meaning

- **Points mean "look here," I'm different.** They stand out on a white page.
- **Lines mean "connect" or "separate."** They are about relationships. Heavy lines feel like stronger relationships, and take more energy to draw. Dotted lines feel weaker.
- **Angles mean "active change."** You change direction when you throw the lines. To see angles your cortex neurons must activate. Angles all around a point illustrate an explosion. The delta actually means change in chemistry.
- **Squares and rectangles mean "formal organization."** You need to consistently repeat parallel lines to make them. They are the perfect symbols for buildings and organization functions. Squares make up the pattern of all the things built on grids and the base map of most data displays.
- **Hollow arrows as combinations mean "active organization,"** putting together the meaning of the triangle and the square. What better symbol for a project!
- **Spirals mean "dynamic unity."** If you make them more circular they lean toward unity. If you draw them like tornadoes they suggest more dynamism.
- **Circles mean "unity"** pretty much the world over. It feels like you are gathering everything together when you make a circle.

Meaning is anchored in our experiences, not in the rules of grammar.

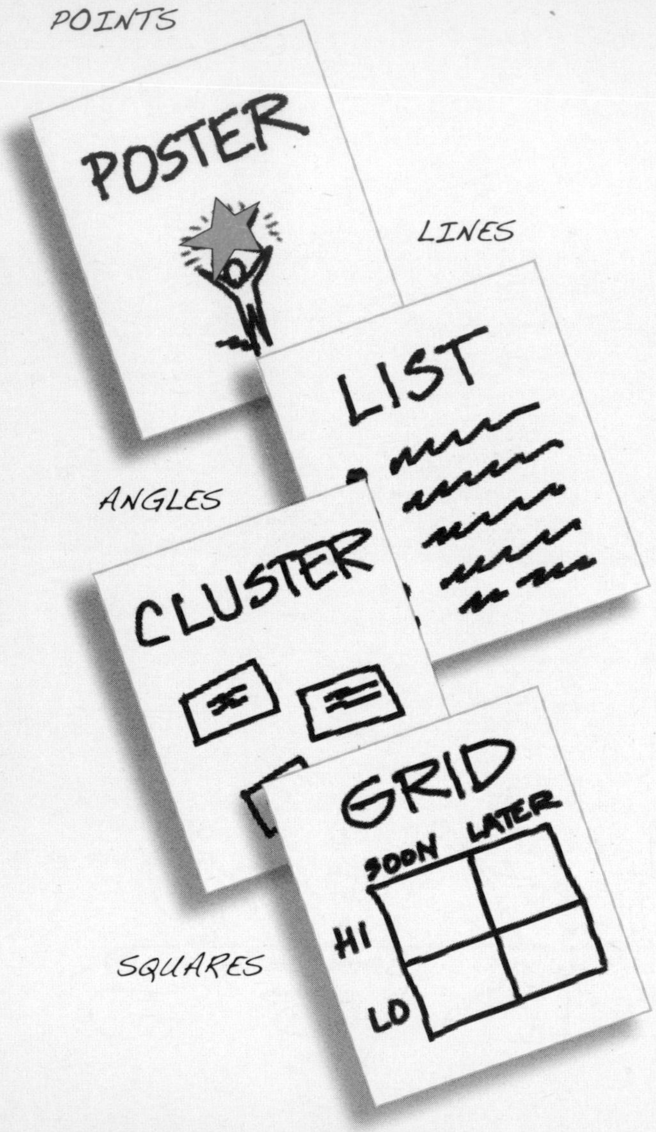

Basic Formats for Visualizing

I remember one day I was working on all these questions about the meaning of shapes and the basic elements of visual language, and I realized that visual language differs from spoken language in a key dimension, which is its ability to be spatial, be it a two-dimensional map or a chart.

I had been collecting examples of how people visualize in meetings for a couple of years and had quite a collection of matrices, outlines, diagrams, organization charts, flowcharts, project plans, maps, bar charts, pie charts, line charts, scattergrams. It was very confusing. I wondered if there might be a basic pattern underlying the spatial arrangement or what I called "formats," just like there seemed to be for the basic shapes.

Because the basic shapes had appeared so quickly and logically, I wondered if that same pattern might apply to the bigger formats, and I was amazed to discover that it did. This was the beginning of the Group Graphics® Keyboard which is explained in more detail in Chapter 9. These are the foundations for visual thinking. At this point let's just take a look at them as a logical progression.

See Drawing as a Process and Not Just an Artifact

My studies suggested that flows of energy and movement are more fundamental than structures and appearances, and I wondered whether, if I looked at drawing and perceiving as processes, the larger formats would fall into some order. They did!

The simplest drawing is a dot on a page. A point means "look here," and I thought, that is a pretty good basic description of the function of **POSTERS**—to make us focus . They use single, punchy images to achieve that, by being different from everything else—just like a dot is different from the white page. A little drawing on a flip chart creates a poster effect.

LISTS are linear in their basic makeup. You make a list by lining up information. It's the simplest of formats to use—one thing after the other. Because speech is also linear, it flows naturally in recording.

CLUSTERS create space on a page. I saw the parallel with angles when I realized that people looking at chunks of information spaced out on a page invariably will begin comparing them, and getting an angle on the information. It's what anyone does with sticky notes.

GRIDS are a step more complicated and require comparing several sets of categories. They are clearly related to the box and rectangle family of basic shapes and are much more formal and constrained than lists or clusters. I was getting pretty excited at this point as I saw the pattern unfold from simple to complex, with the simpler formats able to nest into the more complicated ones, just like in nature!

DIAGRAMS are formats in which chunks of information are linked in branching patterns, as in mind maps and organization charts. The word *diagram* is used for other kinds of formats, but always for this kind, so it felt like the right word. The hollow arrow was a linkage of boxes and angles. This association felt like a bit of stretch, but I kept at it.

It took me a few years to figure out that **DRAWINGS** become dynamic, like the spiral, by inviting an interaction between what the viewer already knows about and the lines in the drawing. Once we catch on to the metaphor, *we* bring it alive by projecting in our experience.

MANDALAS are graphic images organizing everything around a center point, and illustrate the unity of information. It is a Sanskrit word that means "archetype" or universal symbol, and indeed the circle is as close to one as I can find. They are definitely the hardest formats to work with, and the most complex to understand visually, since you have to understand all aspects of the information to see how it is unified.

INTEGRATE WORDS, SHAPES, & IMAGES

Of course a mandala, when viewed from far away, looks like a poster and tends to stand out! I thought this was a nice symmetry—create an octave of choices at the level of formats.

Combining Formats and Graphic Elements

My experience suggests that the basic choices in visual language, and many of the tools and methods described in this book, are about the big frames and formats that organize your display and show people how everything connects together. Once the base format is set (and to write anything on a sheet of paper you will have to choose one or another of the seven archetypal patterns) then the rest is about arranging words, images, and numbers in patterns that make sense, and doing it interactively with the other people in your meetings. This is the new world of tight integration of text and graphics . This is the basic arrangement for board games, computer games, and Lego blocks. In fact, little elements integrated by larger patterns of relationship that grow out of the way things move and interact is the way nature is organized on a grand scale. This feature of visualizing is so pronounced that Dave Gray, founder of Xplane, is writing a book on visualization with Sunni Brown called *Gamestorming*!

So this book isn't about teaching you to draw realistically with any particular skill, or to become a skilled designer, but to use the tools of visual language to reconnect with some deeply natural ways of working, and discover how the process of playing and evolving and doing versions of things—in short, working the way designers work—can unlock your meetings like almost no other process.

3. Four Easy Ways to Get Started

Personal Visualization, Napkins & Flipcharts, Graphic Templates, & Getting Others to Draw

There are many simple ways you can succeed with visual meetings right from the beginning. I've included samples of different kinds of things you can draw yourself and suggest to a group, even if you aren't the leader. It is important to have fun right from the beginning, and get a solid sense of how productive *and* creative working visually can be. This is the fastest way to fuel your imagination about what is possible in this way of working.

1. **Personal Visualization:** The best place to start learning about visual meetings is to have some with yourself—in a blank sketchbook or journal. Most people who really get hooked on working visually keep visual notebooks, and record their meeting and teleconference notes using text and graphics. (So do most people who are good at being creative.) The notebook work will get you over any inhibitions you have about making simple drawings and writing out notes. While you can disappoint yourself, having a meeting with yourself in a journal is a real no-lose proposition.

2. **One-on-Ones:** The next easiest place to begin is in one-on-one meetings, in a restaurant, or a pickup meeting at the office.
3. **Graphic Templates:** Another super easy way to get started is to use graphic templates. This is a term that is commonly used for large, visual worksheets, which are either tabletop or wall-sized. I'll show you some tried and true basics that you can copy and use immediately.
4. **Let Others Draw:** A final and very effective way to get started is to let other people do the drawings. I'll share a number of exercises that are great for getting people to jump right in.

Personal Visualization

In the previous chapter we looked at using journals to play around with drawing and developing some pictographs and ideographs. You might think of this as doodling, which is in fact a great way to free yourself up to be more expressive visually. Paul Saffo, a professional forecaster who has an eye for cool developments, likes to say "paper is brain interface." (He's an active journal keeper as well.) And that is what I've discovered. It's a way to see myself and see my own thinking—in short, to have a meeting with my inner voices. It is also a way to get completely comfortable just drawing or writing out whatever you are thinking. This is a good skill if you want to record what someone else is saying, even if your drawings are simple.

Warm-Up Exercises

Here are some warm-up exercises I've found very helpful:

Paper is brain interface.
Paul Saffo
Futurist

- **Doodle Faces:** Make a number of scribbles on a blank page, then go back and make little eyes and mouths when you see facelike shapes. You might see animals and other things as well. This activity will build up an awareness of how much we project our own understanding into our pattern seeking.
- **Spontaneous Drawing:** Start with a blank page and just begin to draw something. Build on what you started by letting it go to something else and something else, without in any way trying to direct it. While this is very easy and fun once you let yourself go, you might feel inhibited and afraid to make mistakes. Just let it go! No one is watching. Assume that all the wandering around has some meaning and ask your drawing to tell you what you are focusing on in your inner world.
- **Mind Mapping:** A popular way of mapping information is to start with a central idea

and then branch off key ideas linked to that central idea. Then branch off of those, letting your associations extend and extend. My wife sometimes begins poems this way, just associating words in a big branching network, and then writing the poem. I used this format to think out all the things I wanted to share in this chapter.

- **Spontaneous Writing:** This is like the drawing, except you write words. You might find it easier to write a question and then immediately write an answer without thinking about it. It might help to imagine talking with someone and asking the question, and then write down the answer from the other person as if they were there. If you can keep from stopping yourself when an idea arises you will be amazed at what starts coming through.

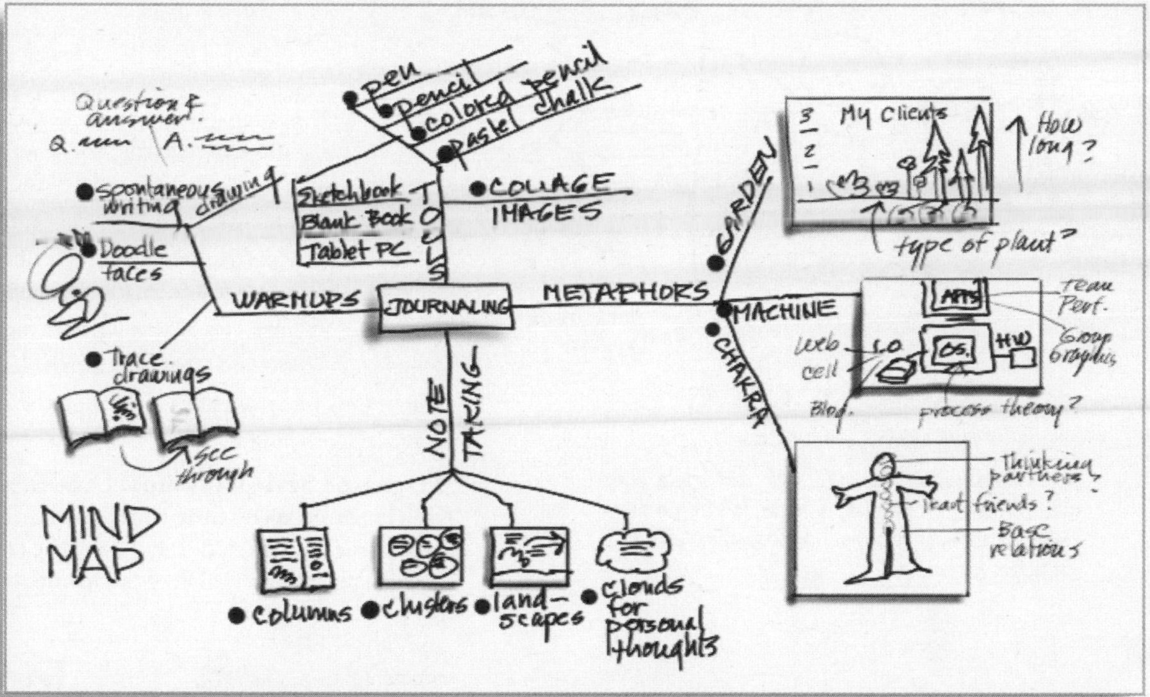

JOURNALING MINDMAP

This mind map was used to think through writing this chapter. Compare reading about these ideas in text with looking at the map and you'll start to feel what some of the differences are in the thinking supported by each.

- **Trace Drawings:** If you draw a picture on one page of a blank sketchbook you will probably be able to see a dim image of the drawing showing through on back side when you turn the page. Look at this shadowy image until you see something and then draw that out. Go for 3 or 4 pages and watch the image migrate. It's like dreaming with your eyes open.

- **Note Taking:** Using visual language to take notes is another very useful practice. By consciously trying different formats for note taking you can become aware of how your

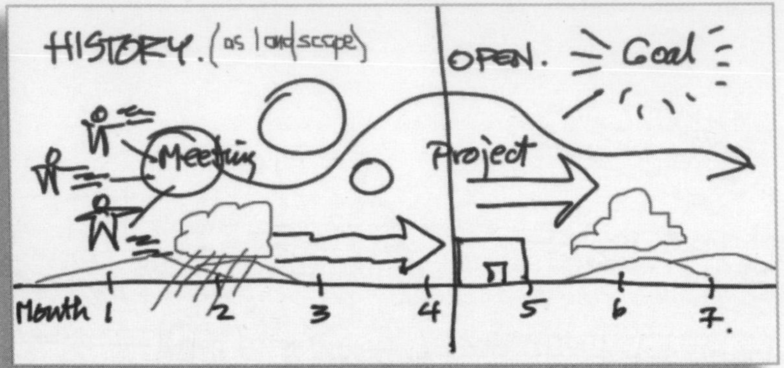

GRAPHIC HISTORY AS LANDSCAPE

A more elaborate kind of history than a peak and valley drawing is to create a whole landscape as you think through a project or something else that has a story over time.

listening is shaped by your intention and sense of pattern. Many of the frameworks shared in this book can be used for note taking, but some are very useful right away as a beginning kind of practice.

- **Landscapes:** Recording a time line like the one on this page this way means mapping your recording onto a landscape, creating a rough linkage between the information and different levels of the landscape. Real life, physical things, and people who are mentioned can be mapped on the ground. Concepts and ideas map into balloons and bubbles in the air. Projects and initiatives might look like planes flying through the air. Goals and visions might map along the top, looking like sunlight.
- **Magazine Style Columns:** Divide a page in half and take notes in columns. Record with lines of text and then, when you hear an image embedded in what people say, do a quick little drawing. It doesn't have to be crisp or accurate, just suggestive enough that you can remember. I think of this format as a magazine style of recording. It's a lot like the format that blogs and other online media are using for layout—basically text and graphics integrated.

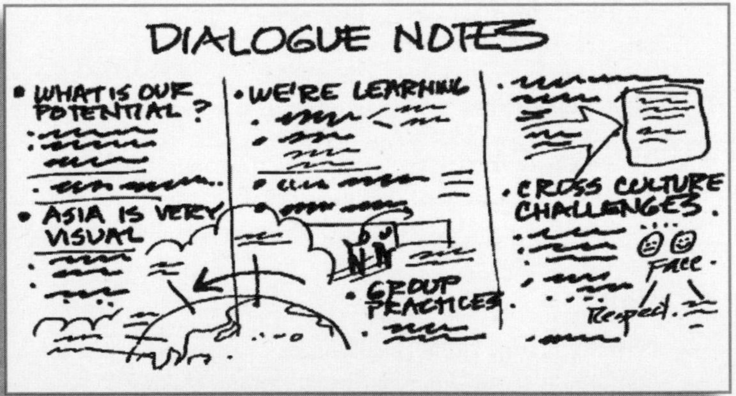

- **Clusters:** Use your journal or sketchbook to record what you hear in chunks of information that go together, rather than lists. Just space out the information and then overlay borders and clouds and divider lines when you see what goes together. I think of these kinds of drawings as "popcorn" drawings. You can practice different things like getting little headlines on each cluster in the same kind of printing, or drawing little icons and pictures when the information is highly visual.

Graphic Metaphors

A metaphor or analogy compares something you know with something you might not know. Have you ever compared your work environment to a circus or felt like your team activity was a hockey game, with the puck being a goal that changes all the time? A great deal of your thinking and a group's thinking is analogous. A recent *Harvard Business Review* article on strategy asserted that 80% of strategic thinking is analogous. We compare how our business runs to Southwest Airlines, for instance, and think about how we might innovate in our business process like they did and perhaps grow more profitable.

For your own practice and thinking, you can do metaphor workouts in a sketchbook. I've described two of my favorites here. Bear in mind that metaphors work if you understand them. If you don't you will then have two things you don't know about—the metaphor *and* what you are reflecting on. I'll expand on these ideas when we talk about using metaphors for idea mapping with groups. For now, just play around to gain insights for yourself.

- **Your Business as a Garden**: Draw a picture of your business or work as though your different clients or work relationships were types of plants. Look at the ones that are most fruitful and illustrate them as kinds of fruits trees of different sizes. Some are ornamental relationships, for image and such. Some are little quickies that don't last long, sort of like vegetables. Play around until you have illustrated all your primary relationships, and then

MY WORK AS A GARDEN

Imagine your clients as plants with different yields. Who are the flowers? Who provides fruit?

MY WORK AS A MACHINE

What is your operating system? What applications do you run?

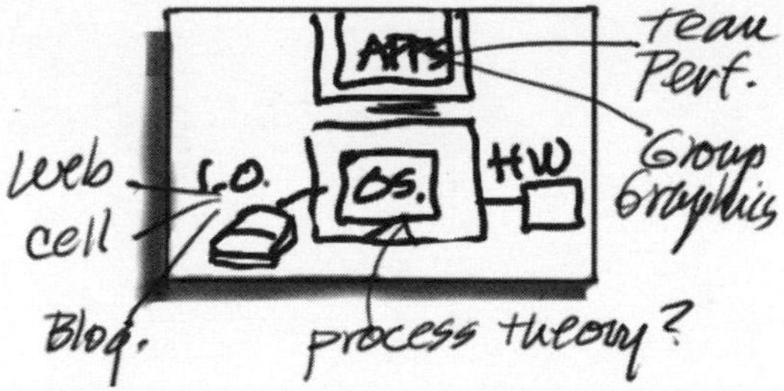

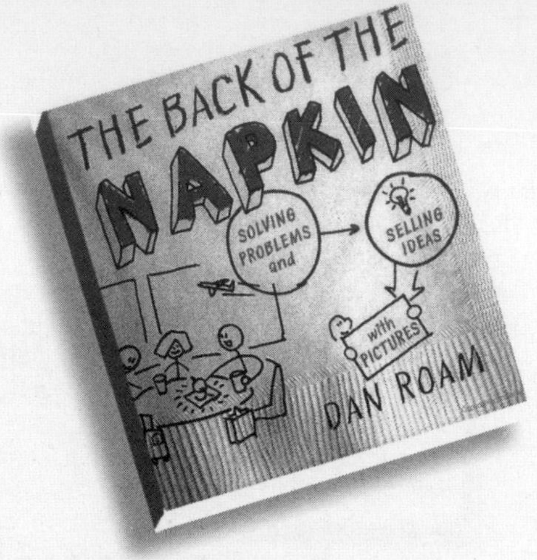

BACK OF THE NAPKIN

Dan Roam's book, *The Back of the Napkin: Solving Problems and Selling Ideas with Pictures, (Penguin, 2008)* is one of the best for showing how simple drawings can do all kinds of magical things to solve problems and sell ideas. He has an expanded edition, too.

think about the patterns that this reveals. If you want to be a little more analytical have the height of the trees indicate how many years you have been in each relationship.

- **Your Business as a Machine**: Pretend your work or business is a computer system. Identify the "operating system" — the core set of ideas that allows you to function (law? sales? design?). Think about the applications you run. These would be the services or methods you provide that have names. What are your input/output mechanisms—your marketing and sales connections? The printer could stand for physical outputs.

Napkins and Flip Charts

Once you are willing to pick up a pen and express yourself, then working one-on-one is a great way to begin experiencing the social power of visual meetings. It's great for things like initial sales calls, times when you are recruiting people to a new idea, meetings you have to discuss a new project, initial clients calls, and the like. These kinds of informal exchanges really come alive if you are willing to use visualizing as part of the conversation.

Just as with your personal journal, there are a handful of kinds of things where whipping out a pen and sketching your ideas or recording what the other person is saying would generate a lot of engagement and understanding.

- **Picture What Success Looks Like:** At the beginning of any project or process you are very likely to have a meeting with someone who is a sponsor or first mover who needs to orient you to what might happen. This is just the right time to pull out a pen and say "Let's draw a little picture of what this will look like when we are all completed and have been very successful." Move around so you are sitting where the other person can see what you are drawing and put a halo of auras around a space on the paper, as shown here. Then simply record a list or cluster of information as the two of you identify items. The halo and the blank space immediately frame the conversation toward the future and the imagination.

- **Picture How You Could Prevent Anything from Happening:** I remember having to lead a strategy meeting with a group of *very* skeptical engineers in a semiconductor company. They were being asked to rethink their operations and reengineer themselves. This was a directive from the top and they were in heavy resistance. I sensed this right away when I reviewed the stated outcomes and agenda for the meeting. So instead of going straight at the agenda, I stepped aside with a flip chart and drew a circle. I then drew some hollow arrows pointing at it. (They could be just line arrows.) Then I turned around and said, "Before we start let's talk a bit about all the ways we can ensure that nothing productive happens in the meeting or this process." I kept a straight face and waited. "We could avoid talking about it when we get back to work," someone said. I immediately wrote it down. "What else could we do?" I didn't give them time to think, and pretty soon we had 8 or 10 items and a lot of laughter. They realized I wasn't naïve about the challenges and the meeting was quite successful.

- **Brainstorm with Bubbles:** The human brain will automatically relate two or three items that are spaced out on a sheet of paper. When you are at the beginning of a project or meeting it's helpful to just identify all the little elements that might make up a successful meeting, and to illustrate these as a bubble chart rather than a list. It immediately activates comparative thinking and sets you up for a design conversation. The items don't have to be arranged in any particular order—just be readable.

- **Diagram a Meeting Design:** The seed shapes reviewed in Chapter 2 are perfect for diagramming out a meeting design. Use circles to indicate the actual meetings and breakout groups. Use squares to indicate documents that need to be produced. Hollow arrows can indicate projects that need to be completed but aren't meetings. Link them together as small and big circles with outputs across a time line, and record with bullet points the different things

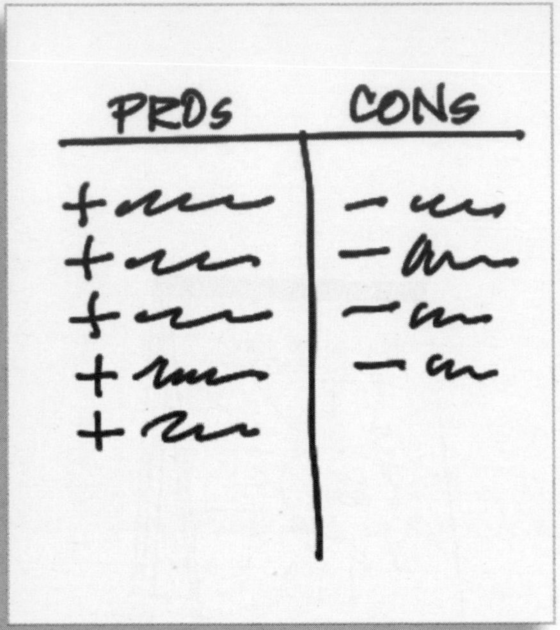

PROs & CONs CHART

The simplest templates are often the most powerful. This T bar graph can be used for many things, like a pros and cons list when looking at a decision. It is also used to do forced field analysis, looking at the forces supporting a change and resisting a change.

you need to do. This informal sketch really provides some traction for thinking.

- **Pros and Cons Chart:** A very simple graphic really helps in a case where someone is confused or uncertain about a decision to make. Make a simple "T" on your paper and label one side "pros" and the other side "cons," then list out everything the two of you can think of. Having the information formatted like this slows the process and lets the decided — be it you or the other person—think about things more holistically. The two lists side-by-side also provide a visual tool a bit like a balance scale. You can see right away which side seems easiest to fill out. That alone will start providing a clue as to which way to move.

Part II in this book focuses in on leading bigger meetings and getting full engagement through interaction, and Parts III and IV deal with simple ways to do larger format visualization. Bear in mind that these simple initial practices remain useful in bigger meetings as well. In graphic visualization, just as in music, the simple basic building blocks become the foundation for everything else, and remain the most useful. Creating simple action lists with people's names on a flip chart is as appropriate and effective a visualization format as you can find.

Simple Graphic Templates

As the use of visual meetings has spread, so has the use of pre-designed graphic templates—basically big worksheets on the wall. These lightly structured frameworks really focus a conversation. Some of the practices I suggest for journaling and one-on-one work are really templates. The peak and valley drawing I wrote about in the introduction is a very simple template. So is the Pros and Cons chart—the T diagram. So is the landscape drawing.

One way to begin getting results in visual meetings is to create a simple template before a meeting. Then have people fill it out using sticky notes or have someone record right on the chart. I was teaching a group of HR trainers in Singapore about these practices, and one had a big organizational learning meeting coming up right after the training. She wanted to engage everyone in thinking about how much he or she had learned about change. I suggested she create a simple template that listed her key questions and had spaces for people to add in information with sticky notes. A black and white version is shown here. The original was in full color and very evocative. She reported that it worked beautifully.

LARGE GROUP REFLECTIONS TEMPLATE

This simple template created by Wendy Wong, senior learning designer from the Civil Service College in Singapore, helped people at a large conference on organizational learning think about additional questions they might have. She simply created spaces for four sets of sticky notes. It was a very successful first venture. She took this picture with a digital camera.

Simple templates as discussion guides can work right away for the following kinds of meetings:

- **Brainstorms:** Where you have a couple of simple questions around which you want people to cluster information.
- **Agenda Planning:** The categories would be • outcomes, •participants, • potential activities, and • agenda.
- **Reflections on Learning:** The morning of the second day of a workshop, training, or off-site might start with people sharing what they learned. Make a template that has spaces for the different things covered in the first day. This is a good way to summarize.
- **Customer or Client Needs:** If you are in a sales or consulting situation you might work out a little template that has certain areas you'd like to know about. It might be things like • desired results, • experience in this area, • tools, • who is involved, and • challenges.

The variations on this theme are abundant. The practice is to think through your discussion area in advance, make a graphic template of the discussion areas, and then have the template help you focus the discussion. One of the advantages of this way of working is that you don't have to be linear in treating the subject. People can hop around between topics and you can hop around

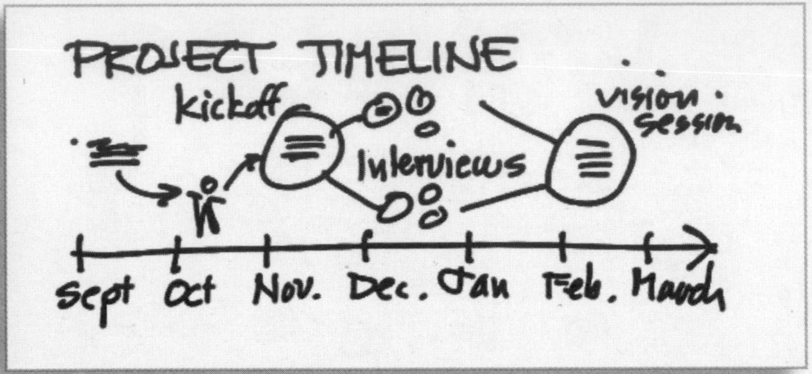

TIME LINES

Simple time lines get everyone to think about projects as a whole, and stretch their imaginations out beyond the immediate pressing issues.

with them, jotting notes or putting sticky notes in the appropriate areas. It also moves the conversation along, because as one area starts to fill people automatically begin to want to have things in the other areas.

More Simple Templates

There are several other kinds of simple templates that come up so frequently it's good to have some in your tool kit. They have a little more structure in the ways the information is arranged.

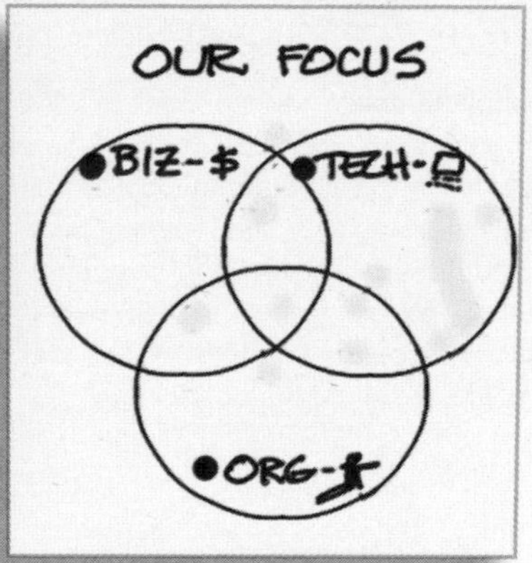

VENN DIAGRAMS

Venn diagrams guide attention into the ways different factors interact. They actually support a whole branch of mathematics.

- **Time Lines:** One of the simplest kinds of templates to use with a group is a simple time line. It is amazing how it changes the conversation to have a visual display of the total amount of time you are talking about. This would be used when you review a project, tell the story of a team, plan out activities for the year, or almost anything that involves time. If you focus on having a title that clearly expresses the purpose of the discussion (e.g., Our Team History), and make the measure clear (hours, days, months, years?), you can be off and running. If you use sticky notes everyone can get involved.

- **Venn Diagrams:** A way of lightly structuring a map that has clustered information is to use overlapping circles. These are technically called Venn diagrams and are associated with a kind of visual mathematics. But you don't have to know about that to see the value of sorting out what goes in one circle, what goes in the other, and what goes in the intersections. On this page is one that deals with common kinds of conversations.

- **Four-Box Models:** Where would a consultant be without four-box models? They are useful because they are so simple and powerful. They break people out of either/or thinking right away, and begin to suggest a range of things. Four-box models take two sets of variables and match them against each other to make four possibilities. They are used for

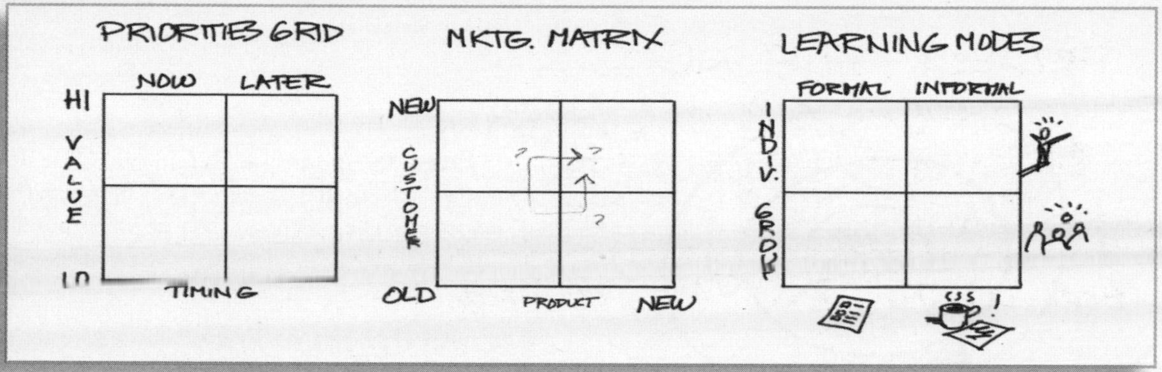

scenario planning, where you want to describe 3 or 4 different plausible futures, for priority making, for analyzing something systematically.

Here are several that are particularly useful. The first is a simple priorities grid. The second is a very common grid used to look at choices for which markets to address. The third looks at four areas where learning occurs in an organization. This kind of template can be as simple as the box and labels, or you can add little pictures to make it more provocative—such as the Learning Modes example here. These are great examples of the kind of fundamental formats that are consistently useful no matter how far along you are in leading visual meetings.

FOUR-BOX MODELS

These simple constructs compare two variables, and invariably spark interesting dialogue and insight. Most every consultant uses them regularly.

- **Time Block Agenda:** Whenever you are planning a meeting there are always constraints on the amount of time you will have. In advance of the meeting, make up a sheet that shows the overall amount of time, and then create marked off blocks of time that show graphically how long an hour or a half hour block would be. This spatial picture becomes the backdrop for figuring out how long you actually want to spend on each agenda item. If you plan a meeting by just listing agenda items, and not thinking about how long they will take, it's easy to keep having meetings that never make it through the agenda. The one shown on this page creates blocks for two A.M. blocks and two P.M. blocks, with breaks already marked in.

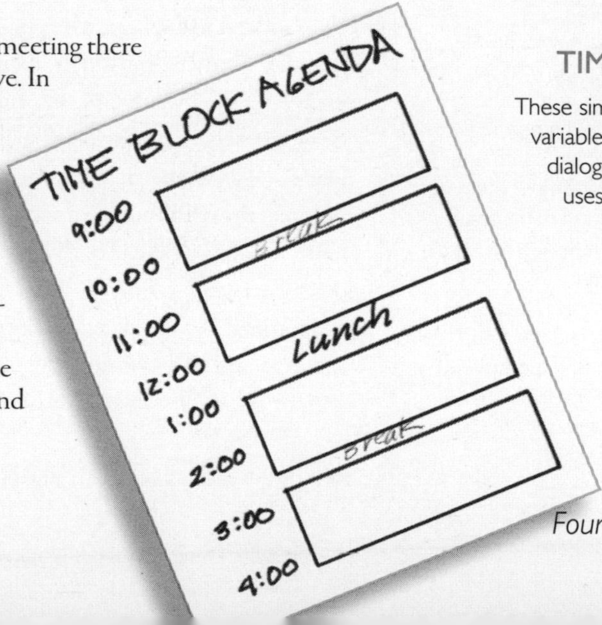

TIME BLOCK AGENDAS

These simple constructs compare two variables, and invariably spark interesting dialogue and insight. Most every consultant uses them regularly.

TARGET YOUR VALUES

I remember a client who wanted to have a good discussion of the values of the company. I made six targets with each of the six value words in the center of each. The issue was having people know what these meant and how they would be translated into action. So the first ring of the target was for the definition and the second ring was for examples of what that value would look like in action in the various different parts of the business. These displays supported a very engaged three-hour dialogue on the subject. The group naturally wanted to fill up all the little targets. The group could also see by where the most writing was where they are the most focused.

- **Targets:** Another simple template is one showing a series of circular rings. Targets like this can be used for a number of interesting things. Drawing circles is *very* easy if you use your arm like a compass and just "stir" around and around before you draw. (Chapter 2 shows you how.)

Getting Others to Draw

A fourth way to get started with visual meetings and have successes right away is to get the people in your meetings to do the drawings themselves! Working with sticky notes and simple templates has the value of getting everyone in on the act. But getting people to actually do drawings themselves invites them over into a different kind of brain-space. It's actually much easier to do than it might seem. Let me tell you two stories about this and you will see how it works.

I was invited to facilitate a meeting with a group of department heads in the City of Vancouver, British Columbia, early in my work as a consultant. They needed to plan for an international exposition that was happening and cooperate in the building of a special bridge and some other things that the city needed. The challenge in Vancouver is that it is the most desirable place to work in Canada because it is the warmest. So in many cases the department heads, once appointed, do everything in their power to stay there, and it leads to a culture of different "silos" and few occasions where they cooperate a lot. This may be different now, but that was the problem as described when I took the job. To break the ice with this group we gave them a simple drawing assignment. We divided them into three groups of five each, gave them large sheets of paper and markers, and said "compare the city of Vancouver to some kind of vehicle that carries people and/or goods, draw a picture of it, and label the different parts!"

We didn't make a big deal out of it, or emphasize the drawing part, or give them time to resist.

DRAW A VEHICLE

Here is one drawing from an assignment to "compare the city of Vancouver to some kind of vehicle that carries people and/or goods, draw a picture of it, and label the different parts!"

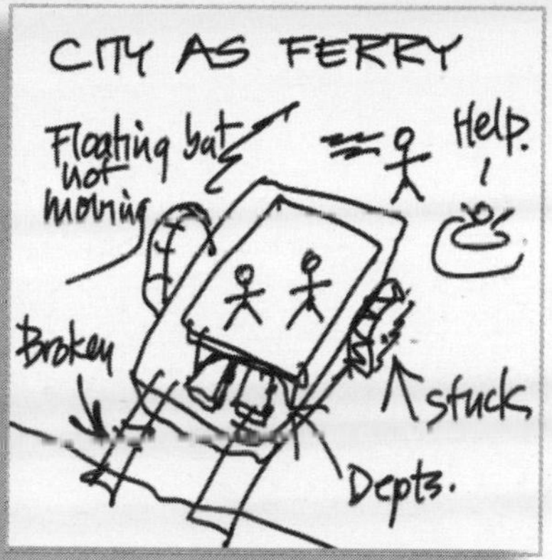

They were off in their groups before they knew it. When they came back they had three of the goofiest drawings. One was a broken down bus and one was some kind of ferryboat. But what I remember most is how hilarious the reports were. Because the exercise was basically impossible to get "right" or "correct" the participants went to humor. To get five people to agree on something in 30 minutes they had to just stumble around, and in the process began putting out all kinds of very true things, but in the form of odd little drawings and metaphorical jokes. By the time they were finished explaining why they drew their vehicles the way they did the meeting was well under way and was very successful.

PROCESS MAP

Here is a sample diagram of a process that has several meetings, represented by the circles. The squares are documents, the arrows are projects, and the bottom line illustrates some resources. My demonstration story at General Motors looked something like this. Each group could, from their drawings, no matter how messy, summarize their new plant story in about ten minutes, with a lot of detail, and no rehearsal.

Comparing New Plant Start-Ups at General Motors

A second early experience getting others to draw was with General Motors and a meeting of several dozen internal managers who were responsible for new plant start-ups (believe it or not, there was a time when Detroit was thriving). Again, this was when I was just starting in this business. It was only a one-day meeting and we needed to cover a lot of territory, and most importantly, share what they were learning from different specific projects. It wasn't a theoretical exercise.

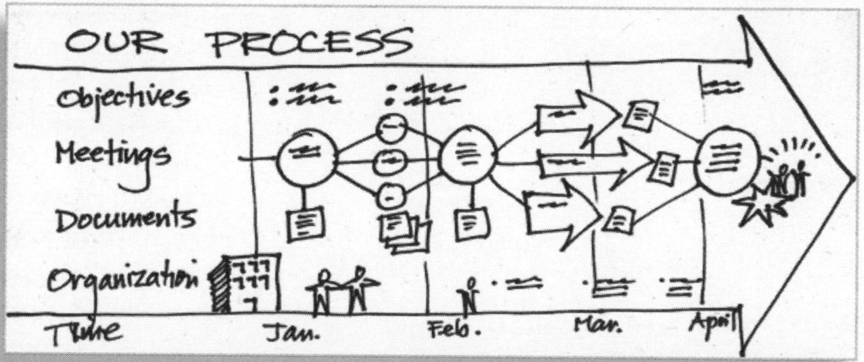

For this assignment I asked each breakout group to draw a time line, and then use very simple seed shapes to tell the story of how they started up the new operation. It looked like the process map shown here. I sketched it out on a large chart using simple squares to represent buildings and reports. I used a simple hollow arrow to represent projects. I showed them how to draw a star person (as described in Chapter 2) for people. And I suggested circles for meetings. "Just tell the story chronologically and make notes about the important steps," I said. I gave them about 45 minutes each to do this. I remember that they came back with five or six of the messiest drawings I'd ever seen, but they were all rough time lines, and they sort-of used the symbols I'd showed them. But what happened next really convinced me of the power of this way of working. Each group could, from that drawing, no matter how messy, summarize their new plant story in about ten minutes, with a *lot* of detail, and no rehearsal. I barely touched a pen.

I personally get very excited thinking that this is a way of working that gets results right from the start, and then has virtually no limit on how far you can extend and apply its methods.

By this time you should have a lot of ideas of how you can get great results with visual meetings without any particular skill at drawing and without being a skilled facilitator. I wrote earlier that leading visual meetings is a bit like playing music. Some are simple sing-alongs with music everyone knows. That is what it is like doing a four-box model with sticky notes. You can also think of a meetings like playing jazz. There is a theme, and some different parts, and you are all committed to playing together and improvising. Musicians need to agree to the key they will play in, and the speed and tempo, and the melody line, but much of the rest is made up. And you can have meetings that are like orchestral music and operas. This takes a lot more design and thinking. Everyone needs to be singing from the same score. I personally get very excited thinking that this is a way of working that gets results right from the start, and then has virtually no limit on how far you can extend and apply its methods.

As this book progresses, I suggest more and more things you can do on top of the basics we've considered in this first section. If you feel the ideas are getting too complicated, skip to the back and look for resources you might engage. If they are too simple read on ahead. However, none of the ideas I share require serious drawing ability or professional facilitation experience. They are all things you can suggest, jump in, and be pretty assured of getting a much more productive result than if you didn't work visually.

II. Engaging Groups & Building Rapport

Why Visual Listening Is So Compelling (& Easy!)

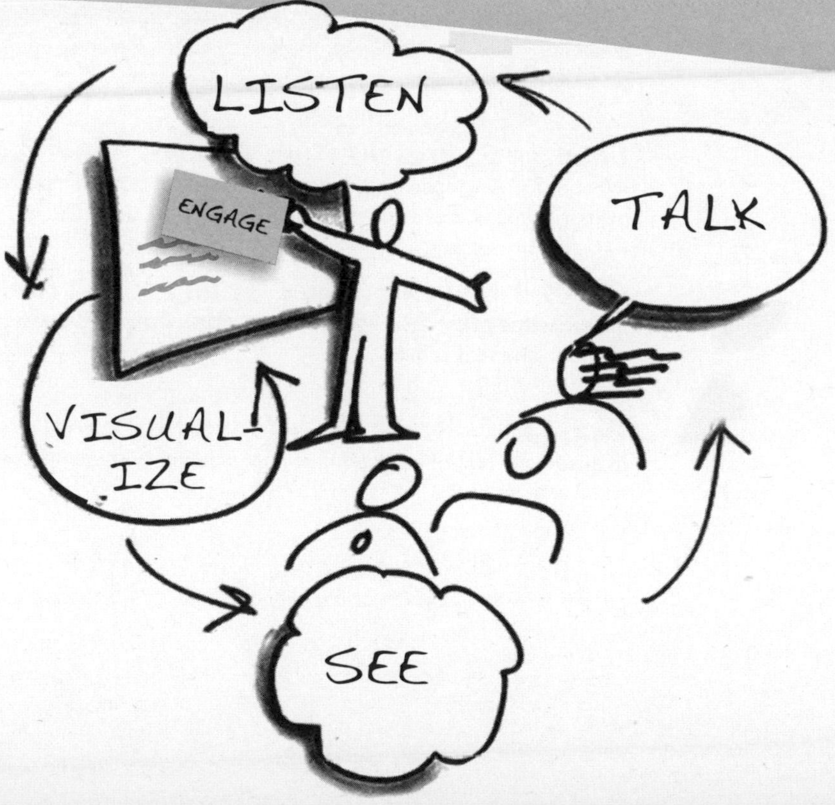

II: Engaging Groups & Building Rapport

Part I described what is possible with visual meetings. This section is focused on the process of really engaging people, the key to truly productive meetings. If people can fully connect with what they are doing, own the outcomes and support implementing whatever ideas they come up with, you and whoever is relying on the results from your meetings will be very happy.

Chapter 4: Getting People Involved Participating in the graphics; why hand-drawn is so engaging; establishing rapport by listening; graphic recording for high engagement; rules of recording; rooms as statements; being receptive.

Chapter 5: Presentation without PowerPoint What pushes? What pulls?; using open metaphors; power of sticky notes; simple templates; freeway maps, geographic maps, and idea maps; when to make murals.

Chapter 6: Consulting & Selling with Graphics Drawing on the same side of the table; agenda planning kits; pitching new bosses; selling consulting; services; discovery processes.

Chapter 7: Hands-On Information Ways of collecting the notes; how to analyze for patterns; practicing in small meetings and agenda design; combining sticky notes and templates.

Chapter 8: Using Images & Interaction Collage; visioning; using picture cards in dialogue; working with cards; sand tray work for organizations.

4. Getting People Involved

Using Pictures to Interact

I remember the first time I really connected with the power of visual meetings to engage people. I was leading a seminar for a group of young people participating in the Coro Fellowship for Public Affairs. They were all placed in internships in different government agencies in San Francisco. One was with the mayor's office, one in city planning, one with the police and so forth for 12 assignments. The founders of Coro believed that people learn best when fully immersed in their own experiences, making sense out of things themselves. As a result staff were not allowed to lecture or present, but could facilitate discussions.

I had gone through the program myself in Los Angeles in 1965 and it had been an incandescent year of learning. Now I was on the staff and wasn't able to be out on assignments. I really wanted to find out what was going on and was impatient with our Friday seminars turning into storytelling sessions that didn't seem to have much depth. One person would talk, then another would tell a different kind of story, basically sharing time, but not really focusing down on anything, and changing topics a lot.

One day I decided to change the way we met. I wanted the Fellows to understand the overall system of government and talk about all the power relationships. I didn't know how we could do this without literally seeing it. So I hung up two long rolls of paper—in this case the end rolls of newsprint. In the early days of working visually we discovered that newspapers couldn't run the newsprint rolls right down to the cardboard core or they would have to rethread the presses. As a result, every newspaper had a supply of roll ends that had one to two inches worth of newsprint paper. Schools would collect these regularly. We found a supply for times we needed flip chart paper. (Now with plotters using large paper most art stores have 3' and 4' wide roles of lightweight, white paper.)

Friday seminars turning into storytelling sessions that didn't seem to have much depth.

The double row was impressive. I had 8 feet of height and about 16 feet of width. I was intending to get a full picture of what was really going on, and interview the information right out of the Fellows. I started very simply. "What's your assignment?" I asked one. "Chief administrative office," she answered. I drew a box about two feet by two feet on the chart. I had her describe a little of what the office is responsible for and guess how many employees. I then asked another of the Fellows where he was placed. "The department of public works," he said. "Is this part of the chief administrative office?" I asked. "Yes," was the response. "How big is it in comparison?" The Fellow thought that it was about one-third the size of the whole so I made a second box inside the first one about one-third as big as the first one and labeled it "DPW." The next person was at the police department, but it was separate from the CAO under its own commission. I proceeded through all 12 assignments until I had boxes all over the big chart that were roughly the size of the number of employees. In the process I had each person say a little about what the different part of the city government did.

MAPPING CITY GOVERNMENT

A Coro Fellowship in Public Affairs seminar transformed when we cocreated a large diagram of all the city agencies and where the Fellows had assignments.

We then looked outside the assignment agencies and began to map some of the other critical units of government. The Fellows had gaps in what they knew, but I wasn't really concerned about that. We were going for the most influential ones and not all the detail. I kept asking questions. I put a symbol in each box where one of the Fellows had a placement. I then began to ask about how the different departments related to each other. I drew heavy lines between parts that worked directly together and dotted lines where there was more of an informational relationship.

Once we had the big diagram we started talking about power. Which of the agencies led others? Were some more consistently in the lead? Who inside the agencies actually had the power to make decisions? Was there a difference between positional power and informational power? During this discussion I stopped recording and we just began sharing what we knew about how the whole system worked.

We'd started working around 9:00. I looked at my watch after a while and it was 11:45! We had gone for nearly three hours without any break at all. Everyone was completely engaged in the discussion and the giant diagram we had cocreated. It wasn't especially elegant or tightly organized, but it had a *lot* of information in one place and we had all seen it go up, so we understood it.

I knew from that day on that this visual way of working was very different from just sitting in a seminar and talking. Giving people a chance to talk is assuredly a key to engagement, even without graphics. But with the visuals we were suddenly having a discussion we hadn't had before, and talking about systems dynamics in a quite sophisticated way—all because we had cocreated the big map. I do not believe it would have been the same discussion if we had been working off a large organization chart that was prepared ahead of time. I believe the act of struggling through the creation of this picture was essential to the level of engagement we enjoyed.

I knew from that day on that this visual way of working was very different from just sitting in a seminar and talking.

Why Are Hand-Drawn Graphics so Engaging?

Pictionary is a fun game where teams compete to guess what a word or concept is from a drawing that their partner makes on a small sheet of paper. A word or concept is drawn from a deck of cards, and each person who is one of the drawers on the team begins to scribble furiously, to communicate the essence of the idea to his or her buddy. If you have ever played this game you will realize quickly it isn't about drawing nicely. In fact a person who spends too much time on the drawing doesn't win. It's about pointing symbolically at what people already know.

Tattoo this principle on your inner brain: "People are more engaged by things that are suggestive than by things that are crystal clear."

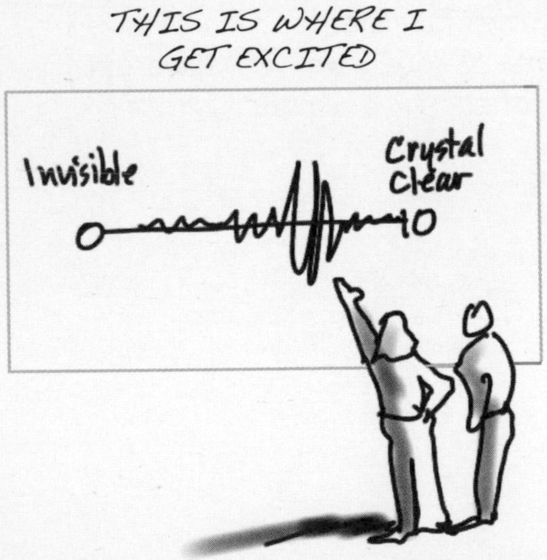

Because our brains are hardwired to detect patterns and fill in the details from what we know already, much of what we see is a "projection." We are literally adding in all the parts we don't see directly, once we figure out what the drawing is about. We do the same thing with language. When you are listening some of your attention is on anticipating what will be said next.

The phenomenon of filling in patterns from small clues is universal across ages and cultures. It is also the reason that hand drawings have such high engagement. Tattoo this principle on your inner brain: "People are more engaged by things that are suggestive than by things that are crystal clear." By engaged I mean paying full attention, looking and scanning, listening deeply, wondering what will come next. When patterns are only partly clear, or emerging in the act of drawing, everyone is riveted on trying to predict what will come next.

Purpose and Trust Come First in Meetings

When people come together in a meeting, be it face-to-face or virtual, there is a predictable pattern of engagement. Jack Gibb, a researcher on group process, worked with organization development consultants Marvin Weisbord and Alan Drexler in the 1960s to formulate a team building model that described this process. According to their research the first question people have is "Why are we here?" This is all about imagining the purpose of the gathering. The second is "Who are you," and an inner question of "what might you be asking of me in this meeting." This is about trust. Then we ask the third question, "What are we doing?" Eventually we ask, "How are we going to do it."

The model asserts that people only progress as they get their questions answered, and back out of the process if they don't. You can infer from this that the key to getting people involved would be to help them answer these questions. The big takeaway here is that humans need to answer the social, emotional questions about working with other people before we can completely focus on the thinking and other work involved.

The engagement process starts even before people come into a meeting room or virtual meeting space. This is the period when everyone is imagining why he or she is having another meeting and wondering who else is coming. In Chapter 1 I included some suggestions for visualizing the purpose of meetings and providing space for people to get oriented even before they gather together. If the name of the meeting points at the purpose in a general way, and a list of outcomes also suggest what is going to be discussed, most people will formulate some story about why they are participating before they even get in the room. The way we understand general statements is to link them with our personal experience. This is a type of involvement, and a standard technique for public speakers, ministers, and politicians.

As soon as people come in the room or enter the virtual meeting space the next question is "Who is there?" Most people are busy feeling each other out and trying to answer the "Who are you?" question early on in any meeting with newcomers. Gibb's research suggests that people revisit this concern every time they come back from a break. Engagement involves our emotions and gut feelings, but isn't just about liking or not liking people. If you work in a business that is running lean and have way too much work to do, going to a meeting can be a tricky affair. You just might get more work! If people are unsure of each

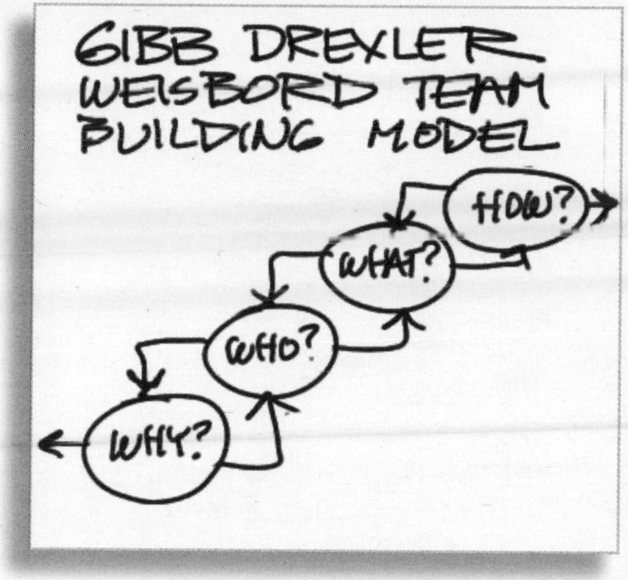

TEAM PROCESS

The progression of stages in group work is well researched in the work of Jack Gibb. Can you see the metaphor built into this model that ends up framing how people think about teams? If you notice a resonance between the little model being used to structure this book and this team model you would be correct. This is a deeply rooted pattern in humans.

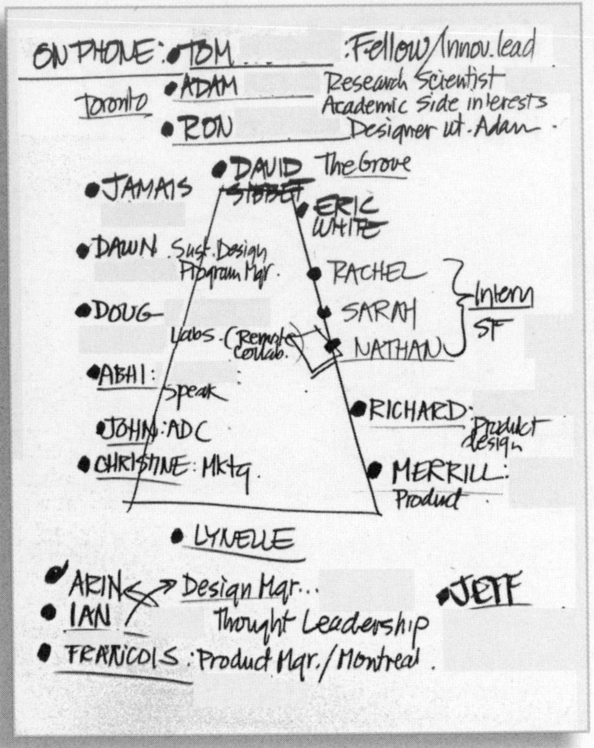

GROUP PORTRAIT

Simple seating charts help everyone get oriented to who is in the meeting.

other or what might be asked of them, the easiest thing to do is to just hide out and not participate actively, or maybe even sneak doing e-mail on a smart phone. If people are on a web conference or teleconference, they have even more chances to disengage and multitask. In community meetings and polarized political situations good engagement becomes even more critical.

Establish Rapport by Listening First, Telling Later

Salespeople know that establishing rapport is a process of showing people you care about what *they* are thinking and interested in and avoiding the temptation to dominate with what you are trying to sell them. It is the same with any kind of other meeting. Listen first and ask for something later. And in a meeting, people want to have a chance to engage in a way that gives them meaningful answers to who else is in the room and what their interests might be.
As a result, facilitators like myself have developed a number of tried and true ways of doing this. Let me describe some of my favorites that you can do:

- **Create a Group Portrait on a Big Mural**: Before people come into a meeting or during the part when everyone is gathering create a bird's eye picture of the tables where people will be sitting on a big chart and put circles where people might be sitting. As the meeting begins ask people to introduce themselves, and go around the chart writing people's names in the circles where they are sitting, and writing down their jobs and whatever else they share. You will have to ask people to spell their names to get them right. You will make mistakes. There will be laughter and it will slow things down, but everyone will be appreciative that you are willing to serve the group by giving them time to figure out who everyone is! This process works just as well on a tablet computer in a web conference.

- **Ask Imaginative Questions:** Add to the preceding exercise a key question that you think would be relevant. For a group that knows itself well it might be a question like "Share something with the group no one knows." This gets everyone involved in wondering what he or she does and does not know about the others. For new groups it might be a question about everyone's favorite activity or vacation place. For a team that will be together awhile you might ask people to share what strengths or gifts they bring to the team, and let everyone brag a little. Remember, if people can figure out the pattern too quickly or assume they already know something, their attention moves to what they don't know—so keep people a little puzzled in order to involve everyone.

- **Have a Weather Report:** A fun way to use sticky notes to start a meeting is to pass them out and ask everyone to write down what kind of weather represents how they feel right now. Are they "sunny and bright," or "fogbound," or "rainy," or "blustery." This is a whimsical kind of thing to do, and assuredly no one is an expert at this process so it will provoke humor, and set up a very engaging field of energy. Everyone will be wondering what the next person will say, and how much he or she might reveal.

- **Graphic Log-Ins:** When people log onto a website they are often asked to answer some basic questions. A great way to get people involved in a bigger conference is to have a large wall dedicated to "logging into" the conference. Create a wall with little monitor-sized squares all over it. When people arrive ask people their name and print it out in the squares, along with their company and title. Then ask, "What is the hottest question you have regarding this topic?" Record the hot topics in red so you can scan all the little squares and see what everyone was most interested in. People invariably hang around the log-in wall reading and introducing themselves to each other.

Each of these activities is similar in that it doesn't involve any presenting, but engages everyone in adding something into the meeting early. Speaking up is a type of engagement, and if everyone gets a chance to add their voice into the meeting at the very beginning the chances of high engagement are much stronger.

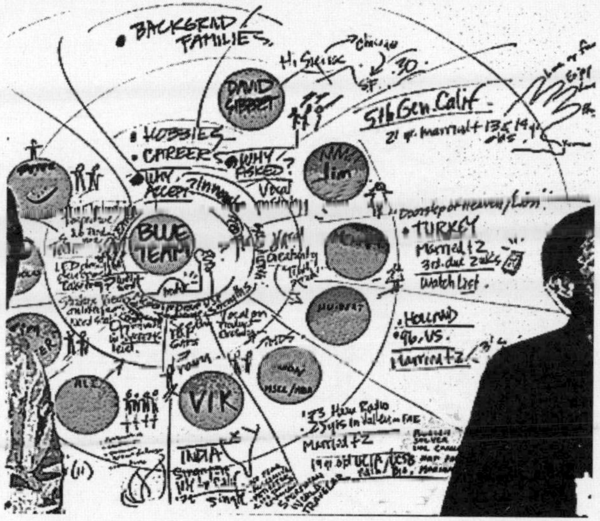

GRAPHIC "LOG-INS"

Teams in an innovation workshop used a target template to "log in" to their assigned team. They shared information that would help them relate to each other over the course of three days of work.

THE RECORDING EFFECT

This cycle predictably and powerfully engages not only the people talking, but other participants who are tracking the connections between what people say and what is recorded.

Graphic Recording for High Engagement

This book is focusing on things you can do if you are not a professional graphic recorder or facilitator. But graphic recording is such a tried and true involvement strategy it's worth considering even if you aren't practiced at it, because it signals so clearly that you are listening and that you heard someone.

The little drawing on this page illustrates what is going on during graphic recording that makes it so involving. Let's look at the process a little more deeply.

When people talk in a meeting, either face-to-face or on a teleconference, one can assume they want to connect and be heard. For sure there are some compulsive talkers who just like the sound of their voice coming out, but most people are well-intentioned. In meetings that aren't visual at all, the only feedback a person gets is the look on people's faces or the way they move their bodies. Now, this signals quite a bit for sure, but anyone who goes to a lot of meetings gets pretty good at not being overreactive. It's pretty hard to know whether you are getting across.

To make things more complicated, it's not that unusual to have someone start to talk right after you finish, about something completely different, with little or no verbal acknowledgment that they heard what you said. This is because people are often rehearsing what they are planning to say while they are listening, and really didn't pay that much attention. No wonder meetings bounce all over the place.

Now imagine a meeting where someone is graphically recording. In a smaller meeting, where this is most effective, and everyone can see the chart where the recording is taking place, a person will talk and the person at the flip chart or template will be listening. After a little lag they start to write or draw something. Now the ratio between what a person can write and how much a person can say is about 1:6 or 1:8 on a good day. This means that the chance of the person recording everything is impossible, but they do get something!

The speaker, if the recorder isn't standing in front of what they wrote, will look at the material and get feedback right away about what got through. This then will shape what they say next, emphasizing things that didn't get recorded, or going on if they see that the recorder got the right idea.

Other people who are listening hear what the speaker said, and then see what the recorder creates a bit later. The pattern-finding mind wants to connect these and begins to try and do that. Whether the recording is relevant and accurate or not, people are drawn into paying a *lot* more attention, and literally getting stirred up in the process. If the recorder misses something there is an impulse to fill it in or correct it. This is an impulse to engage. If the recorder hits the mark and gets what they think is the essence, then they can mentally feel good about seeing the connection.

I invariably experience people engaging a great deal with graphic recording if it takes place as an integral part of the meeting. The key to getting this effect is to get up and do the listening visually, whether it's a polished job or not. If you don't apologize, and let people see what you are doing, they will begin guiding you, repeating when necessary, emphasizing, or even telling you what to draw. And they are completely engaged.

If you follow the rules for recording on the next page you will get good results.

DID I GET THIS RIGHT?

● OUTCOMES

◆ TAKE TIME TO REFLECT ON LEADERSHIP & OUR OWN INVOLVEMENT.

RULES FOR RECORDING

This graphic recording was done during a reflections period on the second day of a Leadership retreat. Each person's comment got some kind of acknowledgment.

- ❑ Use CAPS for TITLES & EMPHASIS & lower case letters for supporting points.
- ❑ Use images for emphasis.
- ❑ Capture key words and use their words, not yours.
- ❑ Write big enough for everyone to read.

- ❑ Use earth colors for text—blue, green, black, and brown.
- ❑ Use bright colors for highlighting—orange and yellow.
- ❑ Use red to emphasize items that require immediate attention or action such as next steps, deadlines, and tasks.
- ❑ Let speakers see what you are writing. Check the accuracy of your recording by inviting participants to give input.
- ❑ Use bullets consistently to indicate new streams of thought.
- ❑ Line bullets up vertically.
- ❑ Leave margins for side comments and polling.
- ❑ Leave space between lines.
- ❑ Overlay circles and lines if the group wants to pop out key information upon review.
- ❑ Number your charts for later reference.

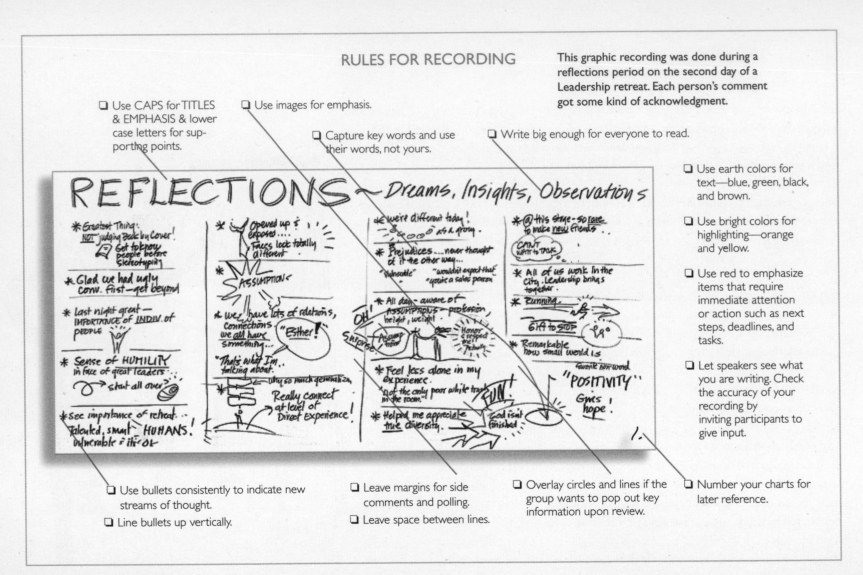

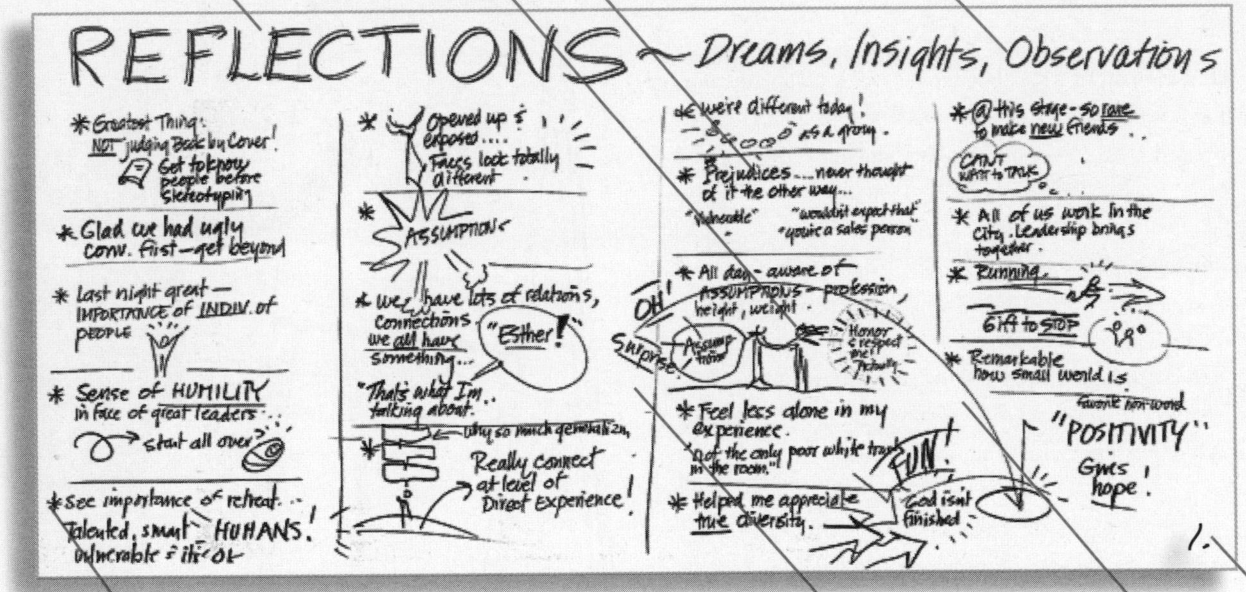

When to Use Graphic Recording

Graphic recording isn't necessary all the way through a meeting. But there are some critical times when recording is exactly the right thing to do. Here is a checklist for times when you might volunteer to record, or plan to record as the meeting leader.

- Listing meeting goals and outcomes. These are good to keep posted.
- Recording expectations of a workshop, special event, or customer meeting
- Creating a group portrait with key information
- Brainstorming options where you need a list of all the choices
- Recording action proposals
- Listing pros and cons during a decision meeting
- Summarizing learning
- Listing persons responsible for followthrough

It is, of course, possible to have recording going on all during a meeting, but it's particularly effective for the kinds of things listed here. Ask yourself, "What would be useful to have up on the wall the rest of the meeting as a reference?" These are the things to visualize.

Using Imagery to Engage

Cognitive scientists agree that our brain processes imagery with different parts than we process language. For most people the left side of the brain is the location of language processing and the right side for imagery. An amazing story about this is Jill Bolte Taylor's *My Stroke of Insight,* a

BLOCKS TO ENGAGEMENT

There are some things you can do without thinking that stand in the way of getting a lot of positive engagement. Here are some of the things to avoid.

- ❑ Substituting your words for theirs
- ❑ Refusing to write because you don't agree
- ❑ Writing so small no one can read it
- ❑ Standing in front of what you write
- ❑ Getting too involved doing a cute drawing
- ❑ Talking back and taking over the conversation
- ❑ Getting upset when people tell you what to record
- ❑ Going too slow and getting way behind

Ask yourself, "What would be useful to have up on the wall as a reference throughout our meeting?"

book she wrote after having a stroke on the left side of her brain that left her unable to process language in normal ways. She has a PhD in neuroscience and was unusually equipped to observe what was happening. Her talk at the 2008 TED conference was a sensation. The sensibility she experienced of having only her right brain working was of a sense of wholeness, connection, and transcendence. She concludes from her experience that all humans have this capability, and that when we work with both sides of our brain fully engaged we have many more chances to engage and work through our difficulties than if we just work with our analytical left brains.

If a key part of engaging people is to engage all the faculties people bring to a meeting, and honoring both the left and right sides of our selves as Dr. Taylor advocates, then using imagery is more than important, it is essential to having a chance at balance and wholeness.

Coro, the public affairs training organization I mentioned earlier, has a very special selection process that is a full day of competitive individual and group interviews. But the whole process begins with sharing a simple image, in the form of some object that has real meaning for the candidate. People will bring keepsakes, bicycles, books, hiking gear—any manner of thing. They have one minute to tell a brief story about what they brought and why it is important. I've been amazed as a judge how engaging this process is, and how memorable.

Several sources are now creating whole packets of evocative photographic and drawn images that are designed for use when facilitating high engagement processes. I describe these in more detail in Chapter 8.

You don't necessarily need prepared cards. I ran a management meeting one time at Old Navy where everyone was asked to bring a picture of his or her family. The introductory activity

PROVOCATIVE IMAGES ENGAGE

Before written books, indigenous people such as the American Indians used imagery to remember their philosophy of life and engage young people in opening up to the natural world. The hawk symbolized, for many tribes, the messenger bird because of its call, and was often associated with the East, the place of the rising sun, vision, and new possibility. I made this paper model of one and have it in my studio as a reminder to look inside for the new messages from my intuition. Having people bring images like this to a meeting —perhaps symbolizing the gifts they bring—can open a group right up.

involved everyone sharing this picture along with a story. Old Navy is a very family-oriented, fun-loving culture, and this was a perfect engagement activity for its planning event. The room came to life in an instant!

Rooms as Graphic Statements—Visualizing Who Is Who

Meeting rooms and how they are arranged is itself a visual statement and part of what can be used to engage people in a meeting. A number of very active get-to-know-you exercises use rooms as spatial displays in 3-D. These work for any size group, but are especially good for larger meetings.

- **Using Rooms as Maps:** Use a room of furniture, or pull back the tables and declare that one wall is north, its opposite south, and the other walls are east and west. Then explain the borders. I've seen this done with a region, a state, or the country as a whole. Once people are oriented have people go to where they live and introduce themselves to the others who are nearby. Then have people move to where they work and do the same thing. Then move to where they like to go on vacation. This kind of activity is guaranteed to get everyone involved.

- **Using Rooms as Mental Models:** Imagine the room being a big four-box model, and describe the axes. I was in a conference where Art Kleiner was giving a presentation on "who matters" in an organization. His research suggested that organizations make decisions based on making

life wonderful for the people who matter. In a follow-up workshop he had people organize themselves in the room where one axis was how big your organization was, from one to thousands, and the other axis was the percentage of time in your entire career that you had been "someone who mattered" in the organization, based on his definition. The resulting arrangement was a powerful graphic image that drove the rest of the exchange.

- **Physical Graphing:** My colleague Ed Claassen and I were training a multinational group in China in team performance and Ed wanted people to appreciate that everyone has different work styles, and demonstrated an activity that they could use with their teams to explore this. He had people line up on several spectra that he defined. First he asked everyone to line up by what part of the day from early morning to late evening they felt they were at their best. When people had sorted themselves out they all looked around. There were ohs, ahs, and laughter as people began to recognize their colleagues. He then asked them to line up based on whether they like to initially work on problems by themselves before engaging others, or like to talk with others at the very beginning. Again there was laughter and recognition. He then asked them to line up if they felt comfortable working with a single focus on one end, or multitasking on another. The possibilities for this kind of "graphing" are numerous, and very involving.

PHYSICAL GRAPHS

Ask people in your meeting to line up based on different kinds of things:

- ❏ Youngest ———————— Oldest
- ❏ Early Risers ———————— Night Owls
- ❏ Finish Early ———————— Just in Time
- ❏ Collaborate ———————— Work Alone
- ❏ Extraverted ———————— Introverted

On Being Truly Receptive

Visualization provides many great excuses for having listening and participation occur early in a meeting. But underlying any of these tools or methods is a more fundamental element, which is what happens to people when they are with others who are truly open and receptive. Humans are very attuned to each other, and pick up on tones of voice and facial expressions at very subtle levels. There are some people who are excellent at faking interest, but most people "leak" their feelings and attitude in things like body posture, rhythms of speech, and other signals.

If you are disinterested, disrespectful, or worst, actually contemptuous of the people you are working with, any of the processes I'm describing could fail. On the other hand, you will be amazed at how people open up if you are truly interested in what they have to say, believe that each person carries his or her own wisdom, and are willing to serve their sharing it by choosing activities that give people space to show up on their own terms in ways that foster listening,

I SALUTE THE GOODNESS IN YOU

Visualization can help you get to this state of receptivity. Many meditative disciplines incorporate this principle. The Tibetans, for instance, have stories about a mythical race of fighters called the Shambala Warriors. They were renowned for their skills and ability to avoid conflict. A core principle was "looking for the rising sun in every opponent." By this they meant looking for the inherent goodness that all people carry, even if 99% of what they were seeing was the darkness before the dawn. According to their myths the opponents would simply lose the will to fight as they entered this field of attention. I read about this story in *The Shambala Warrior* by Chogyam Trumpa Rinpoche and it touched me deeply at one point in my life. I began experimenting with visualizing the rising sun coming up in people's chests as I talked with them. It began to transform my listening.

My own experience suggests it's a trap to assume that technique and tools will solve problems for you if your intention and attitude aren't aligned. Inviting people into their full brains is inviting them into myths, dreams, stories, and visions as well as their judgment, analysis, facts, and problem-solving selves. Our inner worlds are precious things to people, and the ones that animate us aren't shared lightly. To the extent you want to be a part of engaging people deeply and fully with imagery, you will yourself be invited into a journey of reflection and self-discovery.

Keeping this in mind let's go more deeply into some of the techniques for applying high engagement to different meeting settings.

5. Presentation without PowerPoint

Simple Drawings & Graphic Templates

Presentation software, led by the omnipresent PowerPoint, has supported the explosion of visualization in business. "Slides" are almost a required tool for communications in many organizations. People plan with them, sell with them, present with them, and e-mail them to one another all over the world. The easy-to-use graphic tools in presentation software have invited legions of users into visual thinking and visual presentation. And it has led them into some very serious traps if you want truly engaged meetings.

One of the best books on how to use this kind of software is Nancy Duarte's *Slideology.* Nancy designed Al Gore's slide show on global warming . Her company does work for dozens and dozens of the best companies in Silicon Valley. She knows this medium. And bottom line in her advice is to use its power of imagery and simple support for powerful storytelling. Done well, visual presentations in this medium are unmatched in stimulating the imagination of audiences.

PowerPoint Is Push, Not Pull

For all its virtues and flexibility, presentation software in the hands of most people is not a good medium for deeply engaging people, for at root it is a "push" medium. What do I mean by this? In The Grove's facilitation training one of the key principles we teach is having people who lead meetings understand the energy dynamics of groups—they way they move and what motivates people to get involved or pull away from participation. We use a simple model called the "Push/Pull" model to demonstrate the root dynamic. It's a more common language way of talking about a very deep assumption in Eastern philosophy about the yin/yang nature of all existence.

A "push" is anything that asserts itself into a situation, and changes things by adding content, form, rules, guidance, structure, or asking for a decision. In workshops we have facilitators in training stand face-to-face and have one partner push on the other physically, and notice what

POWERPOINT CRITIQUE

If you want to look at the shadow side of overusing presentation software, one of the foremost authors on information design, Yale professor Edward Tufte has written a very engaging analysis on the subject called *The Cognitive Style of PowerPoint®: Pitching Out Corrupts Within*. (Googling "Powerpoint, Tufte" will bring it up right away.)

PEOPLE FEEL *PUSHED* BY....

- ❑ Instructions
- ❑ Dense content
- ❑ Predesigned formats
- ❑ Confrontation & attacks
- ❑ Decisions
- ❑ Evaluation
- ❑ Proposals

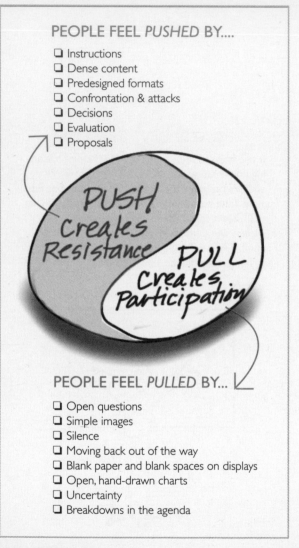

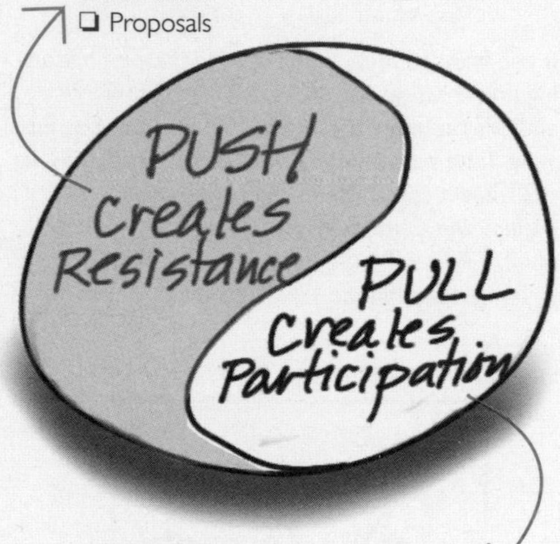

PEOPLE FEEL *PULLED* BY...

- ❑ Open questions
- ❑ Simple images
- ❑ Silence
- ❑ Moving back out of the way
- ❑ Blank paper and blank spaces on displays
- ❑ Open, hand-drawn charts
- ❑ Uncertainty
- ❑ Breakdowns in the agenda

happens. Think about it yourself. Imagine a time someone has pushed you. What do you do? You tense up, you resist automatically, and push back. The same thing happens in a meeting when anyone makes a presentation or a proposal, especially if it is complicated or has implications for action. Our psyches automatically resist and push back.

Resistance isn't necessarily a bad thing. It is a kind of engagement. But if meeting participants are experiencing only being pushed, they will soon feel like pushing back and participating, or the energy will bottle up. Then people get overloaded and they shut down to protect themselves, or begin to challenge the process. This phenomenon is probably what people are referring to when they talk about "death by PowerPoint."

Pulling Creates Attention and Participation

The opposite of pushing is pulling. If you are standing with a partner and he or she pulls, you will also resist, but in a different way. It's not by pushing back. In Aikido, a form of martial art, practitioners are taught to pay attention to attacks, pull back with them and even move the attacker further in that same direction, thereby flipping them over with their own energy.

A "pull" in a meeting context is something that happens that supports people moving in the direction they are going naturally or where they want to participate. Different kinds of things pull attention and participation, as listed in the model to the left.

Pull energy appears when forceful, yanglike movement shifts to open, receptive movement. Ultimately a good meeting leader will be able to do both.

The best presenters with presentation software know how to do this with simple imagery, pauses, questions, audience interaction, and storytelling. Too many slide presentations in business, unfortunately, are a "push" experience, with presenters hurrying through dense content. The participation is not physical and doesn't use all the different modes humans have at their disposal. I want to spend the rest of this chapter sharing some alternative ways that are pretty assured of getting engagement that is actually productive.

Pulling Out Simple Drawings

In thinking about what kind of presentation support you need, check the list to the right and see if you need high engagement and participation. If so, then learning to free yourself from presentation software might be worth the effort. Any organization will spend time every so often stepping back and thinking about its vision and strategy. These kinds of meetings are ones where engagement and involvement is essential. Planning meetings would not be necessary if economic conditions were stable and everyone knew precisely how to do their jobs and get the results they want. But economic conditions are very dynamic and getting more so. Pooling understanding is essential.

In the Future We Will Look Like...?

I led a meeting with the top management of a large, regional grocery chain that was facing the prospect of the big box stores moving into their territory and taking away a lot of business. There were about 15 people in the meeting, and they weren't used to meeting as a group about strategy. They were more operationally oriented most of the time. But it was clear that in order to step up to new competition they would have to operate differently, and moreover, their stores would have to be different. Changes in customer interests were already driving changes—such as the desire to have more actual cooked and deli food available.

TYPES OF MEETINGS THAT NEED HIGH PARTICIPATION

- ❑ Welcoming new team members
- ❑ Initial sessions in a workshop or training
- ❑ Initial meetings with a potential customer or client
- ❑ Brainstorming and design meetings
- ❑ Annual planning meetings
- ❑ Visioning sessions
- ❑ Problem-solving meetings
- ❑ Learning sessions
- ❑ Decision-making meetings
- ❑ Project kickoffs
- ❑ Board/staff retreats
- ❑ Virtual team meetings
- ❑ Workshops

VISIONING WITH OPEN METAPHORS

1. Ask everyone to compare their future organization to something else, another kind of organization, a vehicle, a kind of plant.
2. Break people into small teams and provide a flip chart and markers.
3. Give everyone 20 minutes to talk and rapidly sketch out their idea. It's okay to have more than one idea.
4. Compare the drawings and list the features that people find most attractive.

My task was to help them visualize their new vision with a large Storymap*, The Grove's name for large information displays that let leaders tell compelling stories about organization visions and strategies.

The way I involved everyone was quite simple. I asked them all to pair up and answer a simple question. "In the future, our stores are like ________." I was asking them a very open question, to come up with a metaphor for what their stores would be like. We taped up flip chart paper and provided some watercolor markers. "Do a simple sketch and write out some of the characteristics," I instructed. Thirty minutes later we had 6 or 7 sketches and a lot of conversation.

"Disneyland," one chart was headed. "We are like a county fair," wrote another team. "We are a farmers market," said another. "We are the town square," said another. "We are like a campus," said another. When we shared the simple drawings I listed out the characteristics that each team said they were pointing at—"Experiential, lots of choices, things for the whole family to do, colorful, exciting." We narrowed it down to two—Disneyland and Town Square, and began to work on a vision drawing that would integrate the two.

We might have approached this meeting by inviting in an expert on the grocery business to give a very stimulating presentation on the evolving approaches to store design. I'm sure that people will remember and care far more about their little drawing and dialogue session than the most brilliant of presentations.

Anytime you need a range of ideas, ask people to draw simple pictures of them and create a gallery. You will have guaranteed engagement.

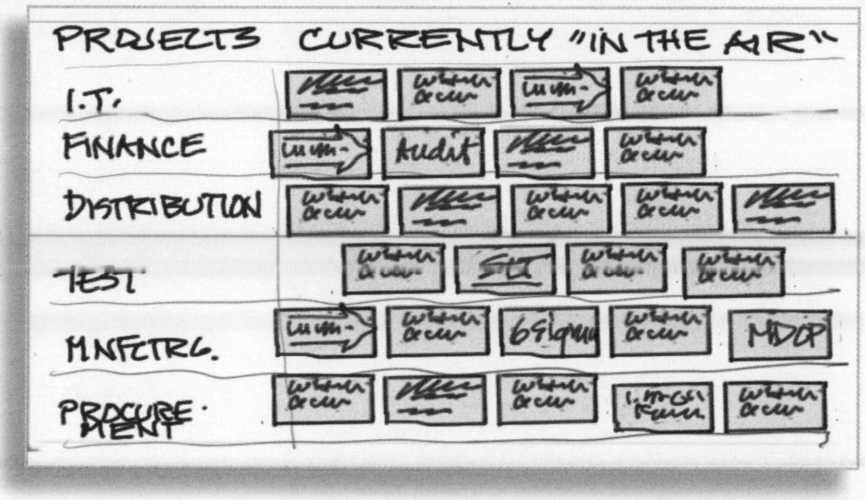

The Power of Sticky Notes to Get Involvement

A large medical equipment supplier had a problem with its operational efficiency. The end to end processes weren't very coordinated and efforts to fix various problems had resulted in a lot of projects getting started by various well-meaning functions. To deal with the challenge top management created a special task force of key leaders in the processes involved and asked a senior HR manager to facilitate the kickoff meeting. The group's scope spanned from production planning to order fulfillment, and all the critical activities that supported those processes including information technology, procurement, manufacturing, distribution, and customer service.

The challenge facing me and the internal HR director staffing the meeting was how to get the group completely engaged and committed to working hard on this project. Several of the managers were competing with each other and not too thrilled with the assignment. The level of complexity was such that no one was sure how to begin.

A very simple activity proved to be the breakthrough in that first meeting. It consisted of creating a huge wall with sticky notes for every project that was "in the air" at the time related to the operational efficiency task. I used the analogy of a flight control center at an airport, and suggested that before we tried to talk about what was needed, everyone should build an agreed-on picture of what was going on right then.

The big display (represented here) has rows representing different functions like IT, manufacturing, procurement, distribution, and finance. There weren't columns, just strings of sticky

CREATE A BIG STICKY NOTE WALL

1. Hang two rows of large paper on a long wall.
2. List all the functions that are involved in your project.
3. Identify all initiatives and projects relating to your subject in each function.
4. When the wall is finished identify overlaps and gaps.

STICKY NOTES

The idea of sticky notes is to have individuals or pairs generate ideas, one per sticky note, related to whatever topic you are working with. If your group is small you can use 3x5 sticky notes. If the group is larger the 5x8 ones are better. If you don't have sticky notes you can always use half sheets of printer paper and tape the sheets up. (Little loops of tape attached to the two upper corners makes a system than allows you to move the sheets easily.)

notes— large 5x8 ones in this case. It took about two hours to complete this display, and when it was done nobody had any arguments any more about the importance of figuring out how to co-ordinate things more closely. Their situation was a snarl of overlapping projects, all begun in good faith, but not coordinated. Imagine an airport with no control tower and you get the picture.

Affinity Charts

Any subject can be analyzed by a group using sticky notes as an alternative to having experts come in and present. You generate items and find the affinities and clusters. Chapter 7 addresses sticky note methods in detail, but let's look at the process here as well. Its advantage is the tremendous amount of information you can generate, and all the activity and movement involved in making and organizing the notes.

There are challenges any time a whole group does this kind of exercise since the items vary widely in specificity and relevance. But all the messiness gets everyone very involved, especially the people who like to see things more organized because they generally can't stand the disorder and wade in to see if they can pull out patterns and connections.

Appreciate that this is just one phase of the larger learning and action process, so don't keep things messy too long. Your next move will generally be to let the group organize the display. There are several ways to do this. You can appoint a subcommittee to do it during a break. You can also ask everyone to begin moving and clustering the items as a large group, invoking a simple rule—anyone can move a sticky at any time. This results in little sticky note contests, where one will bounce around between clusters, but it always sorts out. Add a little more fun by suggesting that no one talk during this process. This gets everyone fully engaged in reading all the information, and avoids getting sidetracked with conversations that aren't relevant.

Thinking activates when you guide the group to identify names for the different groupings they have organized. By the time a group is finished with this kind of exercise, it is completely involved and engaged with the material you need to understand.

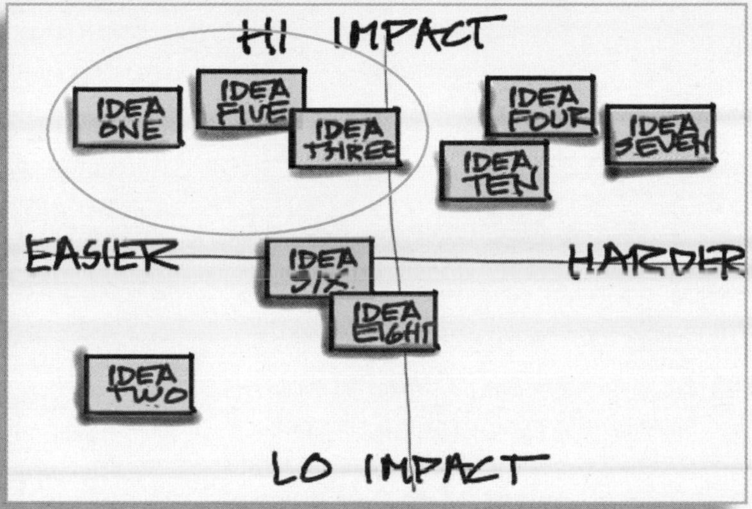

HI-LO GRID

This simple template allows groups to sort their ideas into relevant categories and pick the ones that they think will have highest immediate impact.

Simple Templates

Affinity charts work from the bottom up. A simple template works from the top down, but has similar dynamics. In this case you ask a group to organize a group of sticky notes according to some set of dimensions. This is a good move to make when you are building a decision funnel (see Chapter 17 for a full treatment of using visual meetings for decision making). The basic idea is to sort things out at a preliminary level with some simple criteria.

I worked with an HR team that had about 10 goals for the year on sticky notes and really needed to prioritize and get them focused down to 3 or 4. A free-flowing argument didn't seem like the right way to get agreement. The leader and I didn't feel that voting was appropriate. She wanted the group to really wrestle with which ones would be the very best to take on in light of the company's overall goal, which had been discussed at some length.

I suggested a simple "hi-lo" grid (shown here). The top represented things that would have a high payoff in relation to their company goals. The bottom was low payoff. Then the left side represented things that could be done somewhat easily and the right things that took a lot of effort. We talked a little about what easy and difficult meant, but not that long. The group was then asked to sort the stickies without talking, having the ability to move any sticky any time. In less than 20 minutes they had them sorted and it was graphically clear which 3 or 4 were the most

Process maps are all similar in that they have time on one axis and channels of activity on another. How many channels of activity determines how complicated the map is.

promising goals to take on. They appreciated that the ones that were more difficult could easily be their second- or third-year goals.

Freeway Maps and More Elaborate Templates

Sometimes an issue is complicated enough that some guidance is needed. This is usually why people believe they need expert presentation at meetings. But there is a middle ground between doing people's thinking for them and getting them involved and engaged in an interactive way. This involves using what I'm calling "idea maps" in this book. There are many kinds of idea maps. This type, related to illustrating a process, I call a "freeway map." Its intent was to let the group figure out the substreet patterns.

A semiconductor company I worked with was spending too much on its operations management. This function included all the procurement and provision of supplies to the manufacturing units. They needed to cut millions of dollars from the budget and thought they could do it with a task force. It was a more focused project than the big end-to-end task force at the medical supply company.

In talking over how to run the meeting with the leadership, it was clear that the situation was complicated enough that we didn't need to be stumbling over basics. I asked them whether there was a very high-level view of the operations process that we could draw on a simple flow diagram. They said there probably was. I worked with them with sticky notes to identify these big blocks. Process maps are all similar in that they have time on one axis and channels of activity on another. How many channels of activity determines how complicated the map is. I asked the group to identify the 4 or 5 big channels that would include all the others, and put the big sticky notes where they belonged.

The first meeting of the task force involved presenting this "freeway map." It was big enough and loose enough that we had room to add things, and invited the group to critique the map as a first step. This is a good way to get people involved in information. Ask them to criticize it! It's a bit of a pull strategy applied to diagramming. Once we had the big map roughly agreed to we asked everyone to use little 3x3 sticky notes and put them on the chart. A yellow color meant this part was working really well. A pink note meant this part wasn't working and needed attention. We asked them to note on the pink sticky notes what they were thinking about specifically. (The illustration here uses green.)

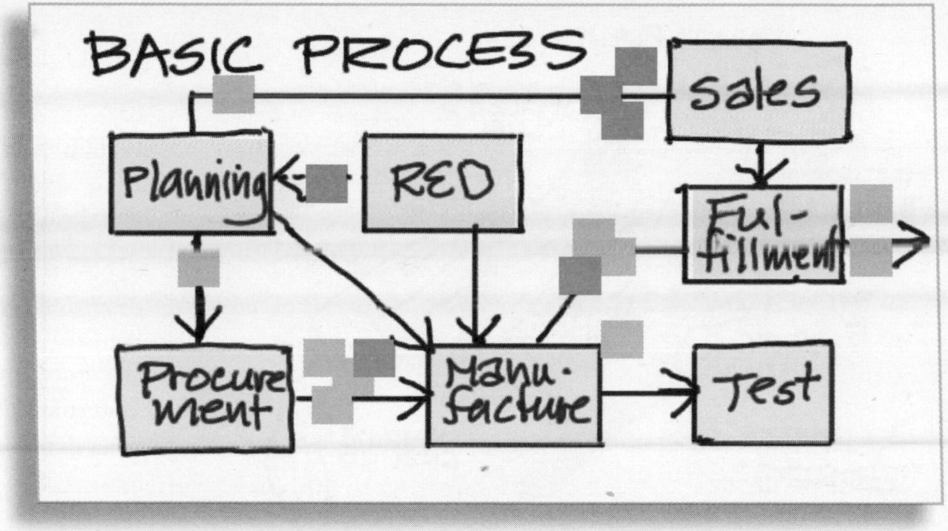

"FREEWAY" MAPS

In examining organizational processes it helps to create a high-level view of the basics before a meeting to talk about what to fix. Then use little sticky notes of different colors to have everyone indicate where things are working and where they need to be changed.

In about 20 minutes the big map was covered with sticky notes. We spent the entire rest of the day talking through the pink ones and making lists of things that needed attention. By the end of the day everyone was completely engaged, and pretty clear about which of the issues were the biggest ones.

Using Geographic Maps

Another kind of idea map is a geographic map that illustrates non-geographic elements like political boundaries and such. I was invited by the National Park Service one time to run a meeting to settle some differences between the team in the NPS that was working on the visitor experiences at Alcatraz and the team that was responsible for preserving the natural environment. The two were at each other's throats, largely because the nesting grounds of the black crowned night heron, an important species on the island, was on the same side as the best view of San Francisco. The park leadership was at their wit's end and needed help.

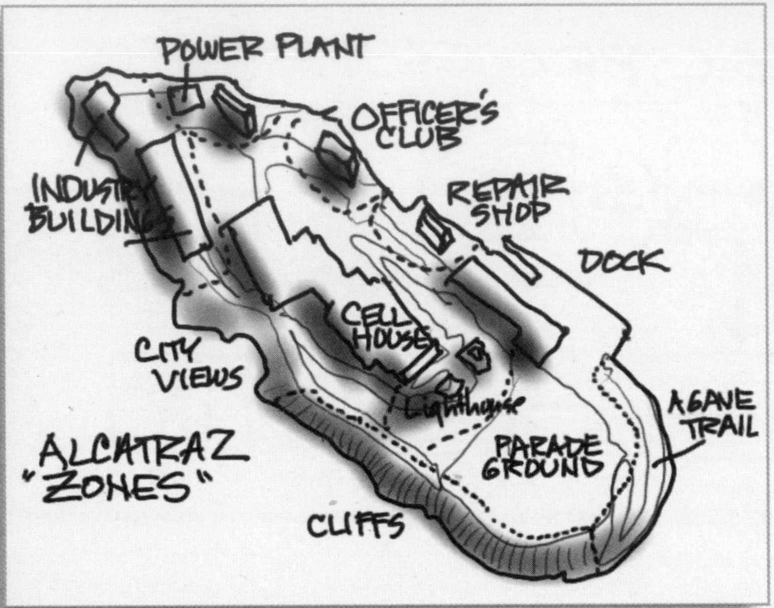

CREATING COMMON LANGUAGE with MAPS

A geographic map like this one of Alcatraz that indicates the different areas provides a group with a common language for talking about physical planning problems in communities and cities.

I know from experience that when people are upset, small annoyances and time wasters can make things even worse. If someone had come in and tried to tell them what to do it would have been a guaranteed disaster. This was not the meeting for any presentations. I also knew that part of what makes meetings a challenge is people having different understandings of situations and different uses of language and even specific words. I wondered if the park groups had a common language for talking about Alcatraz. Did they have any kind of zoning agreements, like any planning department would have in a city? It turned out they didn't really, but there were some common names for the different areas.

I gambled. I felt that if the group could get over the hump of getting everyone aware of the realities of the situation, and be able to talk specifically and intelligently about each side's interest, they could avoid any further frustrations caused by unclear communications. Then their better instincts might kick in and they could work something out. So I encouraged the staff to create a "zoning map" of the island on a large sheet of paper that labeled the different areas in question with specific names, so that when anyone used the names others would knew precisely what area they were referring to. I thought this would do two things.

1. It would keep a picture of the whole island in their minds the entire meeting. This is one of the powers of visualization—showing wholeness and connections.
2. It would eliminate the problem of people getting upset because they misinterpreted what areas others were talking about.

The system worked beautifully and the meeting was very productive.

Using Idea Maps as Presentation Charts

A very interesting visual alternative to using presentation software is to use large idea maps, often called murals, to tell stories. At The Grove we call these "Storymaps" because they support leadership and others telling complicated stories. Look at the list to the right to see all the benefits of working in this big picture way. Hand-drawn murals suggest that ideas aren't fully developed, and can be extended or changed. Murals can also be intentionally incomplete, setting up exercises that involve people by asking them to fill things in. Let me share some stories where Storymaps have been spectacularly successful in lieu of a slide presentation.

Save the Redwoods League

The Grove led a strategy session for Save the Redwoods League, a group that pioneered creating old growth parks along the California Coast. The challenge was involving a large board and an advisory council that was very active. Everyone in the organization was passionate about saving these irreplaceable old trees.. The staff was quite worried, however. They knew that these people were not working with the League regularly and could easily get inspired by all kinds of ideas that wouldn't be feasible given the resources and current commitments. But the meeting didn't have time for a lot of staff presentations about what was going on. It was as much about involving and engaging the board and advisors and getting a clear plan. The way through was to have the staff develop a large presentation mural of everything that was currently going on in the League. It was on a 4' by 8' sheet of paper, hand-draw with markers and chalked up to have nice colors. It only took 20 minutes to present the chart, but it stayed on the wall the rest of the planning meeting and kept everyone aware of the current realities while they were planning. A dividend was the fact that the staff had several meetings before the planning event in order to create the mural. This required them to review their work and get tuned in to what they were doing.

THE VALUE OF PRESENTING WITH BIG CHARTS

- ❑ Big charts keep the whole picture in front of people during the entire presentation, reinforcing big picture thinking, and seeing the forest as well as the trees.
- ❑ Storymaps usually involve picking a graphic metaphor that invites people to use their right brain and storytelling side to understand.
- ❑ Big graphics can be both quite precise and provocative. They combine emotional and analytic values.
- ❑ Big charts do not require linear presentation. A person using them can hop around and backtrack quite easily.
- ❑ The big charts give people something to look at if they aren't particularly interested in the specific items being talked about.
- ❑ Murals can be duplicated in small form as take-aways.
- ❑ The chances of a Storymap getting put up on a cubicle or office wall is *much* greater than other media. Presentation packs mostly go in files.
- ❑ Done well, a Storymap presentation can be remembered and retold by the person hearing it, thereby leveraging the work put into it.

SAVE THE REDWOODS LEAGUE VISION MAP

WHEN TO MAKE BIG CHARTS

The kinds of presentations that are consistently resulting in big charts rather than slideware are the following:

- ❑ **Large agendas** that stay up throughout a meeting and guide meeting leaders and participants
- ❑ **Graphic histories** of how a team or organization got to the point of having the particular meeting you are holding
- ❑ **Context maps** that show the drivers of change in the environment
- ❑ **Overarching visions and strategies** that need to be kept in mind during business planning
- ❑ **Big process maps** used to support process improvement teams
- ❑ **Visual summaries** of current projects
- ❑ **Stakeholder maps**
- ❑ **Murals illustrating a key mental model** being used to organize a workshop or training

At the conclusion of the planning work the League asked The Grove to make a picture of their vision in a form that they could use to continue to tell the story graphically. The mural on this page is the result, and was successfully used for several years.

Media that flickers on and off doesn't have the same impact as media that persists throughout a meeting. The question to ask when you are determining whether a mural is needed is "what needs to stay front and center in people's mind the whole meeting." This is the material to present with murals instead of presentation software.

Creating Your Own Idea Maps

Mural presentations can range from very simple to very elaborate creations. I want to stress that it is more the large size and visual nature of the information than its specific production value that works. You shouldn't feel intimidated about creating your own, or getting teams to create murals instead of slides.

6. Consulting & Selling with Graphics

Drawing Out Customer Interests

If you are a consultant or a salesperson you are aware of how important the initial meetings are with customers. It is here that first impressions are made, assumptions about scope and possibility arise, and trust is established. In sales this would be called building rapport. In consulting you might think of this phase as scoping. Both cases are very similar. In this chapter we will look at using visual meetings to be successful connecting with your customer.

By this point you should be aware of why drawing and visualizing as an active process is very involving. It's rooted in the fact that our minds are all conditioned to find patterns and make assumptions based on partial information. When visualizing is used to listen it provides immediate feedback to how people are heard.

Drawing on the Same Side of the Table

A strategy in negotiations is to try and get on the same side of the table with the other person. If you are taking visual notes during an initial meeting, it is a great excuse to move around so the person you are talking with can see what you are creating. Two people sitting on the same side of a table looking at a sheet of paper or a tablet computer has a completely different feel from sitting across a table. It's a visual symbol of cooperation already.

There are some tried and true initial conversations that benefit from active visualization:

- **Sharing Background History:** Have potential new clients tell you the story of how they got to the point of talking with you. Charting out their story on a time line will involve them right away. People will add in all kinds of things they might not have thought about telling you.

- **Listing Desired Outcomes or Needs:** In a sales or consulting situation asking people to share what they are interested in right up front is always a pretty good idea.

THIS PROJECT STARTED
ABOUT A YEAR AGO

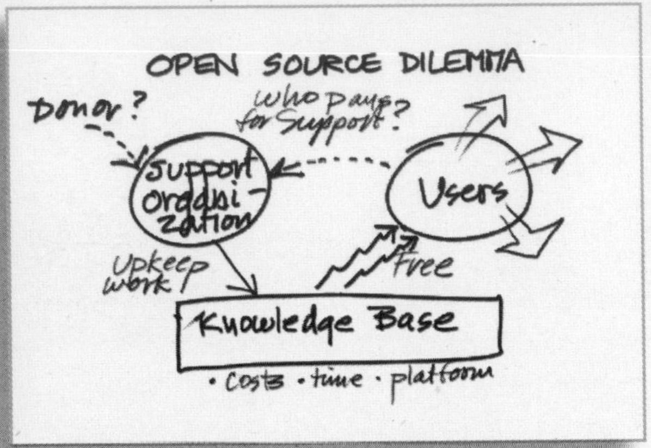

WHO PAYS?

I was sitting in a restaurant in an initial conversation with a nonprofit client about a dilemma arising from having grown very large by making their methods open source. Now they needed to find a way to get support. The question was, who pays for the upkeep of the knowledge base that allows the free services to continue? We drew out this simple diagram to understand the problem.

If you list these things visibly so they see you are getting it right that helps even more. You might even do this on small sticky notes in a journal.

- **Drawing Current Reality Maps:** A type of idea mapping is to illustrate the current situation the customer finds him- or herself in. This can be a very loose kind of drawing, like the diagram on this page.
- **Mapping Potential Solutions:** Customers want to know you can actually help them. But you might not be sure of what is the right approach. It helps in those cases to create a little display of the range of choices available. This is also a way to tell your client about past work if you are a consultant, or the spectrum of solutions available if you are a salesperson.

Agenda Planning Kits

At The Grove we have 19 different graphic templates that are used repeatedly in strategic planning. A few years ago we decided to print these on separate little cards with simple steps-at-a-glance on the back. These cards were so popular with internal consultants that we went a step further to make them a little bigger and include a little overview booklet. The consultant works with the client by pulling out this or that option, describing it to the client, and letting them pick it up and read how it would be done.

When a series of cards are out on the table you will begin to notice that the client keeps coming back to several of them. This is a direct indication of what will work in your meeting. Because the ideas are on cards, it's easy to take the next step and order them in a sequence and begin to look at different possible agenda designs for a process. The card pack is evidence of capability, and doesn't require any kind of formal presentation. In fact, many clients will want to just take the whole pack and look through it themselves.

Customer Interest Interviews

As a way to get new or old customers engaged in thinking through how they can work with you more fully you might work to characterize the services you offer on simple cards. Then ask the customer you are talking with if they would stack the cards in the order of what is most important to them. This is a way to get immediate visual feedback about interests, and have the customer get a feel for your offerings. This kind of activity has a double benefit. The work it takes to break down your services and offerings on cards is a very valuable process of getting everyone on your team to agree with what you are providing. This alone is worthwhile. Then the sharing of these cards with old customers lets them see in a very comfortable way that you may be offering much more than they were used to using.

Pitching a New Boss on Your Value

An internal kind of selling situation happens when a team gets a new boss. The challenge for the old team members is briefing the new boss on what has been gong on without looking like you are unreceptive to his or her new ideas. I worked with a team at Ericsson in Sweden that was charged with doing strategic research for a larger part of the organization. They had done a huge amount of work looking at the general environment and describing the drivers of change. But they knew the incoming boss was very knowledgeable and assertive and were sure he was going to ignore their work. I suggested a visual meeting strategy that was a bit like a judo move.

AGENDA PLANNING KITS

Any time you can break a presentation into little chunks so that your customer or client can play with the different options you are more apt to be heard and get high involvement. The Grove's Agenda Planning kits present agenda choices for planning meetings as well as little cards for the best practices. Here a consultant reviews options with a client, and then works with a design team to organize an initial meeting. (See www.grove.com for more information.)

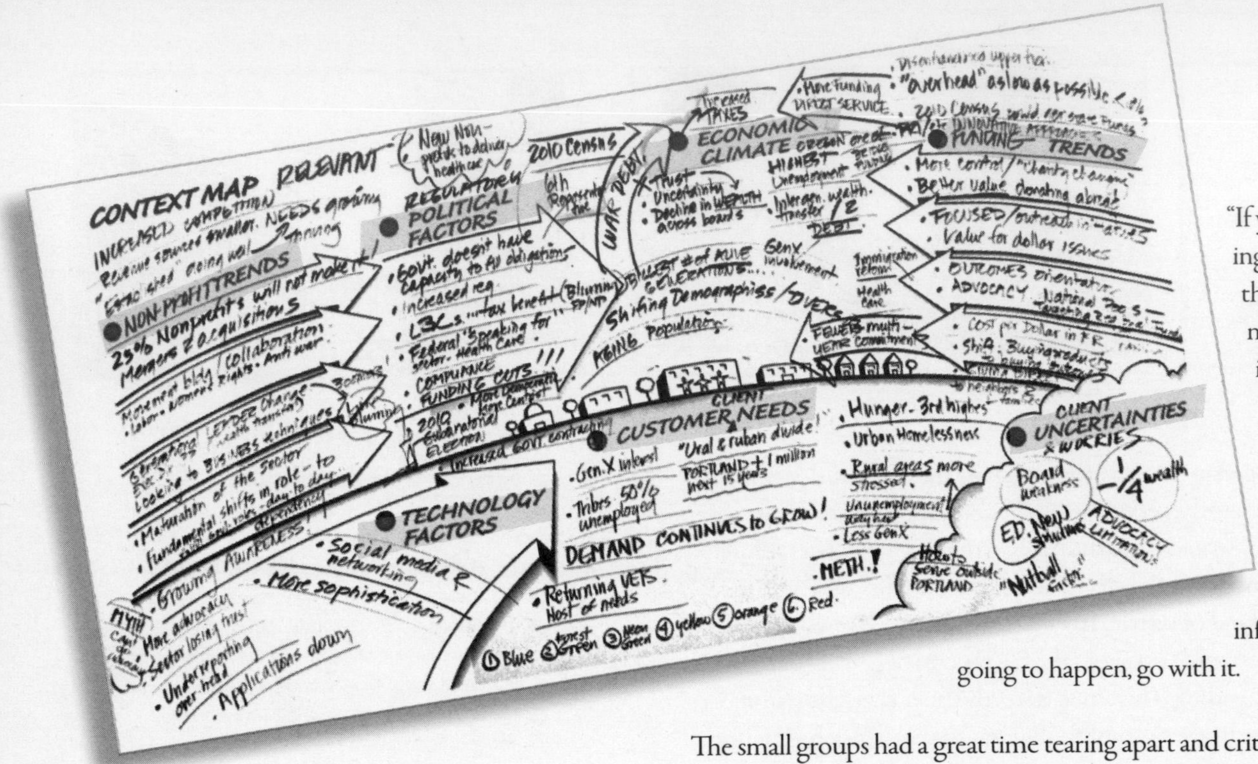

"If your new boss is really interested in showing how smart and knowledgeable he is, then give him and the other new management members (for the boss has already invited in some new players) something to work with," I said. I suggested they draw up their information about the environment on what we called a "context map" and then have small groups at their upcoming planning meeting charged with critiquing and challenging the information. Instead of resisting what was going to happen, go with it.

CONTEXT MAP

This example uses The Grove's Context Map Graphic Guide to illustrate the driving forces in the current environment for a nonprofit support organization. It is very similar to the one we asked the Ericsson managers to criticize. If you work in nonprofits see if you agree with these forces and factors.

The small groups had a great time tearing apart and criticizing the context map, in groups that intentionally mixed the old staff with the new management. Everyone had a chance to share what he or she was thinking, and the group as a whole made a brand new map! Not only did the old team add a lot of value, but thinking got better with the addition of the new ideas from the new boss and his folks.

The Big Whack—Selling Learning Design

In the mid-1990s the PGA faced a dilemma. Their licensing program for golf professionals was being challenged by pros at private courses and special golf colleges that were offering credentialing. Historically they were the only game in town and a golf pro needed to take the courses and get the sign-offs in order to be certified. These courses were often in hotels and taught by other golf pros. They weren't really well designed to create value in and of themselves.

The PGA sought proposals from several consulting firms, among which was one of my clients, the Stanford Research Institute (SRI). The request for proposal said they wanted help to think through doing something about the situation and potentially create a new certification curriculum. An internal team of consultants at SRI invited me to work with them to pitch the PGA for the project. The project would run for several years and involve designing two dozen different courses and a half dozen related training videos. A condition was that the entire result needed to be delivered by existing golf pros and not by special trainers or consultants. The costs of this project were big, and nothing comparable had commanded this kind of investment and commitment. The PGA needed to act, but wasn't about to select a consulting group without a thorough review.

The costs of this project were big, and nothing comparable had commanded this kind of investment and commitment. The PGA needed to act, but wasn't about to select a consulting group without a thorough review.

We knew that the group making the decision were not professional trainers or consultants—they were golf pros. How would they understand what was required from an instructional design point of view? How would we know for sure what they required? How could we communicate our competency? We had a couple of operating assumptions about how to engage the group.

1. We would use murals, not slides, to engage them in a dialogue, not a presentation.
2. The structure of the mural would be a high-level framework that they could fill in.
3. The framework needed to point at something they already understood so they would think of this from a whole systems perspective.
4. We would model listening to them, using sticky notes on our large mural.

We worked a long time on the metaphor and finally had the insight that what they knew the most about was golf! So we mapped the stages of the project on a graphic golf course. A huge golf club represented the pilot program we would design and launch. The ball was the cadre of champions we intended to enroll as potential trainers. The first hole was the first set of courses to be designed and taught by this cadre. The second hole was the next set. And a third hole was the most complicated. Between each hole we would meet with the PGA team to assess the progress and "score" the results, making adjustments as we went along.

We listened! We recorded what they said! We were organized! We got the project. The board repeatedly told stories about how interesting that initial meeting had been.

We called the mural the "Big Whack" and drew it up nearly 24 feet long. We got into the conference room early and had it up on the walls when everyone came in. The visual impression was pretty immediate. They loved it, and loved the ensuing dialogue even more. We listened! We recorded what they said! We were organized! We got the project. The board repeatedly told stories about how interesting that initial meeting had been.

This project was a multimillion dollar event for SRI. Gary Bridges, and Ed Claassen, the project leads for SRI, continued using a visual approach in the check-in meetings. The PGA was very pleased with the result. And those of us on the sales team always gave credit to the "Big Whack."

Customer Discovery Workshops at HP Consulting

In the 1990s HP began to do more consulting on the front end of its projects, using bright engineers in "Discovery Processes" with clients to determine how they might find technical solutions. The entire computer industry was undergoing such rapid change that customers needed much more guidance and help, and were beginning to favor companies that provided solutions. The initial consulting teams were challenged because they were trained as engineers and technical people, not salespeople or meeting leaders. Some key leaders at HP learned about the graphic facilitation work The Grove was doing and invited us to a workshop to show them how visual planning templates worked. They suspected that these lightly structured frameworks might help the engineers.

The Strategic Visioning workshops we subsequently conducted all over the world for HP Consulting showed the engineers on the front line of client relationship groups how to run a workshop for customers that would draw out from them the company strategy and other information that would provide a context for the consulting. They settled on a suite of six basic frameworks.

1. **Graphic History** to record information about the history of their client.
2. **Context Map** to record environmental factors the client thought were important.
3. **SPOT** grid that provided space for listing strengths, problems, opportunities, and threats.
4. **Cover Story Vision** to record the clients' stories about the future they wanted.
5. **Five Bold Steps** template to identify the agreed-on vision and key steps of the project they contemplated with HP.
6. **Graphic Gameplan** to record a potential action plan.

These templates required the engineers to be able to listen and write what they heard in text, but not to draw pictures, yet the results were very visual and allowed both HP and their clients to see patterns in the information.

We have subsequently taught this process to many companies and consultants the world over who want to lead visual meetings, but aren't going to be graphic facilitators or recorders. Any of these formats can be used in a sales situation when you want to demonstrate that you are hearing what your client is saying.

BIG PICTURE THINKING FOR SOLUTION SELLING

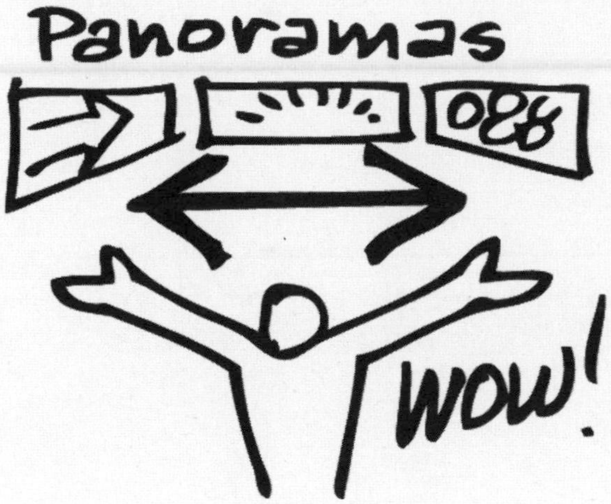

See Chapter 12 for a more detailed look at Visual Planning templates.

Providing Visual Guidance

In both sales and consulting situations the clients may not be aware of what is available. I remember in the 1990s when Bob Johansen, Distinguished Fellow at the Institute of the Future, and I were doing a project for Procter & Gamble working to determine what kinds of features employees would want on the computer workstations that were becoming commonplace. Software for desktops was exploding and many new capabilities were coming online. How could we possibly survey them about something that they might not even know about? Asking them what they wanted without any guidance would have our answers grouped inside the options they already knew about. We devised a simple visualization strategy that worked very well.

For 20 different workstation options we invented little icons and a name for the option that was clear. These were things like spreadsheets, video conferences, e-mail, project management, and other things many people did not know were possible on computers at the time (This is hard to believe now!). We then created a chart with 20 little frames that looked a bit like workstation screens and created a short video explaining them. As Bob verbally described the choices I printed out the name of the option on one of the screens and drew the little icon that pointed at its distinguishing feature. These little icons were then printed on the questionnaire about preferences that we intended to use. Our process was to show employees the video and then have them complete the questionnaire. The process worked beautifully. We learned that if you can create little chunks of information and have them on cards, or know how to draw them out yourself on sticky notes, you can guide your client through looking at what is possible.

LET THE CLIENT PLAY
WITH THE PIECES LIKE
BUILDING BLOCKS!

7. Hands-On Information

Sticky Notes & Dot Voting

This section has already introduced you to many different ways to work with sticky notes and big paper. I want to zoom in a little closer on some of the techniques that will help you succeed with these formats, particularly working with sticky notes, dot votes, and big paper.

As you can see from the different examples I have described already, many of the tools for visual meetings are large graphic frameworks and movable, visual chunks of information, the easiest of which to create and use are sticky notes. This creates a gamelike environment for figuring out patterns that make sense based on the stated outcomes of the meeting. While there are many variations, there is an underlying pattern that works no matter what specific sticky note activity you are leading. It is outlined in detail in the box on this page. Read over the steps listed in the steps-at-a-glance box to the right.

Taking care with the first few setup steps will ensure that people are well oriented and productive. It also increases the quality of the contribution. If you take care of the basics everyone else can concentrate on the work they need to do and not on trying to figure out the activity.

How to Collect the Notes

There are a number of ways to work with sticky notes once you have generated them. Each approach has a different value, and needs to be matched to the meeting outcomes you intend. The most common variations are the following:

- **People Post as They Write:** In this approach anyone can come up and add a note to the board as they generate the ideas. This approach let's people see what is developing and avoids duplicate notes. It also encourages people to get up and down, and generates some energy from all the movement.

GENERAL STICKY NOTE PROCESS

BEFORE

1. Clearly identify the topic that is the focus of the activity.
2. Hang a large sheet of paper or identify a white-board for posting the notes.
3. Create an example of the kind of content you want and how large to write on the sticky note.
4. Make watercolor markers available to everyone.
5. Suggest picking a recorder who will create the notes, if you are using small groups.
6. Explain how long individuals or teams will have to generate notes related to the topic.

DURING

7. Start the process of brainstorming and writing notes.
8. Announce time when you are halfway done, and again when you are three quarters done. (This allows everyone to self-pace.)

AFTER

9. Collect and post the notes.
10. Discuss and cluster, finding patterns.

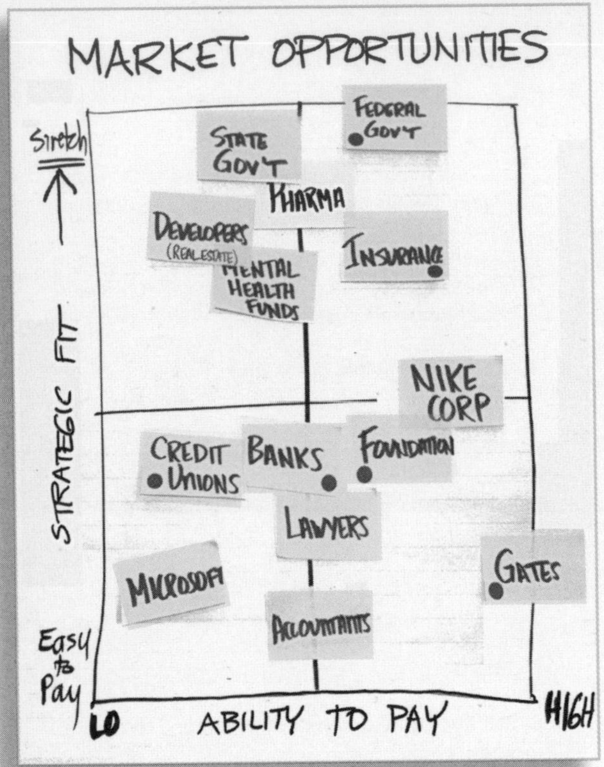

MARKETING OPPORTUNITY GRID

Take two factors, like strategic fit and ability to pay, and ask small groups to identify customers and locate them on the framework. This was created by a nonprofit service organization looking for funders.

- **Everyone Posts as a Group:** At the end of the time period you have provided for creating the notes, let everyone come up to the wall as a group and post their work. You might ask people to cluster the notes in categories, and this will start the organizing process. This approach can get crowded if your meeting has a lot of people, but it also provides a little break where people can talk and connect. Again, the moving around stirs up the energy. This can be very useful if it's late in the day and people are tired.

- **Post the Notes in a Framework:** This approach involves having a template of some sort, like the "Hi-Lo; Sooner-Later Grid" or the example in the illustration here of a marketing grid with strategic fit on one side and ability to pay on the other. You then ask the people generating the notes to post their ideas in the relevant area of the chart. This can be done all at once as a group or collecting and reading them individually and placing the notes by consensus. Your pick will be determined by how much discussion of the material you think would be useful.

- **Collect the Notes by Topic and Cluster as You Go:** If you want to see the clusters emerge with some discussion that everyone hears, then collect the notes one at a time. Start by asking an individual or small group for one of their ideas. Then ask if any others had the same or a closely related idea. Collect and cluster all related ideas on the display. Then ask for another new idea, and for related sticky notes. Continue until you have all the notes. The value of this approach is the items that are getting a lot of attention show up visibly because they have more sticky notes. Multiple people do tend to start bringing up notes themselves and you have to work to control the pace if you want people to hear what the note writer is saying. In a larger group where only some will be able to actually read the notes from where they sit, you may have to hold the note up in front and read it clearly before putting it on the chart. In very large groups having some assistance in collecting the notes makes sense.

- **Collect the Notes by Topic in Columns:** This approach is identical to the previous one above, except you lay out the sticky notes in columns across a big wall or chart. I prefer this way when the focus is setting objectives. As we will see in the next section when we zoom in on visual language a little more closely, a clustering format with sticky notes spaced in a clump will activate a lot of cross comparison. Columns focus people on topic by topic, and visually show the amount of attention a given topic is getting by the length of the string of notes. Because the length is easily compared you can see at a glance which are favored.

Analyzing and Discussing Sticky Note Displays

Working with sticky notes has a big advantage in generating a *lot* of information quickly. Its disadvantage is that people aren't hearing the ideas as they are created, and there can be so many that it presents a dizzy visual array. If it is important for people to know what is on the notes, you will need to have ways to get people to read the notes and consider them carefully. The side box on this page describes how to let groups self-organize the notes. This technique gets everyone to read all the sticky notes. It has a downside in that usually a couple of people start dominating the process.

Another way to get people to read all the notes and think about them is to conduct a poll where people get to indicate their favorite ideas. The most flexible and visually useful way to do this is to use sticky dots, available at any art or stationery store. Dots come in different sizes from ¼ inch up to 2 inches and in many colors. They are an extremely flexible way to create a visual display of what people care about. The items with the dots pop right out as the chart on the last page illustrates. If you plan to photocopy the charts for reference later, make sure to use darker colors. Yellow will not reproduce well.

The chart on the next page is from a planning meeting with an architectural firm. At this point in the meeting the group had listed its strengths, problems, opportunities, and threats on a Grove Graphic Guide® template. I chose to record the opportunities on sticky notes because we wanted

SELF-ORGANIZING STICKY NOTES

1. Suggest that the group as a whole organize the wall of sticky notes.
2. Explain that there are two rules:

   "Anyone can move a note any time to another location"

   "No one can talk"
3. Answer questions such as "Can we move a note back if someone puts it somewhere we disagree with?" by saying, "Yes!" Stay firm about the rules as laughter erupts.
4. Encourage people to "trust the process."
5. Stand back and let the group work. It's quite amazing how the patterns begin to form.
6. End the process when you see that no one is moving notes.
7. Lead a discussion about what to label the clusters.

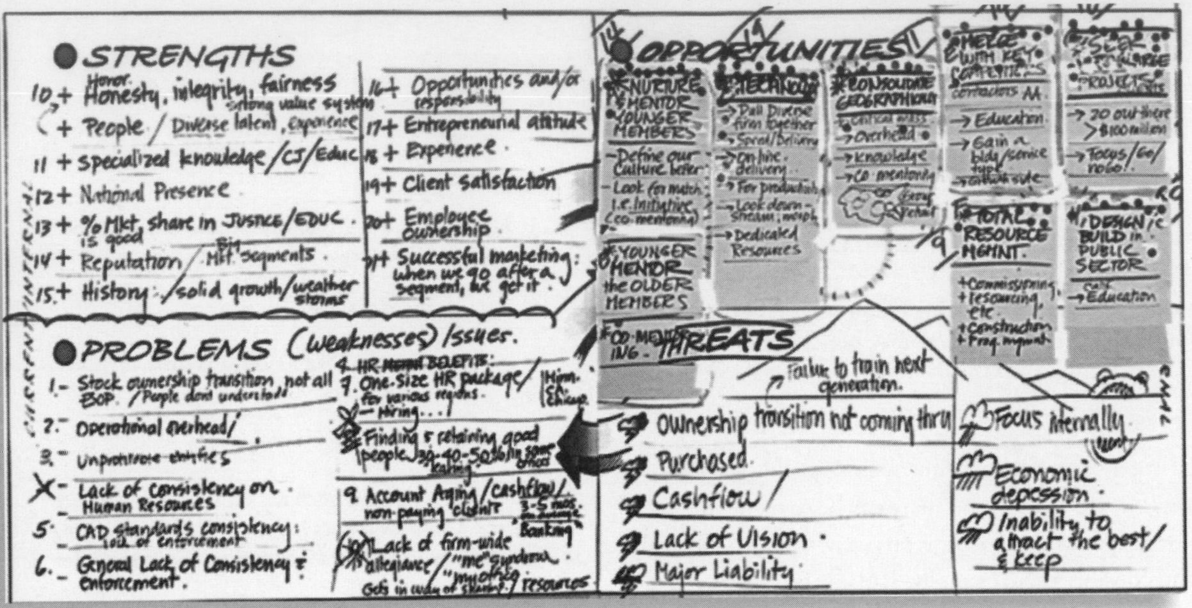

to focus on them and identify the top priorities as a lead-on to visioning.

STRENGTHS
Honesty, integrity, fairness
People / Diverse talent, experience
Specialized knowledge
National Presence
Reputation
History / solid growth/weather storms
Opportunities and/or responsibility
Entrepreneurial attitude
Experience
Client satisfaction
Employee ownership
Successful marketing: when we go after a segment, we get it
PROBLEMS (weaknesses) issues
Operational overhead
Lack of consistency on Human Resources
CAD standards consistency
General Lack of Consistency & enforcement
Finding & retaining good people
Account Aging/cashflow
Lack of firm-wide allegiance
OPPORTUNITIES
NURTURE MENTOR YOUNGER MEMBERS
YOUNGER MENTOR the OLDER MEMBERS
TOTAL RESOURCE MGMNT.
DESIGN BUILD in PUBLIC SECTOR
THREATS
Failure to train next generation
Ownership transition not coming thru
Purchased
Cashflow
Lack of Vision
Major Liability
Focus internally
Economic depression
Inability to attract the best & keep

After all the information was boarded (the sticky notes extended out to the right on the wall beyond the template illustrated here), I had everyone put dots on the ones they thought were most promising. Each of about 40 people had a set of dots that represented one-third the total list. This way the dot process functioned less like a vote and more like a poll. It really helps to let people know that the final decisions won't be made by the numbers, but through dialogue or whatever decision process you have agreed upon.

ARCHITECTURAL FIRM
SPOT ANALYSIS

Looking at strengths, problems, opportunities and threats is a tried and true planning activity. Using sticky notes for the opportunities allowed dot voting and sorting in preparation for visioning work.

Once the dots were on the sticky notes, it was pretty easy to cluster them and reorganize the chart so the ones with the most dots were on the top of the chart, as shown in the picture. These ideas became the springboard for visioning later in the day.

If you need to poll on more than one criteria, then have people dot vote with two or more colors. One might be what they are most passionate about, and another color might be what might get the best result for the organization. You can invent many other combinations since this way of working is very flexible. Sometimes you might not have sticky dots to work with. The same process can work asking people to make little dots with their markers. This relies on people using the honor system to only cast a certain number of dots, but still provide the visual target.

Practicing in Small Meetings and Agenda Design Sessions

If you aren't used to using sticky notes the place to practice is in your own workspace, a small conference room, or even a restaurant. It is possible to get similar results working small—with a flip chart–sized paper and little sticky notes. It is also possible to work flat right on your desk or table. If you want to photocopy your charts work on 11"x17" or A3-sized paper and tiny sticky notes and put them directly in the copy machine if you have one.

Most big meetings are preceded by smaller meetings to design the agenda. This is an excellent place to use sticky notes, trying out different arrangements of activities central to meeting design. The process is very straightforward. Use a time block template as your base display. Then create little sticky notes for all the things you want as outcomes, and all the different events and activities you can imagine doing to reach those outcomes. Once you have identified all the elements, talk about the things you can't change, like meeting times, meals, special speakers who have already been invited, and the like. Around these constraints arrange and rearrange your sticky notes. If you are working with a meeting sponsor or design team, they will have suggestions. You can make suggestions. Eventually it settles.

I used this process a bit differently one time to solve a workshop design problem. I was facilitating a meeting for the top personnel and organization managers in a large multinational to see if they wanted the program offered around the globe. I wanted them to "own" the process and be involved and suggested to my British sponsor that we leave the third day open for their design. He would have none of it, fearing criticism for not being prepared. After much argument I finally proposed that we create little posters on half sheets of paper that illustrated each potential activity, and then involve the top managers in helping us pick the ones they wanted and organize

GENERAL DOT VOTE TIPS

- ❑ Give people dots equaling one-third the number of items you are assessing.
- ❑ Specify where to stick the dot on the sticky note or information on a chart. If the dots are all placed in a similar location the visual effect is clearer.
- ❑ Discourage multiple votes for a single item. Explain that this is not a vote, but a poll to assess interest, and the decision will come later.
- ❑ When all dots are placed count them and write the number with angled slash lines top and bottom to make the vote numbers look different from anything else on the chart.
- ❑ Get help to count the dots if the chart is large.
- ❑ Step back and lead a discussion about what the dots tell the group.

ACTION OVERVIEW TEMPLATE & STICKY NOTES

A RE-AMP work group from Illinois uses sticky labels and a simple template to identify all the past and future global warming prevention actions they have taken and will take on a company specific, city, county, region, and state level.

them. This worked so well it is now a standard technique for doing group process design we call "Activity Block Agendas," since it works with a large time block template.

Looking at Global Warming Actions in Eight States with RE-AMP

One of the more inspiring uses of sticky notes, dot voting, and templates was the annual meeting of the RE-AMP project in Ames, Iowa, in 2008. This project is a consortium of over a hundred non-government organizations and 15 foundations that have banded together to collaborate in cleaning up the global warming pollutants in the energy industry in the upper Midwest. The project began in 2004 with grants from the Garfield Foundation and has grown steadily in influence and effectiveness as the members learn to embody their slogan of "thinking systemically and acting collaboratively."

The Grove has been supporting this project since its first year, and has helped them work out visual ways of seeing what they are doing in their big annual gatherings. In 2008 we wanted to get a comprehensive assessment of activity in the eight-state region. North and South Dakota, Iowa, Minnesota, Wisconsin, Illinois, Michigan, and Ohio all have delegations at the meeting for a total of about 140 people. How would we get them to see what everyone was doing?

Before the meeting, as a result of our design teleconferences, we designed a 4'x8' template for each state. Our idea was to have the different state groups all work together in a big meeting room to cocreate their reports in parallel. We figured this would give the state groups a chance to meet together, and let people who wanted to kibitz across states to move around. The templates consisted of a simple grid with different colored bands. The picture on the facing page is in gray scale, but the originals were in very pleasing pastels, created on a large plotter. The template turned out to be quite intuitive for the participants. Their actions naturally broke down into rows of things they were doing, visualized as a landscape. They worked "on the ground" with specific coal companies and cities. More generally they were also doing things with the PSCs, the Public Service Commissions that regulated energy rates and such. They were also working even more comprehensively with state legislative bodies and with agencies. It was appropriate to have these overarching the other rows.

We wanted each group to identify tasks they had completed in 2008, ones they were starting in 2008, and tasks they planned for 2009, the following year, so the columns were labeled accordingly. In the meeting itself we asked each group to write their actions on postcard-sized, white, crack-and-peel mailing labels. We then asked them to add some colored dots to indicate the specific area the action was targeting—coal, energy efficiency, transportation, clean energy creation, or global warming cap and trade issues, the names of the RE-AMP working groups . We posted the instructions using slides on a large screen. This is what the instruction screen looked like (with the names of the colors added since this is a gray-scale image).

Participants were totally engaged in the process of filling out these templates. On the prior page is a picture of the Illinois state group working on the template. We gave the entire room an hour for the task. We then gave everyone a chance to move around and read each of the state displays, calling time at 5-minute increments so people could shift. At the end of a half hour each state then presented from their display. The total activity lasted two and a half hours and left the group at lunch with an unparalleled, big picture view of what was going on. If anyone was unconvinced of

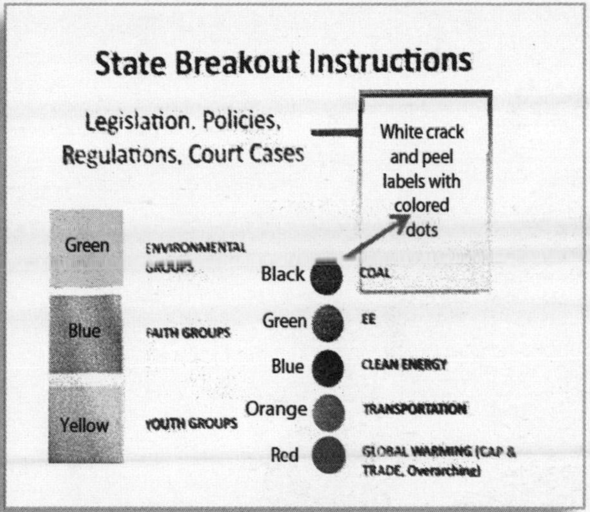

STICKY NOTE & DOT INSTRUCTIONS

We wanted to see three clusters of actors—environmental groups, faith groups, and youth groups—so we had each use a different color sticky, requesting they put their specific group name next to the actions they worked on. The white crack and peel labels would describe the action, and the colored dots the target of the action, as shown above. The final charts were very dense but readable, a bit like a good road map.

the sweep and growing excitement of this effort coming into the meeting, they couldn't escape the power of the big room ringed in the large displays chock full of actions completed and contemplated. We digitally photographed all the displays and provided a book to all participants with each sticky note in color and readable! What was remarkable about the RE-AMP application was the fact that there were no facilitators for any of the groups. It was completely self-organized using the tools that had been prepared for them. This is a good example of how the combination of techniques described in this book can result in improvisations and extensions.

The Power Is in the Engagement

Letting people get their hands directly on information with sticky notes is pretty simple, and that is its beauty. The power is in the involvement you get. You also get an energy bonus. Any time people are physically active in a meeting they are moving their bodies. This translates directly into more energy flows in the group. The more energy, the more power you have to change minds and relationships.

It is common to add energizer activities to workshops and trainings, and large sales meetings and other events. But often planning and decision-making meetings do not engage people this way, and are actually real challenges if you want people to stay focused and involved. It gets worse in virtual meetings. On web conferences one should change things every five minutes or so, and work extra hard to directly engage people if you want their full attention.

We'll return to the value of moveable media in the section on visual thinking. For now, reflect on the value of immersion and persistence of information as a key to high engagement. Big embraces! Moveable moves! Both have a lot of pull power to ensure high participation.

8. Using Images & Interaction

Collage & Picture Cards

Providing people with images and information in moveable pieces is another way to generate the same kind of energy that sticky notes tend to generate, with the difference that you are adding content to work with. Collage refers to the practice of using images from magazines and books to create new combinations that express ideas and feelings. Picture cards are sets of single images usually printed and laminated for re-use that work a lot like games, and can be used in clusters as well as individually. I've touched on these before but want to explore how to actually use them in a little more depth. They are a terrific way to get a group working visually if you or they are a bit inhibited about drawing.

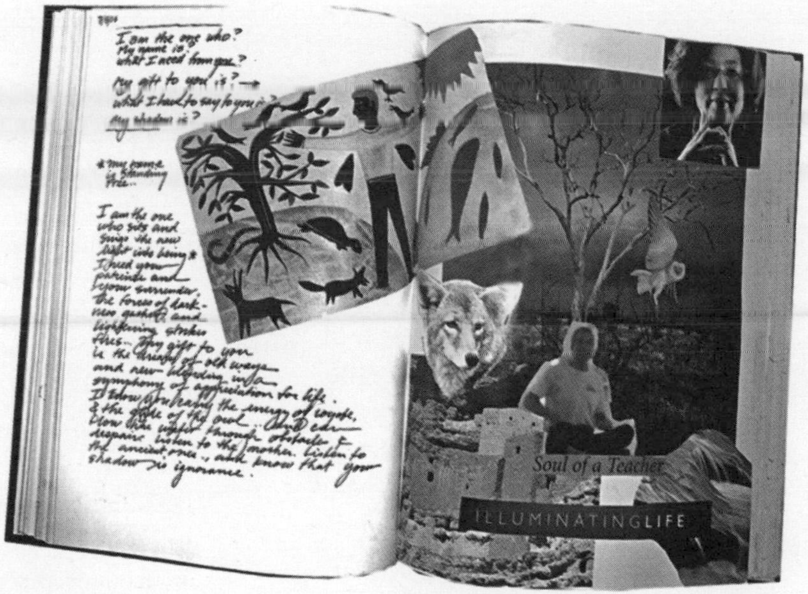

COLLAGE IN JOURNALS

This is what I created in my sketchbook journal as part of a self-discovery exercise at a Facilitation Mastery Workshop. See www.soulcollage.com for more information on this technique.

Personal Visioning with Collage

Let's start with collage and a personal story. My colleague Laurie Durnell, director of The Grove's consulting group, loves to do Soul Collage. This is a set of practices for using imagery from magazines to explore inner direction and interests. The term is copyrighted by Seena Frost, a psychologist who has developed a whole literature about this technique. I was personally touched by this in a simple exercise Laurie led in one of The Grove's Facilitation Mastery workshops.

The process is quite simple technically. Laurie collects magazine imagery from many sources. They are images from nature, work, travel, technology, family, literature, mythology—a very broad selection. She includes words and headlines from ads and stories as well. She brings these images with her and leads exercises exploring personal directions, when that is appropriate. This day our instructions were to create a small collage of images that spoke to us about our deeper purpose in life. "Trust what you pick and work rapidly," she said. I think we only had about 20 minutes to complete our picks and paste them up.

Laurie then asked us to quickly write a statement that included completions of the following questions: I am the one who ____. My name is____. What I need from you is____. My gift to you is____. What I have to say to you is____. My shadow is____.

I believe that full engagement means body, mind, soul, and spirit. If this is true, then balancing our thinking selves with our other sensibilities is desirable, especially in situations where people need to change their ways of working and their relationships with each other, and need to do this with respect for differences.

These simple questions pulled a wonderful statement from me that I still return to for inspiration. We shared them in circle at the end of one day in the workshop and moved into dinner in a very different place than when we began, engaged at a level of depth and subtlety evoked by the imagery. I include this example because it demonstrates how much can happen with collage imagery in a short period of time, how words and images can inform each other and stimulate a great deal of insight.

The wonderful thing is that collage works with whole groups. Rich magazine imagery, so abundant in most places, taps that side of us that dreams, works symbolically, and constructs stories about our deepest meanings. I believe that full engagement means body, mind, soul, and spirit. If this is true, then balancing our thinking selves with our other sensibilities is desirable, especially in situations where people need to change their ways of working and their relationships with each other, and need to do this with respect for differences. Collage opens us up.

Using Collage for Visioning

Following the economic collapse of the credit system in late 2008 many organizations' business models became invalid. The means of support changed radically. One client I worked with supports nonprofits on a statewide basis with consulting and technical services. They needed to rethink their whole way of working in order to survive and thrive.

A key part of an initial workshop in which the entire board and staff met together to envision their future was a visioning activity using collage in combination with a Grove Graphic Guide called the Cover Story Vision. It consists of imagining that a major magazine has featured your organization on the cover and then imagining what that cover story says. The template has room for big headlines, sidebars (a magazine term for feature stories in inserts), quotes, images, and a cover. Because everyone is familiar with magazines, no one stumbles over the metaphor, although picking which magazine can be a bit of a discussion. We encouraged them to pick magazines they would be proud to be in.

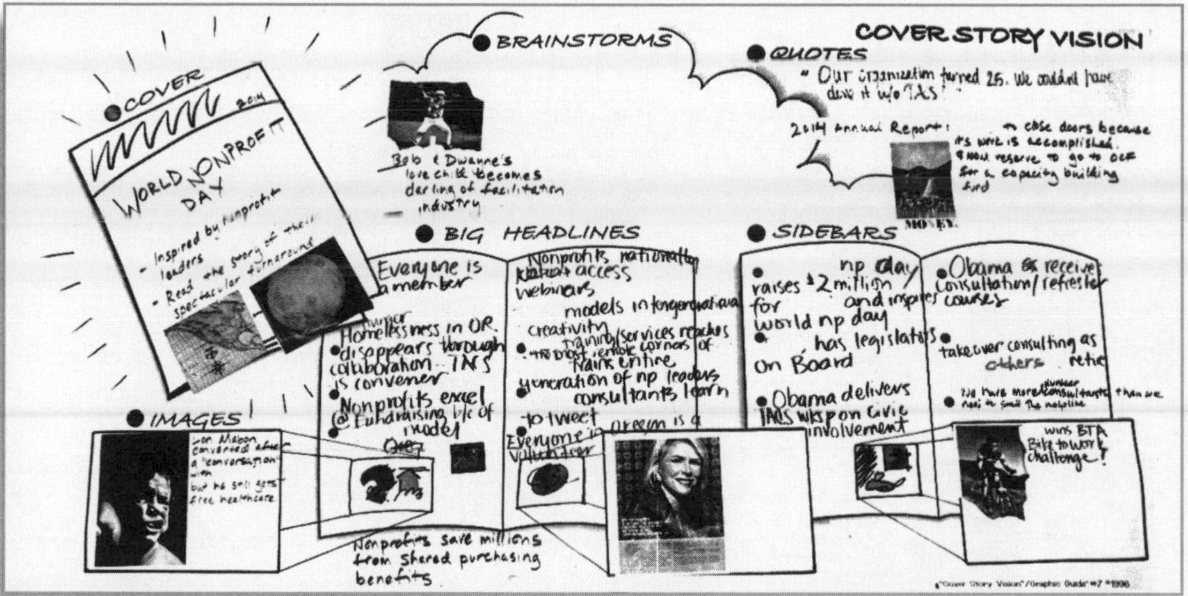

Because the situation in the organization was serious and people were a bit discouraged, we felt that using collage imagery would help them get to a state of visioning that would go a little deeper, than just having an imaginary discussion, so we brought several boxes of magazines and let the groups work with the images as well as markers on the templates. An hour later we had five powerful displays. Each group then presented, telling the story of their future in the past tense as though it had already happened. The energy lifted considerably as people began to work with the raw imagery, and exploded in laughter and good feeling during the presentations. They did share a dream and it was suddenly alive again in the midst of the challenges.

COVER STORY COLLAGE

Using collage in combination with templates balances the evocative power of imagery with the organization of the graphic framework. This one is a vision collage from the offsite of a nonprofit support organization working on developing a new business model.

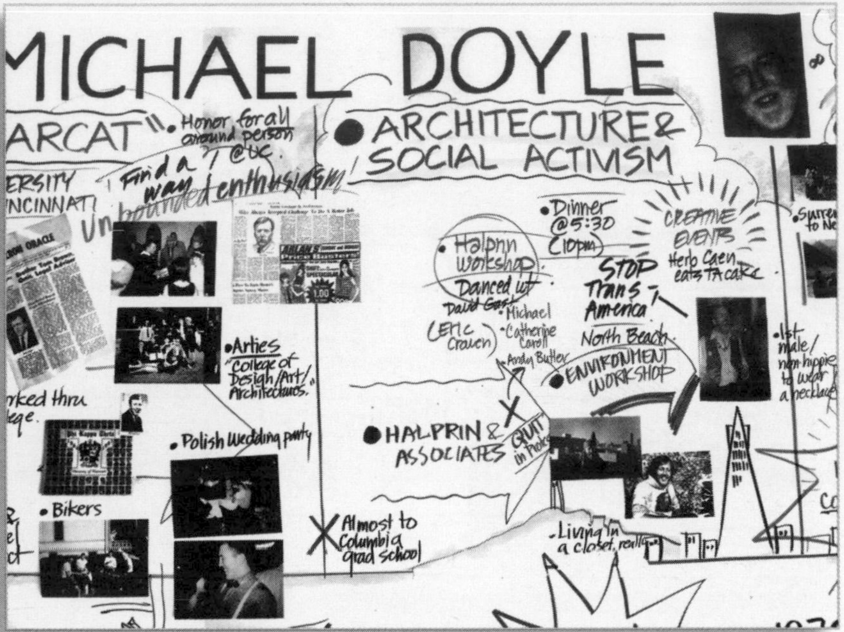

REMEMBERING MICHAEL DOYLE

When Michael Doyle died the consulting community of the San Francisco Bay Area turned out to remember him, with a 32-foot-long collage of pictures and memories. Michael was my mentor in the early days of learning facilitation.

Other Uses of Collage

I've used collage in a wide number of settings with similar results:

- **At the memorial of a consulting colleague** who led the professionalization of facilitation in the 1970s, Michael Doyle (coauthor of *How to Make Meetings Work*), everyone was asked to bring images and photos and artifacts from his life. The memorial consisted of people coming up and telling their stories and adding their photos and memorable images to the time line. The mural was a centerpiece for hours of conversation after the formal part of the program was over.

- **Staff and board of the Baltimore Aquarium** were asked to bring their own magazines with imagery and created beautiful visions in advance of planning for a new aquarium project. By asking each participant to bring relevant imagery we were able to begin the thinking about the event much in advance of the actual meeting.

- **The IT department of Agilent Technologies** was asked to bring images from the three years it spent cloning every computer program at Hewlett Packard when it spun off into its own company in the 1990s. It was a feat of historic proportions that the leadership wished to acknowledge by creating a graphic history of the event. The meeting began by asking everyone to collage all the artifacts everyone brought onto a huge time line, which became the springboard for telling the story. As people posted all their artifacts the meeting buzzed with storytelling and reflection.

Primary Power of Collage

Collage imagery is very powerful to the people who select the image. This is because the image itself isn't where the meaning lies, but in the connection between the image and what it evokes in the person who relates to it. People who do Soul Collage as a regular practice keep their work for years and find continuing meaning as they reflect on what the images mean. The same happens with groups, but a little less powerfully, unless the group has spent a lot of time agreeing on the images they include. Collage functions much more as an engagement and inspiration tool in group settings.

The power of images, be they a picture or a set of words that are very evocative, is in their simplicity and flexibility. This also opens them to many different interpretations. For communications about organizational visions and goals, the images need to be associated with words if you want to assure they are communicating consistently.

GO SLOW TO GO FAST

I remember Michael Doyle teaching us facilitation, saying "go slow to go fast." He believed you either took time engaging people up front and having everyone understand what changes or plans they were making, or you would have to spend the time later during implementation catching everyone up—a process that greatly slows down the process of getting results.

Using Picture Cards to Stimulate Dialogue

As visual thinking has spread, tools that supply ready-made imagery to support dialogue in groups has grown as well. At a conference launching a new network on business visualization called VizThink, one of the main events was a challenge event where three different methods were used to solve the same organizational problem. They were:

1. Graphic templates
2. Mind mapping software
3. Picture cards

I was leading the template group for a group of about 20 who volunteered to join us. A similar number worked with a person using software that allowed the meeting leader to type and link chunks of information in big diagrams. But Christine Martell, who has a whole company based on picture cards called VisualsSpeak, worked with several hundred at once! Each table had a deck of laminated images. They varied in size from half sheets to whole sheets and covered a wide range of subjects. Participants were invited to think about the organizational challenge and then intuitively select images that spoke to them. These were then "played with" to create a combination that might suggest a solution for the client. The power of Christine's process was in engaging and opening up that many people all at once. The challenge was getting closure in a short period of time. As we will see in the next section, working with large charts and templates is hugely efficient in getting groups to focus and work with large, complex amounts of information, which is what the challenge event required.

PICTURE CARDS

Christine Martell's VisualsSpeak cards come in packs of different sized imagery to support all the kinds of dialogue you might want to support. Here are a few of the images, reproduced by permission. (See www.visualsspeak.com/ for more information.)

The ability of the picture cards to engage is undeniable. Teachers have used card systems for years with children, to break a topic down and allow combination and recombination. Tarot cards have been used for divination and personal exploration since the Middle Ages. In the facilitation field the Institute for Cultural Affairs has worked with imagery in this way since the mid 1970s, developing an entire approach that includes imagery, cards, and many other techniques called the Technology of Participation (TOP). This group is grounded in nonprofit and cross-cultural work and found that imagery is a powerful bridge.

Picture card exercises can be turning points in dialogue and problem solving for groups that are very stuck. As I've argued throughout this book, visualization provokes both sides of our brain, and imagery wakes up the right side directly, because that is where we process images. It is also out of our visual sense that we see connections between things that may seem unrelated otherwise. But the consistent usefulness of the single imagery tools is in provoking dialogue, for the images need to be explained, and the ways to do this are quite broad!

How to Work with Cards

Here are some of the things that will work right away for you if you want to encourage high engagement and rich dialogue in your meetings using image cards.

- **Introductions:** Spread the cards around on the floor or a table and ask everyone to pick an image that calls out to them as they enter a meeting. Then during introductions have each person share their image and why it spoke to him or her.
- **Problem Identification:** When a group seems stuck in talking about a problem, and you want to go into the underlying causes, take a break and ask people to pick an image that represents the problem. Then have pairs talk about their picks and share insights with the group as a whole.
- **Appreciative Inquiry:** Ask people to think about what is working in the project or situation you are addressing, and pick images that represent the quality they would like to see supported and encouraged.
- **Organization Change:** Ask people to pick an image that represents a change they would like to see. Have people discuss their picks in pairs or small groups, and then share insights in the larger group.
- **Solution Finding:** Ask people to look at all the images and intuitively pick images that point toward a solution to the situation they are working on. Again, discuss in pairs or at small tables and then share insights.

FUNCTION OF IMAGERY
by Kenneth Boulding

At an International Forum of Visual Practitioners conference Virginia Hamilton, a top executive in California's workforce development system, shared her experience with picture cards. She cited Kenneth Boulding, author of *The Image: Knowledge in Life and Society* (University of Michigan Press, 1956). Boulding is credited with cofounding General System Theory, and was a prolific writer about social psychology, economics, and interdisciplinary philosophy. Virginia shared a series of assumptions Boulding makes about imagery and its usefulness in change work as she has experienced it.

1. People operate out of images.
2. Images govern behavior.
3. Messages shape images.
4. Images are held by values.
5. Images can change.
6. Changed images change behaviors.

IDEO METHOD CARDS

IDEO, an innovation and design firm, developed a set of 51 Method Cards as inspiration for practicing and aspiring designers, as well as those seeking a creative spark in their work. Here is an image of some of them. (See www.ideo.com/news/ideo-method-cards.)

- **Behavior Change:** An edgier activity might be to ask people to pick images that represent behavior they don't like and an image of what they would like to see. This more negative approach might be just the angle you need to throw people into parts of themselves where they aren't so rehearsed so they show up more authentically. Virginia encourages groups working this way to explicitly discuss the values that lie behind the images people pick as way of getting into the foundation material.

IDEO's Method Card deck provides both concepts and images to stimulate thinking. It includes a rich set of ideas for doing things like "bodystorming," which is role playing and physically acting out solutions, or the one shown here "A Day in the Life," which encourages spending some time being like your customers.

Don't wait to get a set of formal cards to try this approach. You can easily make your own cards by mounting images on cardboard. Art stores also sell plastic sheets for laminating images if you want to protect them. Having sets of images that are focused on the areas in which your meetings fall might be an advantages.

Sand Tray Work for Organizations

I want to conclude this section on using visualization for high engagement by sharing my experience with 3-D imagery, inspired by the sand tray work of Jungian therapists. Carl Jung used imagery centrally in his work and so have his students. He was a student of archetypes, the kind of images that have universal meaning and appeal and seem to be deeply embedded in the human psyche. Jung was especially fascinated with dreams, which often are dynamic quilts of imagery that seem to have a language all their own. In the process of developing techniques for allowing people to access these parts of their sensibility, Jungian therapists have developed a technique called "sand tray therapy" that has had a powerful influence on my own reflective work as I work to engage my many buried selves in dialogue with my conscious brain.

I was introduced to this approach years ago by some therapists trained in Jungian techniques . We worked with two small trays about three feet by four feet in dimension and six inches high, filled with sand. They had blue bottoms that you could see if you pulled the sand away, making symbolic beaches and lakes. They also had shelves full of miniatures of all sorts — princesses and toads, goblins, trees, little crystals, machines, animals of all sorts — literally hundreds of images embodied in dollhouse-sized, 3-D figurines and objects.

LEADERSHIP IDEAS IN FIGURINES

Working with little figures in a tray of sand is like working with collage in 3-D. Everyone gets to respond and tell stories and share new ideas sparked by the symbolic elements.

The process of using sand trays is similar to collage. Users are asked to think about something specific, like a relationship, and make a little arrangement in the sand that represents it. You have to work quickly, much more quickly than you can think about consciously. Little figurines jump into your hand and onto the tray just because you like them. In about 10 minutes you will have a little arrangement. The rest of the session is spent talking about these very different "pictures." You may be asked to speak as if you were this or that part of the arrangement, and notice things. The approach is non-judgmental. You look for sparks of insights, and *wow*, do you get them.

During the '90s a consultant named Gillian Barton was doing sand tray work with a business

THE GROVE ON LEGOS

Emil Tin, an intern at The Grove in 2007, encouraged Kara Nichols and me to join him in a Lego® block exploration of The Grove's organization. You won't make much sense out of this photo, but the several-hour dialogue was rich with insights and exploration. You can see how we blended the Lego activity with drawing on the chart.

called the Idea Factory in San Francisco as a way of stimulating conversation about strategy and innovation. Of course! This made immediate sense after my experience personally. We immediately tried it out at The Grove and had several fascinating dialogues. It took us into territory we would never have gone otherwise. The picture on the prior page is of one of the trays where we explored our images of "good and bad leadership." You get to figure out what it means! At the time it sparked a rich exchange.

When you begin to understand the role of imagery in our deeper way of making sense of things it becomes apparent that all kinds of media can work as support for dialogue and engagement if treated as a doorway to insight. Imagery allows people to engage at a fresh level. John Ward, the consultant who uses kinesthetic modelling that I wrote about earlier, called his original practice Knead to Know. He used clay and led our Grove team through a process of playing with making little shapes and figurines that represented our values. The dialogue that emerged over several sessions gave rise to The Grove core values that we follow today.

Another variation of using 3-D imagery is the work Lego is doing applying its toys to organizations. They have a consulting wing that leads strategy sessions using Lego blocks to visualize organizational problems and solutions. One of their associates attended a training of ours and we spent some time learning how to construct meaning with the little blocks. I haven't tried collage, sand tray figurines and Lego toys all together yet, but I bet it would be fun!

III. Graphics for Visual Thinking

Mapping Ideas & Finding Key Patterns

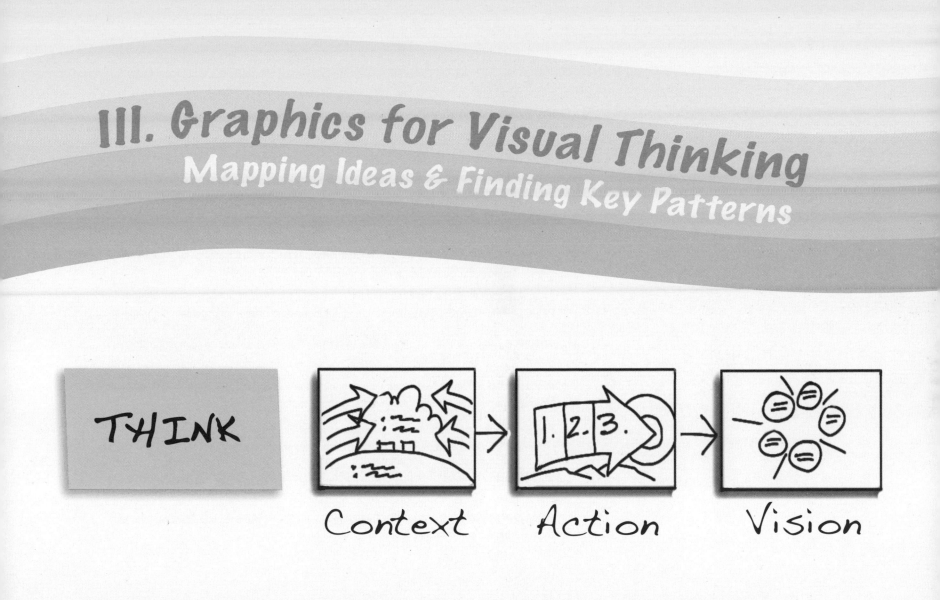

III: Graphics for Visual Thinking

This section reviews specifics tools for writing on the wall, problem solving, storyboarding, visual planning, and all the ways to get groups to think together and generate breakthrough insights and meaningful plans.

Chapter 9: Group Graphics® How visual meetings are like jazz; the Group Graphics Keyboard; examples, applications and tips; the theory behind the Keyboard.

Chapter 10: Problem Solving How to understand problems and root causes; graphics for simple brainstorming and problem solving; solving wicked problems; understanding systems.

Chapter 11: Storyboarding & Mind Mapping Creating narrative flows with storyboards; thinking in branching patterns.

Chapter 12: Visual Planning Using graphic templates to guide visual planning; The Grove Strategic Visioning Model and Graphic Guides; creating decision support rooms.

Chapter 13: Multiple Groups & Gallery Walks Working with breakout groups; handling report-backs; managing large displays; gallery walks for seeing the big picture.

Chapter 14: Digital Capture Using digital photography for documentation; reporting formats; tips for processing chart photos; using graphics to link data online.

Chapter 15: Visualizing at a Distance How to work visually with web conferencing software; working with tablets; supporting interaction online.

9. Group Graphics

Seven Ways to Write on the Wall

Any time you face a blank page or chart you will have to choose how to begin. This involves understanding the basic patterns I talked about in Chapter 2 in regard to the Group Graphic® Keyboard, and its seven ways to write on the wall. These are the foundation formats out of which all the other variations emerge and the keys to visual thinking with groups.

How Jazz Works

Let's begin with a metaphorical side trip that will make all this talk about process more understandable. I personally like to play the piano and have always wanted to play jazz. I grew up being required to have traditional piano lessons with sheet music. I became fairly proficient but eventually rebelled, coming back to playing in college and starting over, making up my own combinations and pieces.

One day I wandered into a small music shop and found myself surrounded by tall piles of sheet music of all kinds stacked on several tables with narrow aisles in between. I came around to the front, overwhelmed. There was an older man who I assumed was the owner. "Can I help you with something," he asked, peering over his glasses. I was hesitant, but said softly, "I'd like to learn how to play jazz." The man looked at me up and down and didn't say anything. Then he reached under the counter and pulled out a book and plopped it on the counter. "Learn your scales," he said, and went back to his reading.

This was a turning point in my understanding of process. I'd expected to be guided to some pieces of jazz music. What he had given me was a book called *Hanon's Exercises*, a book of scales and runs that would exercise my fingers in all the kinds of patterns the hand can make playing a piano. There were no jazz pieces in the book! Why did he give me that one, I wondered? I think I now know. If I simply learned sheet music I would be tied to that one interpretation. By learning the basics I was stepping through the door to true invention and improvisation.

THERE ARE SO MANY CHOICES. WHERE DO WE START?
TO DOs
GANTT
ORG
MATRIX
SHBONE

Visual Meetings Improvisation

The examples in this book are like the simple finger exercises that you can combine improvisationally. The formats I describe in this chapter are like the different scales in different keys. The pictographs, ideographs, and words are like notes. Visual meetings aren't all improvisation. I do like sheet music and you will get great results in visual meetings just applying some of the activities I am recommending in the Steps-at-a-Glance boxes. But if you want to really understand how visuals work most flexibly, learn the keyboard. My hope is that understanding these basic patterns will do for thinking what the piano actually did for music. It allowed musicians to collaborate across boundaries. I imagine the Group Graphics Keyboard can empower conceptual jazz. It certainly has in the network of visual practitioners trained by The Grove over the years.

Thinking about Graphics like Music

So how do you shift to thinking about graphic displays as a process rather than just a pattern? It means starting by understanding that what we are describing is a relationship, not an object. There are two key relationships embedded in any visualization process:

1. **Creative Process:** The relationship between you and what you are putting on the display as you create it
2. **Perceiving Process:** The relationship between the display and people who are then using it to make sense of something

It turns out there are only seven basic kinds of relationships! By relationship I mean more than just a static connection. I mean the dynamic interaction between you and the display, and the meeting participants and the display. Visualization is always about *both* the perceiver and the perceived, and both are ways of thinking.

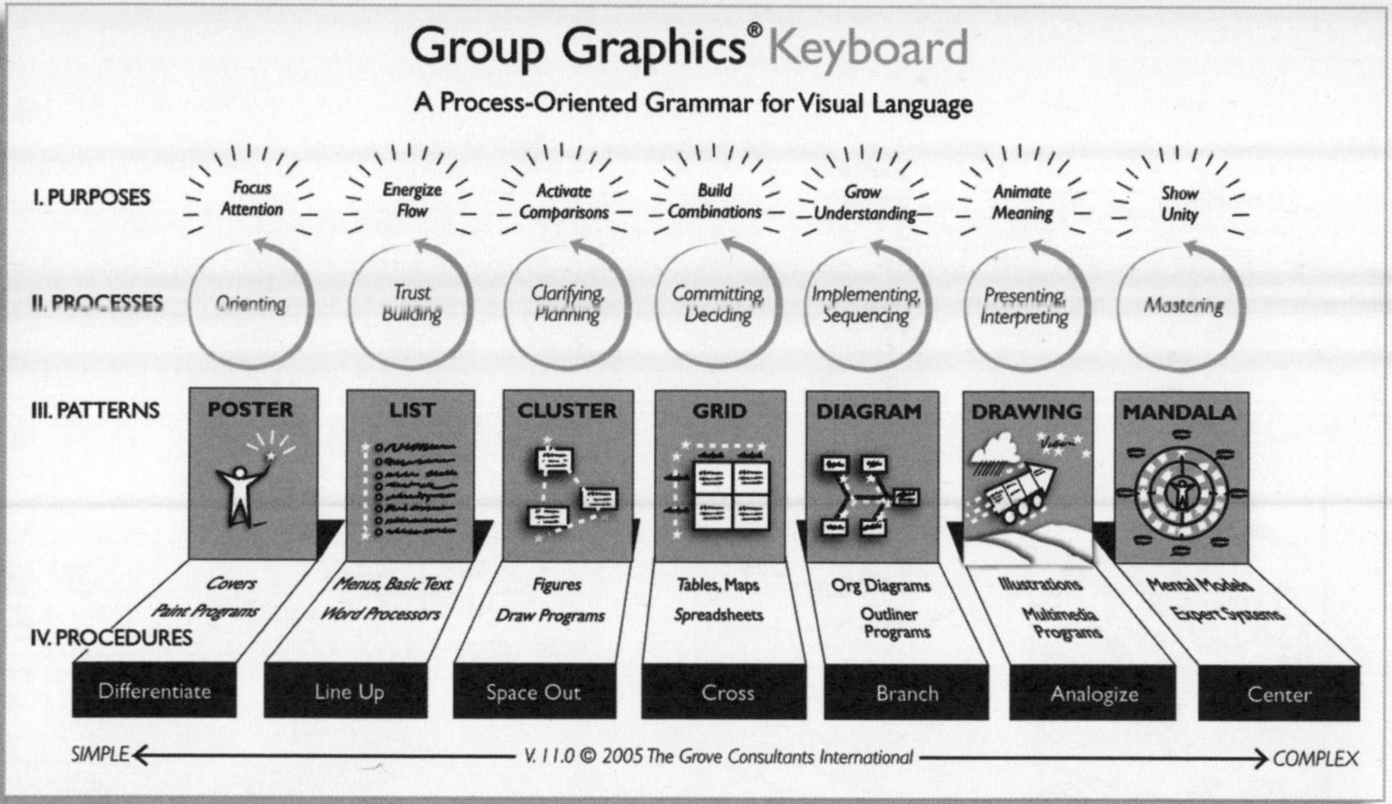

Here is a chart that shows you the full keyboard of patterns, the purposes they serve, the process they embody, and the procedures involved.

Don't let this visual overwhelm you. On the next page is a spread that will illustrate this same concept from the point of view of someone walking into a room and seeing a lot of charts on the wall. This spread is then followed by individual spreads on each format, so there is plenty of support for understanding. If you can learn to see the big patterns that underlie all the detail, the design of the big formats gets clearer and the welter of choices simplifies a great deal. Watch a designer sometime. They squint at their work to see the big pattern, purposely knocking out the detail. Then they zoom back into the detail. Macro-micro-squint-focus—this is how our brains make sense of the whole. After you learn the basic seven, the rest is combinations, just like in music. That is what the subsequent chapters are all about. Think conceptual jazz!

GROUP GRAPHICS KEYBOARD
This framework organizes all graphics into seven archetypal processes with the simple ones on the left and the more inclusive, complex ones toward the right.

THE GROUP GRAPHICS® KEYBOARD

POSTERS

Focus Attention

If you want to focus attention and orient

...differentiate...use strong, single images

LISTS

Energize the Flow

If you want to model listening without imposing structure

...line up the info

Activate Comparison

If you want to bubble up unconnected information, and get people to start making connections

...space out the information

GRIDS

Build Combinations

If you want to see combinations and formal relationships, and support decision making

...cross categories

DIAGRAMS

Grow Understanding

If you want to explore links, extensions, and organic systems of organization, or want to design a process for moving forward

...connect with branching

DRAWINGS

Animate Meaning

If you want to enliven your graphics and bring them to life with analogies that participants can understand

...use graphic metaphors

MANDALAS

Show Unity

If you want to think about how all parts fit together in a unified whole

...center all the information

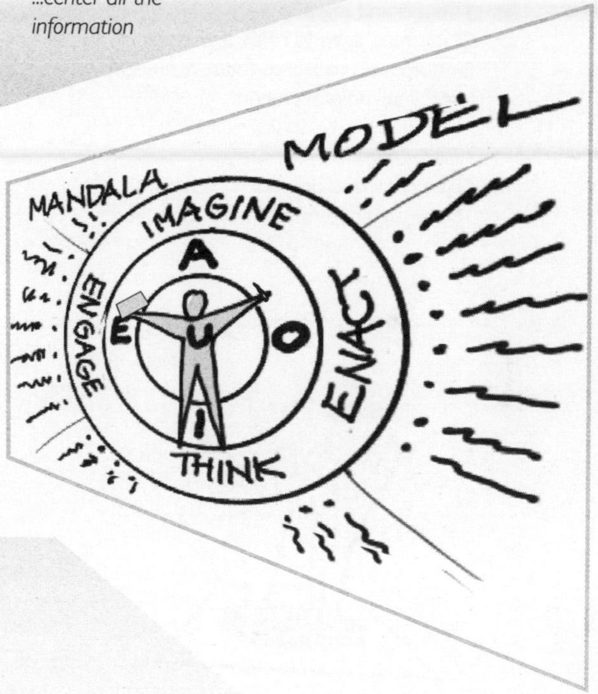

SEVEN WAYS TO WRITE ON THE WALL

These seven formats are organized so the simplest is on the left, and the most inclusive and complex on the right. The simpler patterns can nest in the more complex ones, like in nature. The ones you choose to use depend on the intention you have for your meeting or activity within a meeting. Under the names are seven generic properties of each pattern that suggest the purposes of each type of display. The next pages zoom in on each in detail.

Posters Focus Attention

POSTER

BEST USE
- Meeting titles
- Themes and logos
- Outcomes, agenda, roles, and rules
- Conceptual models to focus trainings
- Special acknowledgments

LIMITATIONS
- Can only make one point well.
- Too many posters take away the effect.

The simplest format is a chart that gets attention by being different from other things in the room. Big, single images or titles create a poster effect. Their purpose is to focus attention on a clear, central theme, and generate the potential for something to happen. Although one single image can be considered a constraint, you still have many choices in how you get attention. Color, spacing, exaggeration, and other graphic elements stand out if they are different from their surroundings.

If you study professionally produced posters, like the kind that are on bus stops or on billboards, you might notice that if the overall concept is strong and differentiated enough, then details can be added to provide more information for those who look a second time. On large charts you make, your big titles for different key parts of the meeting should stand out and be readable around the room, clearly different from anything else you record. If you need to include a lot of words, use one illustration to tie them together and create a poster effect, or treat the words themselves in a very graphic way that gets attention.

Imagine participants walking toward your meeting down a hall that is some kind of neutral color, with little bulletin boards, and having them encounter a life-sized cutout like a movie billboard. Most people would look at it. If it is holding a sign with a big title of your meeting that points right at its purpose—then you will have grabbed a participant's precious attention right at the start. If they walk in the room and a large title or outcome statement is on a blank sheet of paper, they'll notice that as well and spend a little more time imagining the purpose of the meeting.

This is the "poster effect." It's the process of getting people to look where you need them to look. Posters make a point!

THEME AND TITLE POSTERS

As people gather for meetings there is always a period when people are introducing themselves and getting settled. If you post a large theme poster that indicates the purpose of the meeting, then people subconsciously start thinking about things before the formal agenda begins.

The covers of books and the first slides in computer presentations are title posters. Their purpose is to focus attention and orient people to the general purpose of the contents in a broad way.

SINGLE IMAGES

Individual, colorful images stand out, especially if your meeting has a lot of other recording that is mostly words. As the number of charts increases, so should the boldness of your posters if you need to focus attention. The poster on the left announced an evening of storytelling at the Leadership Spring Retreat in Baltimore.

Lists Energize the Flow

LISTS

BEST USE

- Brainstorming
- General recording
- Minutes
- Agendas
- Expectations
- "Parking lots" for deferred items
- Process suggestions
- Inventories and options
- Agreements and actions
- Next steps

LIMITATIONS

- Hard to compare items.
- Several hours of listing becomes a visual blur.

ISN'T SPOKEN LANGUAGE LINEAR?
ALL THESE TABLES OF CONTENTS ARE LISTS!

Writing information one line after the other in a linear fashion is the easiest way to get a flow of exchange going with a group without imposing much structure. If you don't know where the group is heading and want to devote your attention to having the group and you get to know each other, then listing is the best way to begin. Everyone understands this format.

Within lists your emphasis can move between headings in ALL CAPS and supportive points in lowercase lettering. If you know that you will return to the list to rank items or review, then leave enough space in the margins to make additional comments, dot vote, or communicate a spontaneous activity. Pre-made agendas and outcome charts are usually lists.

Western cultures read from right to left and top to bottom. You can assume patterns of order that follow that convention. If there are borders and lines that reinforce this linearity they function, like roadway markings. A line under a title means it isn't part of the list that is below. A line connecting two shapes indicates connection. Graphic artists use borders and connecting lines that surround and connect information on a page to guide the reader. This linear kind of perception is fundamental, and is directly facilitated by this format. It doesn't drive our scanning, but affects it.

I've been interested to see how magazines experimented with tables of contents when graphic computers became common in the 1990s. *Wired* magazine got quite adventurous in presenting its contents in spatial ways. But after a few years they went back to a more linear approach. Why? I suspect it is because human beings find linear flows of information easiest to scan. Almost invariably agendas and tables of contents, to do lists, and things we need to read smoothly are organized in a linear pattern. We also remember events in chronologies, and tell stories that way. Our waking days are spent with one experience after the other moving through time.

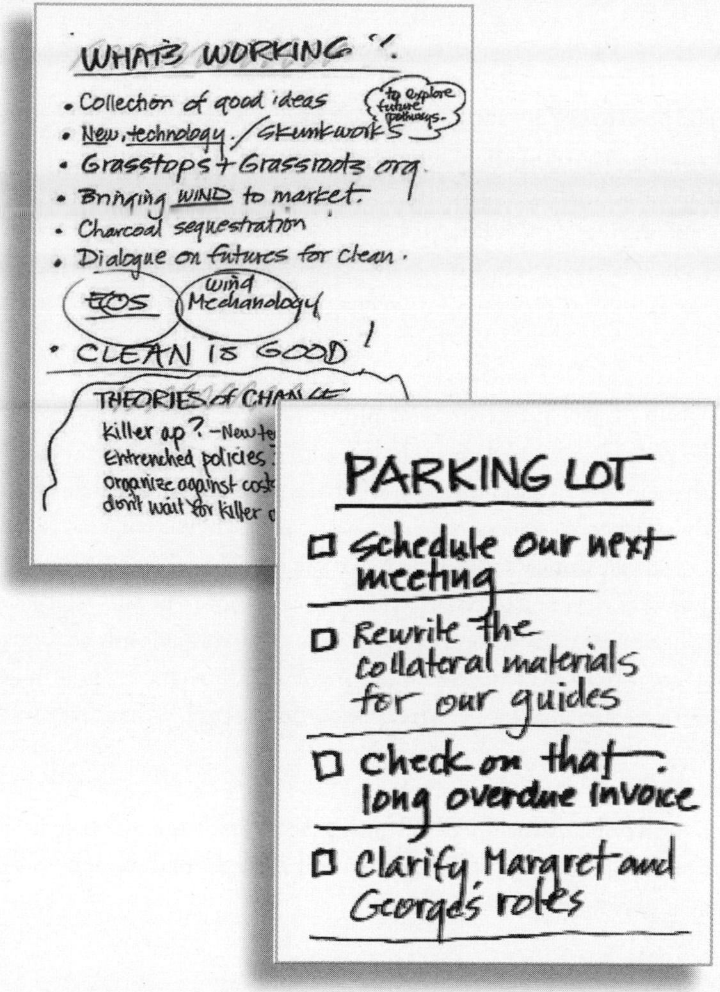

GENERAL RECORDING

When you don't know what is going to be said or where a discussion is heading, then listing or the following format of clustering are the best choices. With listing, if people indicate main subjects, then create headings, like the "what's working" lists to the left. If you don't know the subject, simply leave a bit of room between items and in the margins so you can come back and underline or add bullets if an item turns out to be a topic heading. When you begin, learn to use one consistent color for main heads, and two alternating earth colors for supporting text. Develop a consistent bullet style, as well.

PARKING LOTS

When items are raised in a meeting that are not on topic or need more attention later, a well-used facilitator practice is a "parking lot" list on a side chart. This can be referenced later to make sure all items are accounted for. It's best to keep it simple and clear.

Clusters Activate Comparisons

CLUSTERS

BEST USE

- Brainstorming themes and options
- Recording discussions that hop around among a lot of topics
- Loose design
- Visioning
- Context mapping
- Nonlinear thinking processes
- Drawing out customer interests
- Orienting students to a new field
- Identifying potential team goals

LIMITATIONS

- Sacrifices sequencing to grouping.
- The chronology is hard to follow.
- Can seem messy.

Humans inhabit space, and need to understand it just to walk into a room and get a seat. Relating to things in a spatial way is more complicated than just flowing along. To even see a shape our eyes have to dart around in something called a stochastic process. Our sense of seeing things clearly is a process of assembling many, many little snapshots, so seeing things spatially is inherently active. A display that has chunks of information arranged spatially requires active exploration. This is the reason that sticky note processes are so engaging, as I hope I made clear in Part II on engagement.

A wall full of sticky notes is an iconic cluster chart with information spaced around without connections. It's the preferred format if people are bubbling with information and you want to interact in a free flow with them, but also stimulate some initial thinking about how things will eventually fit together. The *absence* of connections drives participants to make all kinds of associations as they interact with the display and compare its contents. Clusters can be very loose, or can reflect clumping of first and second levels of information in a more formal way, as shown in the example here and on the next page. Sticky note processes can start randomly and move toward organization and categorization through rearrangement. The movement this format supports is an outpouring of creative sharing—a virtual popcorn of energy. We naturally want to find connections.

When connections aren't on a display their absence actively pulls people's attention and in the relationship we actively make comparisons. Remember what we learned about push-pull in regard to overall energy patterns.

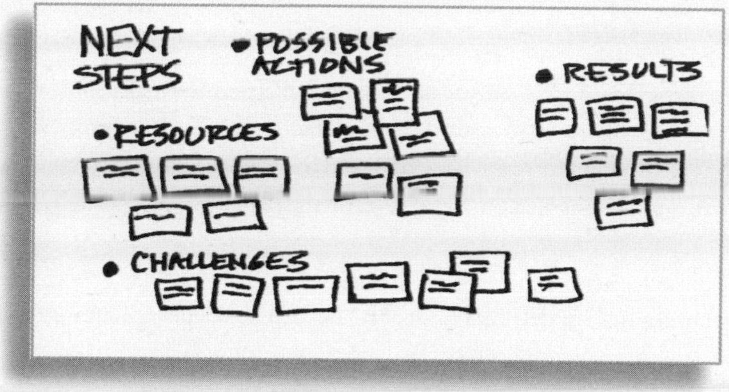

AFFINITY CHART

Walls of sticky notes are sometimes called affinity charts, where meeting participants themselves generate many items, usually writing the notes themselves (it helps to provide a model so people write clearly). There are several processes for then making sense out of the array (see Chapter 7). You can ask people to group the stickies either silently or through discussion. When the categories become clear, write labels and circle the stickies that have an affinity to one another.

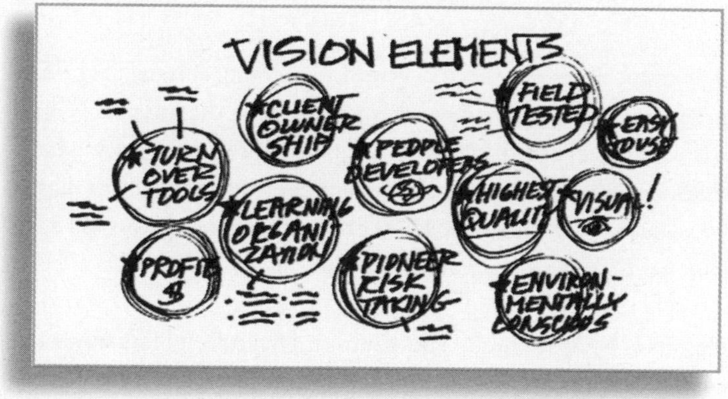

VISIONING CHART

Use clusters when a group is looking for vision themes after a visioning exercise, and doesn't know how it all fits together. Use a separate circle with a star bullet and clear caps for each theme, then add additional comments around the bubble. If you record something every time someone speaks, the vision will begin to "develop" like old-style film.

Grids Build Combinations

GRIDS

BEST USE

- Evaluation
- Project and agenda design
- Organizing tasks on a team
- Calendaring and roadmapping
- Mapping numeric data
- Mapping geographic information
- Forced comparisons
- Perception stretching

LIMITATIONS

- Categories must be clear.
- Doesn't reflect the process of the group.
- Hard to adjust once you've set the frame.
- Constrains improvisation if the discussion moves off topic.

WHAT ABOUT DATA CHARTS!
BUDGET

If your group needs to compare proposals, analyze information, and perhaps make some decisions, you might chose a grid or matrix as a format. Moving through this kind of pattern is more constrained and deliberate than other formats. To understand the combinations, categories need to be very clear. Once categories are agreed on, a grid is very helpful in working through all possible combinations by comparing the categories.

Simple grids, like many conceptual models, may have only two categories per column and row. More complex grids, such as those used for project budgeting or responsibility charting, require more effort. If you choose to work in this format, be prepared for a slow process. One very helpful facilitative move when working with a grid is to lead the group through category decisions by using sticky notes. Once the categories are clear, budgets, project plans, maps, and data displays become very powerful.

Grids underlie all the geographic maps we use to navigate. In a meeting context the gridding of time against agenda items gives us a formal framework for controlling the process. People who run large meetings for a living actually create "tick tock" agendas or "window panes," which are grids that have the times down one side, and rows of different considerations across the top—usually the activity name, a description, a note about the process being used, who will do it, what equipment or materials are needed. These tools act like scripts.

I think of lists and clusters as being the archetypes for our right and left brain ways of working. The left brain, as described in most literature on the subject, handles linear, logical, sequential information. The right brain handles spatial relationships and imagery. The grid combines listing and clustering. Having both linear and spatial qualities on one chart is definitely more complex than either separately.

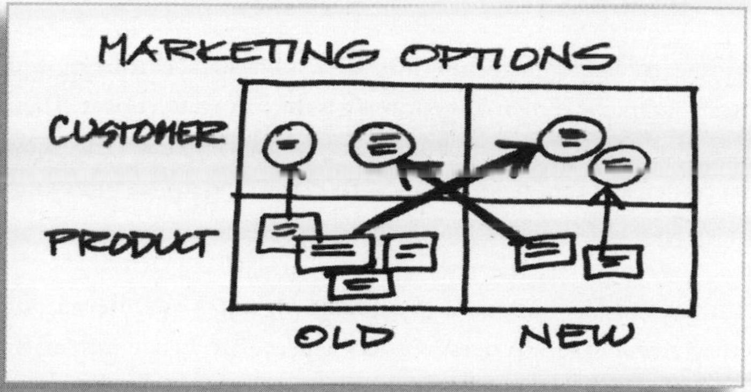

FOUR-BOX MODELS

Four-box models that compare two sets of simple categories are useful to move a group to a more comprehensive, analytical understanding of a subject. The example to the left was used to analyze marketing options of a large multinational. Scenario planning formally combines two or more sets of variable forces that have a clearly identifiable range of possibilities. Portfolios often use this structure. Use sticky notes to support the group doing "what if" thinking.

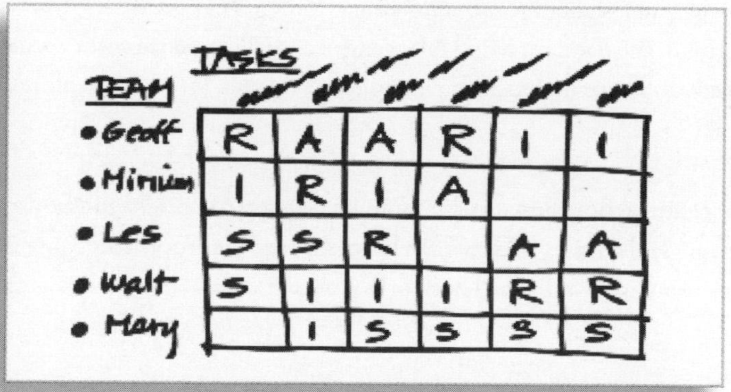

RESPONSIBILITY CHARTS

A very disciplined way to clarify what everyone on a team is doing is to list critical tasks on one axis and names on the other and identify what kind of responsibility each has for each task. One way to do this is to use the RASI model, asking who is Responsible as leader, who has Authority for signoffs, who Supports, and who needs to be Informed. Decide on each person's relation to each task. Be prepared for a real work session if you head into this territory.

Diagrams Grow Understanding

DIAGRAMS

BEST USE

- Process mapping
- Mind mapping
- Systems analysis
- Finding root causes
- Decision trees
- Flow charting
- Organization charts
- Note taking

LIMITATIONS

- The process is slow and complex.
- No natural stopping place.
- Items must link into the overall structure.
- It is hard to show multiple connections.

I NEVER IMAGINED
THAT MANY CONNECTIONS

If you want to support a group moving thoughtfully through a subject and examining connections and relationships in an organic way, then diagramming is the format to choose. The word "diagram" is sometimes used for any kind of chart, but it is ***always*** used for charts that show connections. The process of creating and reading diagrams starts slowly, and moves more energetically as the pattern becomes clear.

Branching patterns are the way the deep structures of the mind organizes itself. Because organizations are living systems, diagramming their processes is very appropriate. Diagramming is also the language of systems thinking. In fact, you could make a case that systems-level understanding is fundamentally about visualizing connections you can't experience directly—something that requires making displays.

For teachers diagramming is an excellent way to encourage students to take notes. You will learn something about this in the parts on Mind Mapping. I actually used this process to think through parts of this book, and have included an example in Chapter 11, which explores this whole idea at some depth.

Now in the twenty-first century more and more people are coming to understand how powerful networks are, and increasingly diagrams of networks have become common. Engaging groups in seeing patterns in their own knowledge and networks is a terrific interactive way to strengthen this way of thinking.

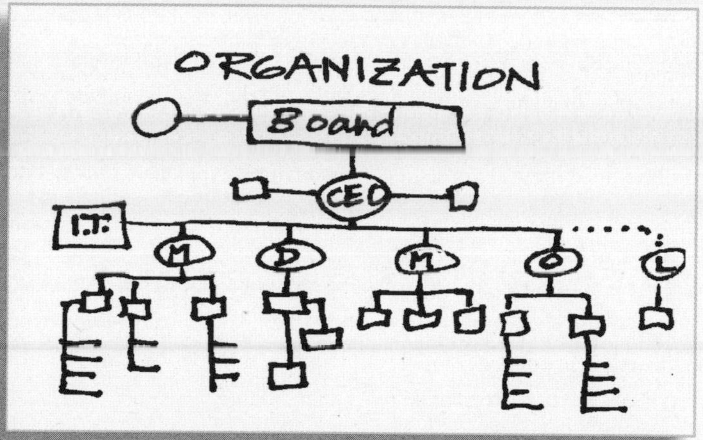

ORGANIZATION CHARTS & SYSTEM MAPS

Traditional hierarchical organizations have a pattern like that on the left. But they can also be shown as organic systems. Causal-loop diagrams are one of the core tools of systems analysis. Organization charts can contain a grid structure underneath, and become quite elaborate if you play with different line qualities representing different kinds of relationships, and different shape boxes representing different kinds of functions.

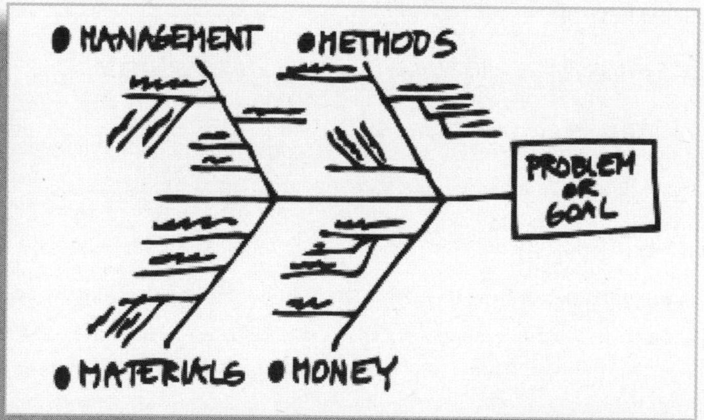

FISHBONE DIAGRAMS & MIND MAPS

Start with a central idea as the head of the "fish" or in the middle of the chart. Then create a topic as a branch in any direction. Add the major elements of this branch as sub-branches, and then break those down into finer elements. This is an enormously flexible format once you get going, and can be quite creative and elaborate. Diagrams can incorporate underlying grids, as the one to the right shows with its four categories.

Drawings Animate Meaning

DRAWINGS

BEST USE

- History charts
- Environmental scans
- Visions
- Innovation sessions
- Action plans and roadmaps
- Understanding systems through metaphor
- Overviews of a field of knowledge

LIMITATIONS

- Requires experience with the metaphor.
- Can blind-side thinking if the metaphor doesn't include an important element.
- Maps are not the territory; metaphors are not reality.

If you want your group to come alive with an immediate appreciation of the big picture, add a graphic metaphor to your display that the group understands and that is appropriate to the subject you are addressing. People will project their understanding into your charts and bring alive all the dynamics that are difficult to draw. Be prepared for meetings to develop a lot of energy if you've connected with the right metaphor.

The keyboard metaphor I've been using for this chapter is a "drawing" out of what you know about music and improvisation and applying it to dynamic meetings. If you have any experience with music, then it should be immediately apparent that any number of "compositions" or processes is possible given the seven basic formats.

Metaphors may be added to any of the prior formats to enliven them. For example:

- A poster could be a big keyhole.
- A list could be drawn to look like a rolled scroll by adding a border that curls.
- A cluster could look like popcorn or little clouds.
- A grid could be drawn to look like a screen, or a group of farmers' fields.
- A diagram can be a tree, a web, or a river system.

It's important when working with metaphors to realize that they are bound to culture and the experiences of the participants in your meetings. They can be obstacles as well as enablers if they keep you from seeing important things. This is why using multiple displays and different formats becomes so important.

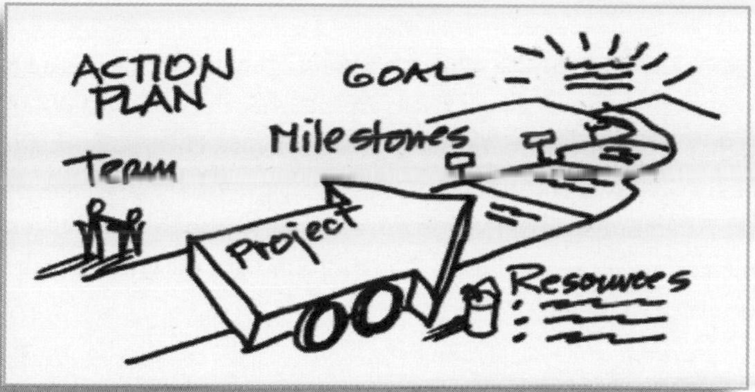

JOURNEY METAPHORS

For action planning, a journey metaphor shows a project heading toward a goal. In a more elaborate drawing you can illustrate action plans as journeys over different kinds of roadways and skyways and waterways, depending on the types of challenges a group is facing. Working out these drawings is a wonderful way to think through implementation issues at a holistic level.

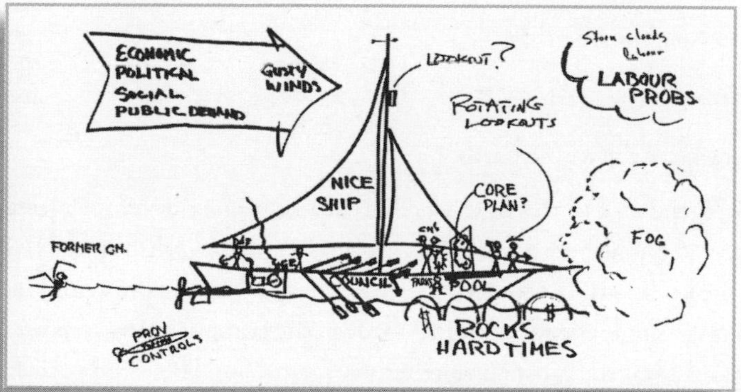

VEHICLE METAPHORS

This chart was created by a city council asked to compare its organization to a ship or boat. The teams generated images and compared them. This stimulated real insights—in a humorous context—about what was or wasn't working. Metaphor work can also be used for visioning, where teams pick other organizations, machines, plants, or animals that represent their desired future. Imagery often makes it easier to discuss tough or sensitive issues.

Mandalas Show Unity

MANDALAS

BEST USE
- Introductions charts
- Visions
- Mental models
- Pie charts for financial data
- Radar diagrams for multifactor analysis
- Target charts to show unified focus
- Constellation maps

LIMITATION
- Complex and challenging to read.
- Sometimes everything isn't unified.
- Writing in a circular pattern can be difficult.

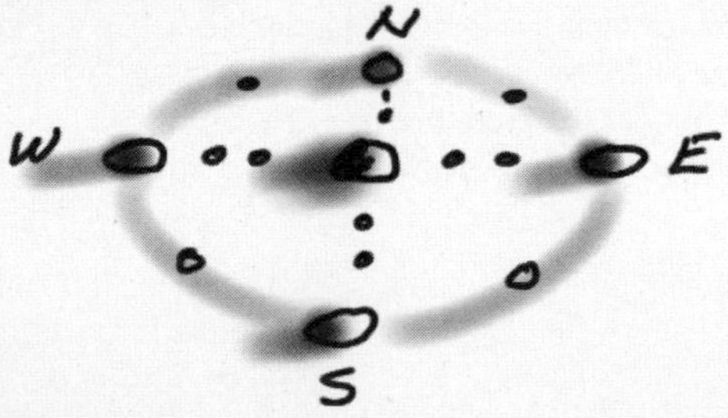

If you want to support group thinking about a subject in a holistic, unified way, and want to move around a subject with a balanced understanding of all its aspects, then the circular motif of the mandala format is the right choice. The word "mandala" is Sanskrit for archetype (something everyone knows) of which a circle is the most universal. It's the shape of Tibetan tankas, the medicine wheels of the Native Americans, and the Mayan sun calendar. It's also the most common format for illustrating mental models, seeing financials in the round on a pie chart, and showing multiple factors on radar diagrams.

In organizational work, mandalas are often used to present an integrating framework for a change process, or set of management principles, or to portray a group working together as a team. As the most complex display format it can embody the simpler ones.

- It can contain lists, illustrate clusters, radiate out from its center in constellations.
- It can have a grid overlay like a dartboard.
- It can show diagrams.
- It can also be a drawing of the whole Earth.

Richard Hackborn, the legendary HP manager who led the laser printer division to great success in the 1990s and later served on the board, came by a Group Graphics workshop at HP one time when I was presenting the keyboard. A month later I saw him again and he presented me with a circular drawing with every single component HP made in the computer divisions arrayed in a circular pattern. "You said it was the most comprehensive format and I believed you." It was a pretty powerful example of how stimulating this keyboard idea can be.

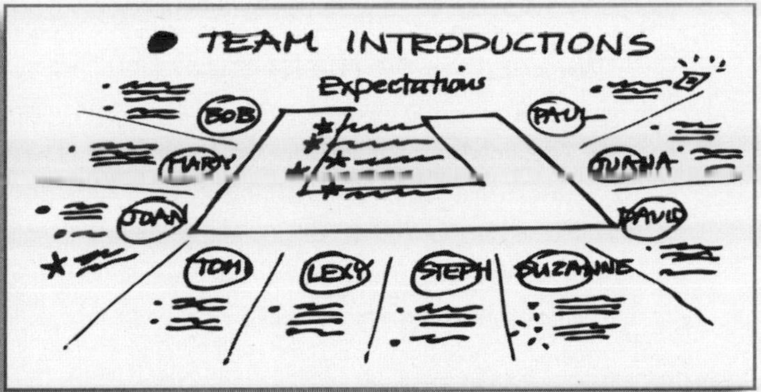

TEAM PORTRAITS

A great way to begin a team process or a workshop is to illustrate everyone in a circular seating arrangement, with information about each person radiating out from his or her name. The information you map can be tuned to what you want the group to know about each other. Lead the process slowly to make sure you have the correct name spellings and have captured the information people are sharing. It says, "We are one."

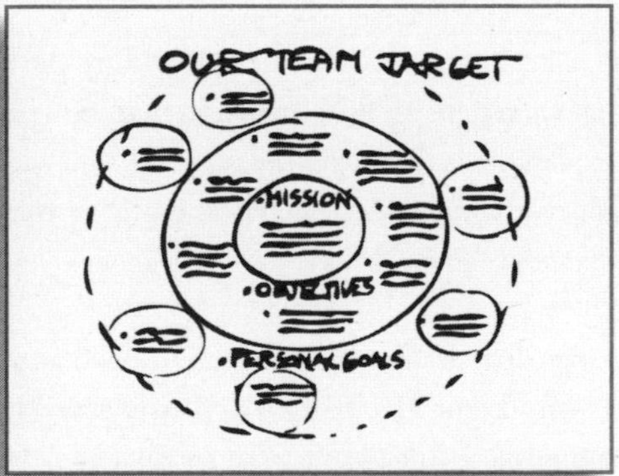

TARGETS

Action plans and game plans usually aim at clear targets—objectives that are Specific, Measurable, Actionable, Relevant, and Timely (SMART). Here the target contains three levels of categories that allow a group to explore different aspects of its goals.

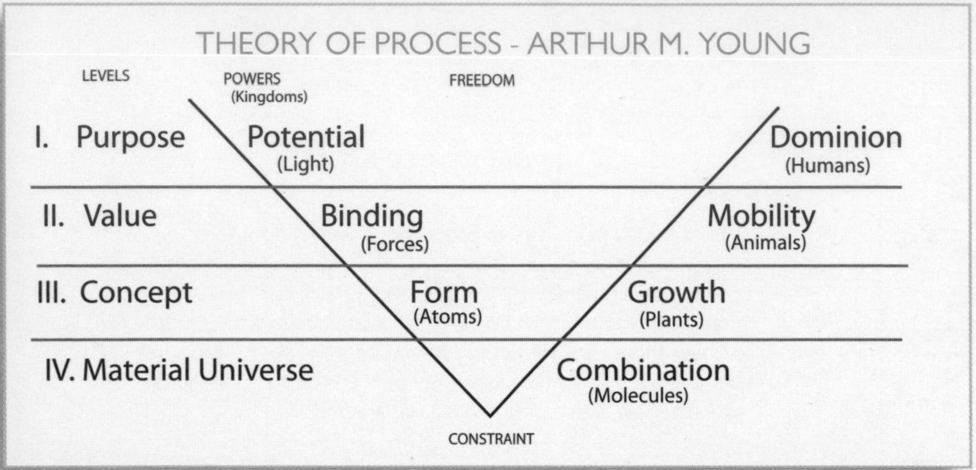

THE ARC OF PROCESS

When Arthur Young described evolution, he used a framework of seven stages that move from freedom to constraint and back to freedom. He called this the "Arc." For a complete explanation see his seminal work, *The Reflexive Universe* (Delacourt Press, 1976).

Background on the Keyboard

In developing The Group Graphics Keyboard I was guided by Arthur M. Young's description of how natural systems organize themselves. If you don't like theory skip this part and read on about all the different applications to specific kinds of meetings. But if you do like theory, there is some of the best available under the keyboard structure.

Science itself describes evolutionary process as one of gaining increasing complexity, with increasingly efficient means. In this sense plants are more evolved than crystals and minerals, animals are more evolved than plants, and humans more evolved than animals.

Young guided his students to appreciate that under the mineral world are the building blocks of molecules, atoms, fundamental forces and light itself. Young was a mathematician and physicist trained at Princeton, and favored explanations that cover the most ground with the simplest distinctions. He perceived that science itself had discovered how complex things in nature grow out of combinations of simple subsystems.

When Young described evolution, he used a framework of seven stages that moves from freedom to constraint and back to freedom. Light, as unconstrained as anything in nature, becomes a negative or positive force when it binds into one direction or another as electron or proton . Forces become atoms when they constrain themselves to moving around a center, an identity that even has a specific number. Atoms become molecules by binding themselves together in webs of interconnection that make up our physical world.

In a metaphoric way I saw that lists as recordings of the flows in discussion act like informational forces, recording directional sequence. Sticky notes seemed more like atoms, with grids associating with the molecular, crystalline world. This kind of metaphoric thinking is discouraged in formal science, but Young encouraged it in his students, because he believed that things were not unified by the way they look or appear, but by the way they move as processes. He was thinking the way a person listens to music, for the resonance and harmonies.

The rest of the keyboard made even more sense from this perspective, since the world of plants, animals, and humans in the evolutionary schema do have material form that we can see, and the processes by which they develop create distinctive patterns.

Branching Patterns Provide the Architecture for the Plant World

When a display moves to a branching pattern the same thing happens in information that happens in the biological world . Understanding grows as you branch your perception out from a core idea. Young points out that the entire world of plants is based on branching patterns, starting with the DNA sequences that are at the heart of all living matter.

YOU SAY BRANCHING,
I SAY FRACTAL !

In my field of organization development, I was aware that some of the original theorists like Ludwig von Bertalanffy were actually botanists developing tools that would help them think about living systems. One of these is causal loop diagramming, a way of displaying the relationships between elements in an ecosystem in branching patterns. Peter Senge and his colleagues at MIT and Innovation Associates were among the first to make this kind of systems thinking accessible to large numbers of people. It's evolved into the Society for Organizational Learning and Senge's *Fifth Discipline*, a classic work regarding the learning organization. Senge consulted with one of my clients, the San Francisco Foundation, in the mid 1980s. Martin Paley, the executive director

I came to realize that what people mean by systems thinking is thinking about how things really work beyond the realm of our direct experience, and that at a deeper level organizational systems that act like living, dynamic organisms are very related to the plant world.

at the time, was part of a thought leader group organized to test the applicability of systems thinking to organizations. Martin brought Innovation Associates to the foundation and the entire staff including myself went through several systems thinking workshops.

What was the first thing they trained us in, you might wonder. It was causal loop diagramming! I was deeply involved in applying my Group Graphics work to organizations by that time and was fascinated that it seemed to require this visualization technique to even understand what they were saying about stocks and flows and positive and negative reinforcement cycles. The way this thinking gains traction is by recording different facets of experience on some display, and then, and only then, can a person begin to look at the connections. I was doing this with the Coro Fellows! I came to realize that what people mean by systems thinking is thinking about how things really work beyond the realm of our direct experience, and that at a deeper level organizational systems that act like living, dynamic organisms are very related to the plant world.

The keyboard came alive as I saw the similarity in the other branching formats that are tried and true tools for visualizing about organizational processes. Some of the ones I write about are:

- **Critical Path Charts:** Showing how tasks connect over time on complex projects.
- **Vintage Charts:** Used by technologists to show the evolutionary progress of a technology through various versions.
- **Organization Charts:** Used to show formal reporting relationships.
- **Fishbone Diagrams:** Used in quality improvement to analyze root causes of problems.
- **Mind Maps:** Used to illustrate any arrays of connected ideas—now supported by many kinds of software.

- **Process Maps:** Diagrams to show the flow of a meeting.

Discovering the Key to "Drawings"

When first developing the Group Graphics Keyboard I was so excited about the clean distinctions between poster, list, cluster, grid, and diagram that I wanted the full keyboard to be that crisp. I originally thought that the way displays would animate, and reflect the evolutionary jump from plants to animals in nature would be to embody movement and timing like flow charts. But flow charts are really just grids with time on one axis. This wasn't a clean difference. I went back to my fundamental assumption that it is the relationship that jumps to animation and not the display. With that perspective I appreciated that when a graphic metaphor is added to any of the prior kinds of displays, the interaction between viewer and display moves to a new level. It does, literally, animate, as the viewer projects his or her experience into the simple lines that point at it. I called this fundamental format "drawings.

As I explained in the two-page spreads discussing the keyboard formats, the richness that comes with graphic metaphors has a requirement, that the viewer have experiences with the metaphor! If not, there are two things that aren't clear—the metaphor and the thing it is explaining. It therefore becomes very useful to think about what kinds of experiences everyone in your meeting or group has! Here are four that seem to work worldwide.

- **Landscape Metaphors:** Everyone has experience in nature at some time, and knows the ground is down, the sky is up, and weather is in between. Using this metaphor to map information is universally understood.
- **Journey Metaphors:** Many people think of planning as a kind of journey. We are in a particular place. We want to go somewhere, our destination. We plan how to get there—the

SEEING THROUGH THE LENS OF METAPHOR

When you look at drawings that are "about" something, you associate the graphic metaphor with what you already know. The more overlap, the richer the animation. The shadow side of this effect is losing sight of the fact that the metaphor is not the thing itself.

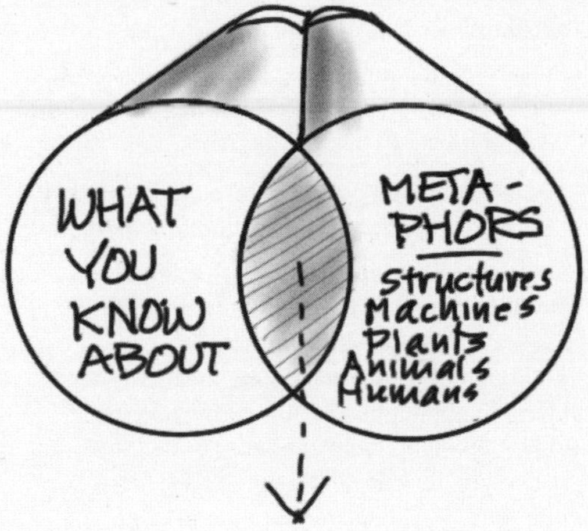

THE EVOLUTION OF SOFTWARE

As the first widely accessible graphic computer, Apple's evolution is a parable about the Group Graphics Keyboard.

- In the beginning was MacPaint—single image ads.
- Next came MacWord—the lister.
- Then MacDraw—the cluster program!
- Business viability required Excel—the grid-based spreadsheet.
- MacProject and Omnigraph allowed diagramming, and could generate views as tables (grids), clusters, or lists.
- PageMaker and PowerPoint allowed animation through pagination, and later actual animation.

No interfaces had circular displays in the beginning, except special dashboards, radar diagrams, and rare AI interfaces. Now programs such as The Brain can array data around a central theme at the click of the mouse. It is interesting that Apple's new iPad, as an interface to the great cloud computing environment, reaches toward integration of all these ways of perceiving.

journey. Mapping an action plan on this kind of time line is perceived as making common sense because this pattern is so universal.

- **Vehicle Metaphors:** So many people own and drive cars, or take buses and trains, that comparing organizations to vehicles is widespread, and useful. The widely different kinds of vehicles make this a rich vocabulary for exploration of organizational models.
- **Human Metaphors:** Comparing one kind of organization to another is another rich area for visualization. Are you thinking about business as sports, farming, engineering, war making, family, or community? All these kinds of metaphors can become the organizing principle for displays.

Coming Full Circle

I associated the circle with unity and wholeness from the beginning of this process of designing the Group Graphics Keyboard. What puzzled me was my experience that the circle is actually very simple and easy to draw, especially if you use your arm like a compass and "stir" the shape onto the paper. But I again went back to thinking "relationship" and appreciated that seeing an entire range of information as unified is indeed the most challenging and complex process one can undertake when thinking about anything.

Technically, creating text in circular patterns on the computer was one of the more difficult challenges, so the early formats never did pick up on that. But I did notice that in the evolution of the computer software, it precisely mirrored the keyboard patterns. When I saw this I knew that I'd come across a way of thinking that would have long applicability.

10. Problem Solving

Getting Unstuck & Thinking around Corners

The project driving Interaction Associates (IA) when they were Coro's next-door neighbors in the early 1970s was called "Tools for Change." IA had a grant from the Carnegie Foundation to study how teachers and educational systems could learn from designers and architects to apply all the methods creative people use to solve problems. Their team actually published a booklet with dozens of strategies, and these were quite influential in shaping what we tried in the Coro Program. In a way, visual meetings started with visual problem solving.

Problems are things that won't work the way we want them to. This can be as broad as a situation where there is a big gap between your aspiration and current realities, or it can be as simple as having something you rely on break. You may have a problem that a certain piece of software has a bug, or that a storm has closed down transportation, or there isn't enough money in your budget to hire the staff you need. Whether problems are full catastrophes or small annoyances, they all spring from a common source—a mismatch between expectations and reality.

In meetings that focus on problem solving, visualization is a true power tool. It's no accident that designers, architects, and engineers, who think of themselves first and foremost as problem solvers, all use visualization centrally. This chapter shares some of the most tried and true applications. We will begin with the basic problem of having a group understand what the problem is.

Problems as Given; Problems as Understood

In the 1950s William J. J. Gordon, working in the Arthur D. Little Invention Design Unit in a research and development function, developed a systematic way of brainstorming and problem solving using small groups, recording, and skillful use of metaphors called Synectics. This is still a methodology that is taught, but like many powerful approaches, has gone mainstream. The

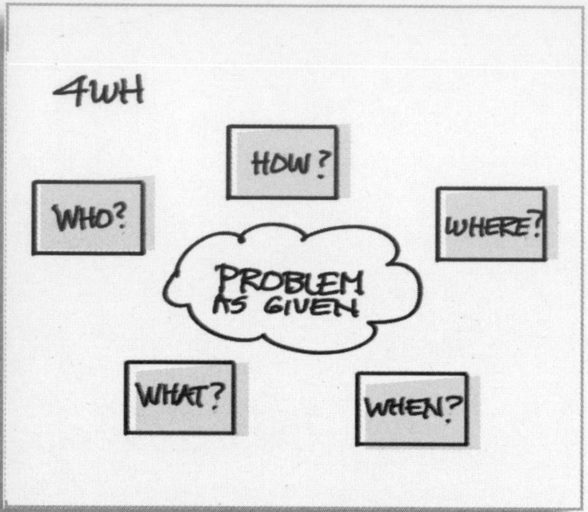

THE 4 WH TOOL

This the traditional tool a journalist uses to explore a subject he or she intends to write about. It's a great set of questions to understand a problem as given.

Synectic approach advocates beginning a problem-solving process by understanding the problem! This sounds like pretty common sense, and it is! But it is amazing how many times meeting participants will dive into problem solving with people proposing solutions before they have stepped back to analyze what the problem really is.

The simplest way to understand a problem is to ask the people who think there is a problem to describe it and take notes on a flip chart. If you are a salesman you might engage your potential client with what they think their challenges are. This is another word for problems for most people. If you are a teacher spelling out a problem for your students, you will surely encourage them to ask questions about it before jumping to answers.

There are also some more structured ways of going about asking questions that will help you understand a problem. I've sorted the following common tools using the progression of formats described in the Group Graphics Keyboard. You can see that since the generic display formats I explained in the previous chapter are simply different ways of looking at information, using different formats will reveal different facets of a problem. Following are the names of these approaches as used by people who run problem-solving meetings.

- **Exploring Images:** In Chapter 8 I explained how sets of image cards could be used to support dialogue about organizational issues and problems. They can also be used for simpler problem solving. Have people stand around a good collection of images and each pick one that represents the problem as they understand it. Then have everyone share what they saw in the simple images and record the insights.
- **Four WH:** When I was trained as a reporter in journalism school we were taught to ask "who," what," "when," "where," and "how" questions. We held off on the "why" questions

because those are interpretive and don't drive attention to the facts of the case. (This tool was also a key way we trained Fellows in Public Affairs at Coro to interview people about how government works.) Again, you can record these in lists, or use sticky notes and cluster the answers around the problem statement.

- **Pareto Charts:** Quality teams are encouraged to research incidents of recurrent problems they are analyzing, and create a chart that categorizes the items and graphs them by their frequency, most on the left and least on the right. The resulting chart will visually demonstrate where the bulk of the issues lie. Applying the 80/20 rule suggests that 80% of the problems can be dealt with by treating the biggest 20% of the items. (This chart is a grid, as you can probably tell.)

- **Fishbone Diagram:** The Total Quality Movement in the 1970s and 1980s (which has evolved into many kinds of quality improvement training,) popularized the fishbone diagram as a template for understanding a problem. These are also called Ishikawa Diagrams after their inventor in Japan. The drawing looks like a fish, with a head that is the problem, and bones that are the contributing elements of the problem. (There is a picture in Chapter 9 in the Diagrams spread.) These can also have bones. When analyzing a problem to understand it, you brainstorm with those people involved in all the different bones and then try to find a root cause to the problem. For any kind of physical systems problem this kind of analysis is extremely helpful.

- **Forced Metaphor:** A way to use drawings to understand a problem is to force a metaphor, and explore how what you are looking at is like something completely different. Having several small groups draw out their answers allows for cross comparisons. I shared a story about the Vancouver city officials comparing their city to a vehicle as a team-building activity, and a grocery chain management using metaphors to explore their vision.

- **Five Whys:** This approach goes right at the question of why people think there is a problem, and what the underlying problems might be. (You can use a mandala format

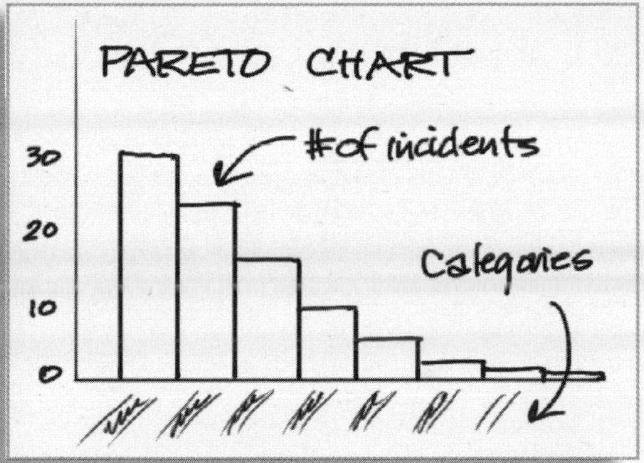

PARETO CHARTS

In quality improvement, teams are encouraged to track the number of specific types of problems that arise in a production line, for instance, and then plot the causes on a bar graph with the most frequent on the left. This shows graphically where the root causes of the inefficiencies probably lie.

RULES FOR BRAINSTORMING

The intention of brainstorming is to gather as many ideas from a group as possible, without shutting down or scrubbing out ideas that seem off the mark. In fact, brainstorming is all about jumping out of our normal ruts. The generally followed rules are:

- ❑ Suspend judgment
- ❑ Speak out whatever occurs to you
- ❑ Don't edit—be willing to have lame ideas
- ❑ Write down all ideas
- ❑ Work quickly

List brainstorming by itself doesn't guarantee you will generate breakthrough thinking. It takes combinations of efforts, including sleeping on ideas and asking your subconscious to go to work!

during a session to draw these out, using either markers or sticky notes.) If someone says, "the problem is we aren't making enough money," you could ask "Why?" They might say, "Our sales are down." Again, "Why?" "Our salespeople aren't reaching out to new customers and our old ones are oversold." "Why?" "We don't have any lead generation activity in new markets." "Why?" "The salespeople are only evaluated on the number of calls, not the number of calls to new customers. It's easier to call the old ones." You can see how this can drive very interesting analysis.

Brainstorming & Solution Finding

Once you have explored the nature of a problem and searched for central causes, the next steps are to find and evaluate solutions. Once again visual meetings are an important way to do this. There are two general kinds of problems that require different approaches. One set of problems is the common kind that faces any project team or group trying to invent or innovate. They are the problems that arise from needing a better way to do something or fix something.

The traditional problem-solving approach, as illustrated on the facing page, is a process of moving from understanding the problem to implementing solutions. The process moves steadily from learning to solution finding.

As you lead meetings associated with this kind of process you would probably take notes on a flip chart or use one of the sticky note approaches I described earlier to represent the problem. It then helps to review success criteria for a solution. Sponsors and clients can provide this or the group as a whole can discuss the quality of ideas they want to generate. At this point brainstorming solutions can happen in a number of ways:

- **List Brainstorming:** Simply write down as many different ways of solving the problem as you can think of.

- **Brainstorm "How To" and "I Wonder" Statements:** Support brainstorming by thinking of how you might do something, and what you wonder might be possible.

- **Create Sticky Note Walls:** Have small groups generate a wall of sticky notes related to the problem, and then link together narratives about potential solutions, illustrating these with rearranged sequences of sticky notes.

- **Hold Vision Breakouts:** Have small groups visualize a complete solution to the problem on a blank sheet of paper or simple templates, then come back together and share their ideas.

- **Improvise:** Improvisational actors are great at making things up and creating unlikely associations. You might treat your problem like a theater sports assignment and actually act out a solution in that spirit. Sometimes our right brains get in the way and we need to consciously jump over to the other side.

Evaluation Options

Once you have a lot of options to look at, use your success criteria to rate and rank them. There are several ways you can do this:

- **Discuss and Propose:** Review the criteria you visualized earlier and review all the options you just identified, and hold a general discussion about which solution would be best. Ask people to make action proposals and list these on a chart.

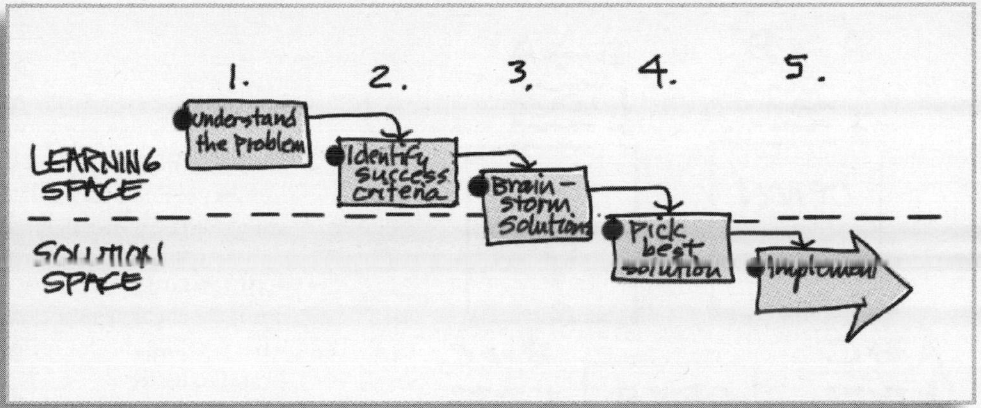

GENERIC PROBLEM-SOLVING PROGRESSION

This progression is good for ordinary problem solving that deals with issues where expertise is relevant and the situation you are dealing with has understandable rules. Having this chain link together is very dependent on careful documentation. If it is graphic and visual, the chances of people linking the whole chain are much improved over working with large text-based piles of information or inches of slides.

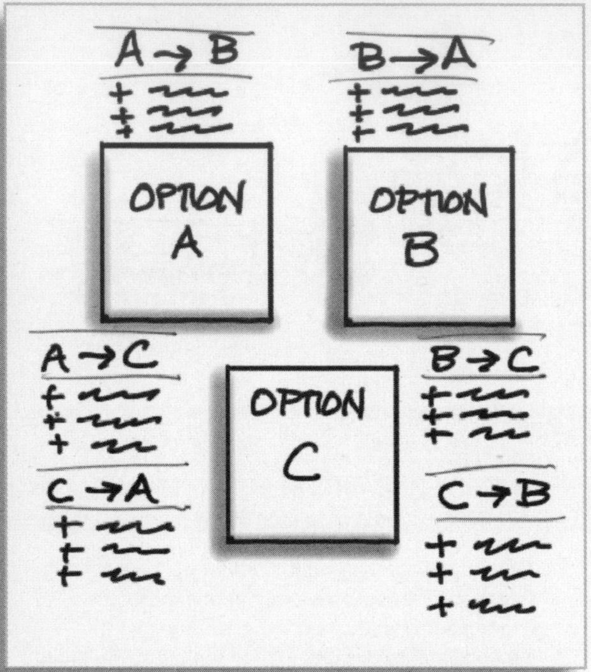

COMPARING PAIRS

When people have strong stakes in different options, use a negotiation strategy and look at the advantage of each in comparison with all the others. It takes a while and lets everyone loosen up a little from their positions. Then see if you can find a solution that merges the best elements.

- **Dot Voting:** After you have reviewed the criteria, give people sticky dots (one-third the number of items) and ask them to dot vote the ones that seem to be most relevant. A variant would be to use different colors for different criteria.
- **Comparing Pairs:** Post your most favored solutions on sticky notes or flip charts and compare them against each other. List what you like about Option A over Option B, and what you like about Option B over Option A. Then compare B to C, and C to D, and B to D and so forth.
- **Decision Matrix:** List your options on one side of a large matrix chart and your criteria along another and check off everywhere the criteria are met. If you use numbers, you can indicate a range of compliance and calculate the solution that seems to be the best fit.
- **Hi-Lo:** Transfer your options to sticky notes, and sort them out on a grid where a high-low axis is vertical, and an easy-hard axis is horizontal.

Chapter 17 on decision making explores this phase of your meeting in more depth. When you are working with organizational problems where people have stakes in different solutions, then different kinds of negotiation strategies allow people plenty of time to get their position acknowledged and let go enough to consider other solutions.

Wicked Problems

The traditional problem-solving approach doesn't work with "wicked problems." Many social and political problems are of this kind, and meetings that are called to address them are messy and complicated. But physical problems can be wicked as well, when parts of a system are so interconnected that a solution in one area changes conditions and solutions for other areas, or it is a unique occurrence that has no pattern or precedence.

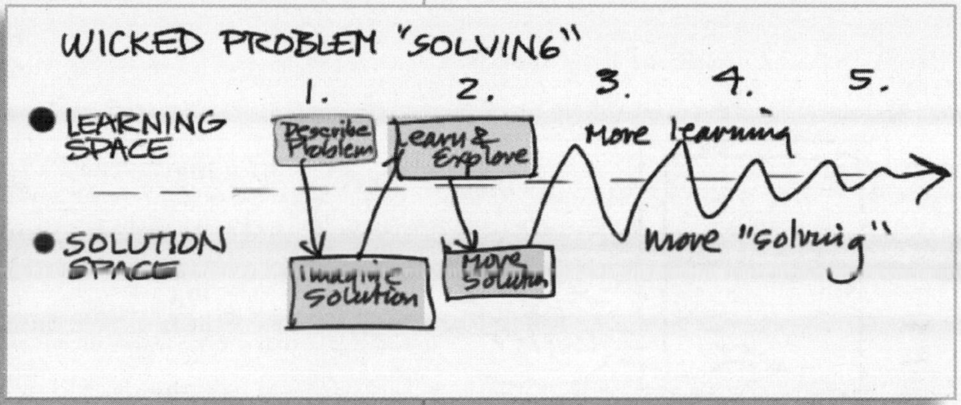

Wicked problems deserve a book by themselves, but here is a simple visual depiction of the wicked problem process that can be a great help to groups and meetings that find themselves in the face of them. It shows the same flow of work over time moving between the learning space and the solution space, but suggests that both occur from the beginning in decreasing spirals of attention, instead of in a neat waterfall sequence, until a solution is implemented at the end that "satisfies." One never gets a complete and clear solution like one might with simpler problems. Just asking people in your meeting if they think they are trying to solve a wicked problem can shift the perspective to a more open, solution-finding orientation.

WICKED PROBLEMS ARE ONES WHERE...

- ❑ The problem is ill-defined.
- ❑ Conditions impacting the problem are dynamic and changing.
- ❑ Different stakeholders with different interests enter the process as it unfolds.
- ❑ Solutions for one part affect and change other parts.
- ❑ There are different and changing criteria for success.
- ❑ There is no defined solution.

The Trim Tab Factor

I'm a collector of stories that deal with the more general problem of people feeling like they can't influence situations because they are too complex or they don't have enough power. Buckminster Fuller, a renowned inventor (the geodesic dome) and optimist about human beings' ability to solve problems through design, believed that the we could learn to change systems from the way rudders turn big ships.

Large ocean liners have rudders that are many meters tall. When the ocean liner is moving, many tons of water push on each side as it moves through the water. The question is, how does the crew actually move the rudder? I will pose this question to groups and people guess it's connected with a very large steering rod, or they won't know. The answer is actually quite simple. Out on the edge of the rudder is a much smaller little rudder. When this little rudder sticks out into the rushing water on one side or another, the power of the moving ocean pushes on this little "trim tab"

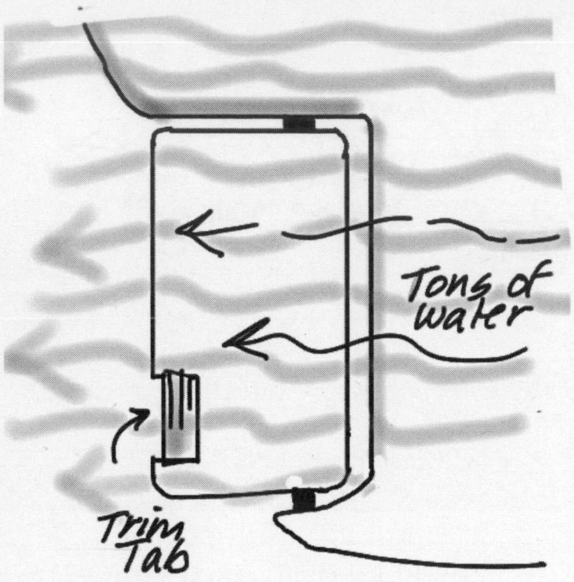

TRIM TAB THEORY

Buckminster Fuller, the inventor of the geodesic dome, believed you should use the forces of nature to work for you, like the trim tabs on a big ocean liner rudder or an airplane wing.

and turns the bigger rudder. It does not take a great amount of energy to move the trim tab. This story is a story of leverage, and it encourages people to look for those actions they could take that will move the larger system with its own force. It is a kind of engineering judo.

When it comes to that class of problems called "systems change," the trim tabs are those levers of change that use the forces already at work in the system to push the change.

Causal Loop Diagramming

Consultants trained in formal systems analysis use a very sophisticated visualization strategy to uncover the core dynamics of a system and find the trim tabs. If you want to explore this kind of approach further, there are resources listed in Chapter 23. This is not a simple kind of analysis, but is a powerful way to get people to think differently. I'll tell a story about how it was used to get a new perspective on the challenge of cleaning up global warming pollutants, and then refer you to some software that can help you do this kind of work if you are interested.

Scott Spann, founder of Innate Analysis, preceded me as a consultant to the RE-AMP project in the upper Midwest that I wrote about at the end of Chapter 7. It began with several dozen non-governmental organizations and foundations there that were concerned that funding for renewable energy was making no difference. In 2004 Scott interviewed dozens of experts on the energy industry and mapped the way in which they said the energy system worked. He developed a composite causal loop diagram in special software that had something like 175 different nodes, all influencing one another. He then conducted small group critiques of his maps with self-selected experts from energy, environment, economics, and transportation perspectives. When I joined the project in early 2005 to facilitate a strategic planning process to take action on the analysis, I found that the group has become very clear that four things drove the entire industry, and those four needed to be dealt with together or nothing would change. On this page is a simplified 16-factor chart I created from Scott's more detailed analysis, for the purpose of explaining to the many people we needed to involve going forward.

Finding the System Drivers

While complete analysis was complicated and difficult to share visually, the simpler depiction (shown here) of the result turned out to be quite important in shifting everyone's perspective. It became clear that people's interest in retiring existing dirty energy (coal) was a key variable. This factor was linked with the strength of the demand for new cheap coal energy (there were 25 new power plants being proposed in the six-state region). A third factor was energy efficiency. Without an increase in energy efficiency, it was unlikely the energy system could handle even the basic base load requirements, let alone support growth. A final factor was the amount of support available for new sources of renewable energy, like wind and solar and geothermal.

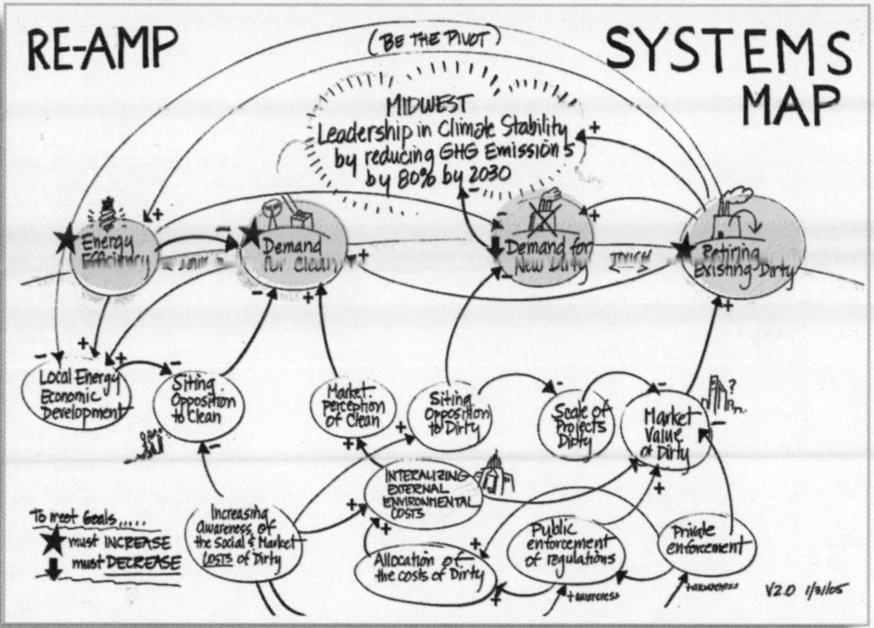

CAUSAL LOOP DIAGRAM SHOWING FOUR DRIVERS OF CLEAN ENERGY

The RE-AMP project in the upper Midwest used systems thinking to focus in on the four drivers of change in the electric sector regarding clean energy.

The diagram shows the four drivers, and the supporting causes. This is harder to read in black and white than in color, but if you study the diagram you will see that some lines have a plus sign and others have a minus sign. The ones with a plus mean that when the source factor increases, so will the one it is pointing to. A minus means that an increase in the source factor will decrease the impact of the other factor.

If you are interested in systems mapping, check out Isee Systems at www.iseesystems.com. As of the writing of this book it provides both Stella and I-Think software that allows anyone to do this kind of causal loop analysis, for both environmental systems and business systems. The software will actually complete the calculus based on variables you can insert and modify, and run models of the system at work with different kinds of graphic output. (Stella was a program developed in conjunction with the work at MIT that inspired Peter Senge and his work on the learning organization. The *Fifth Discipline Fieldbook* identifies many generic systems loops that function like archetypes.)

Thinking around Corners with Kinesthetic Modeling

The barrier to any kind of good problem solving is the way in which our brains lock in on patterns that we understand. Since remembering and predicting are underlying functions of our cortex, and task orientation drives perception to a great extent, if you want to get people in your meetings to think originally these habits need to be disrupted productively. This is one of the powers of visual meetings, in that visualization can educate groups to whole new patterns of understanding, and thus drive new perception.

The examples I've provided so far all work quite powerfully, but there is an additional way you can jump people out of their mental ruts, and that is to introduce fully immersive experiences that precede the work with the charts. You can work visually in 3-D!

John Ward, who I mentioned earlier, calls himself a Visual Thinker. He was trained as an industrial designer, but evolved through his own business experience to working with organizations. He helps them think through organizational issues using modeling, literally with clay and other materials. John's passion is getting people back to what he calls "original thinking." Going to the senses and the body is what jumps people out of mental habits," he believes. He uses string, macaroni, tape, cardboard—any commonly available materials—to get teams to model their organization and then harvest their creations for insights.

John has some strong opinions about how to make this approach work. "People should be silent while they work," he says. "It takes the body as a whole to engage." He gives people short periods of time to model and then takes as much as a day to debrief. After people construct their models he asks them to notice the images and constructions and talk about them without trying to make any interpretations, keeping people as close to the experience of the image as possible. Only gradually does he let people move to making associations and telling stories that relate back to the presenting problem.

KINESTHETIC MODEL OF THE ECONOMIC ENVIRONMENT

Small groups at a VizThink conference made models of how they thought the network might respond to the economic collapse in late 2008. Yes, that is me and John Ward in the background, along with a participant.

John has led everything from biotech companies working on business development to a "worm summit" looking for advances in vermaculture. I experienced a session of his at a VizThink conference in San Jose in February of 2009, following the economic meltdown of 2008. The problem he posed to us was how the VizThink community might be affected by the economic downturn. This page shows a picture of the creation one team made. The dialogue that followed the creation and describing of the 3-D patterns was very hard to contain. The workshop was scheduled for two hours; people wanted to go much longer. For thinking around corners, kinesthetic modeling is a real mindbender.

Design Charrettes

Very complex problems may require whole systems of meetings to generate fresh ideas. A process that designers and architects have used for years is to compress planning into a short, intense period of time called *charrettes*. This is a French term for wagon. The architects of old, when they were called upon to present to the king, would make last minute changes *en charrette*—on the wagon. Let's look at a case where a whole series of meetings were used to do some truly innovative thinking about how science is taught to the general public.

Reinventing the Natural History Museum

When the California Academy of Sciences (CAS) decided to rebuild its facilities following an earthquake in 1987 that damaged some of its structure, the director at the time believed that the real challenge (read problem) was to reinvent the whole idea of natural history museums, and their historic reliance on dioramas and boxes of curiosities. To that end CAS invited four design firms, only one of which had prior museum experience, to meet together and team in designing the first twenty-first century natural history museum. The Grove got the job of running the week-long design charrette. We fielded a team of four of us—two to facilitate, and another team to create real-time documentation of both text and graphics generated by the design teams.

California Academy of Sciences invited four design firms, only one of which had prior museum experience, to meet together and team in designing the first twenty-first century natural history museum.

The process involved a series of immersive experiences. Each was led by a CAS expert, and was followed by a group design session and a full group sharing session with reflections. Then another round would begin. Although we didn't describe it this way at the time, this design challenge was truly a wicked problem in the sense I described earlier.

Our first exercise followed an initial tour of the actual CAS museum. We asked all the designers to interview some children at random that they encountered out on the floor, then come back and brainstorm some exhibit ideas, working in groups that mixed up the four firms. Right away everyone was thrown off his or her normal patterns. Not only are children guaranteed to have surprises, the cross communication between the firms was stimulating.

We then went to Half Moon Bay, and following a naturalist-led field trip through a coastal redwoods ecosystem, teams again had a chance to brainstorm potential exhibits. This time they were encouraged to model them out using cardboard, straws, tape, and other media.

A third round invited the designers to change groups and draw out some concepts that integrated ideas from the first two rounds.

The evening of the second day we had a design huddle to assess the progress. Everyone was getting pretty tired with all the stimulation. The program scheduled a trip to a tide pool the following morning with another of the Cal Academy staff. But the CAS staff was a bit overwhelmed at this point. CAS had been a very stable, slow-to-change place for years and years, and suddenly being thrust into a design charrette seemed to be stressing the group.

"Why can't we see the CAS staff as a tide pool and look at ourselves that way, and skip going to the beach?" I asked in the design session. I explained that we could use a very old rock that one of the geologists had found the day before as a "talking rock" and have the CAS staff sit in a circle inside a circle of the designers, and answer a very simple question "Why do you work at the California Academy of Sciences." Our design team loved the suggestion!

Within 15 minutes of the CAS staff beginning to tell their stories the designers were in tears. These were people from New York and London, pretty experienced in corporate events design, planetarium and aquarium design. But they hadn't encountered the depth of commitment and passion they heard from the CAS staff. This institution is one of the leading research organizations in the world on the challenges of global warming and ecosystems survival, in addition to being a museum, planetarium, and aquarium. No one working there was just holding a job. They were educating the next generation in a race to survive!

Needless to say the design thinking of the four firms went to a whole new level. If you want to see the result, visit the new CAS in San Francisco. It is truly a breakaway design.

CALIFORNIA ACADEMY OF SCIENCES POSTER

Tomi Nagai-Rothe at The Grove made this poster for the California Academy Design Charrette, a gathering of four design firms tasked with reinventing the natural history museum for the twenty-first century.

EXHIBIT PROTOTYPE

Designers working on the California Academy of Sciences used collage, cardboard, and other media to represent exhibit possibilities in their design charrette. If you are interested in the results, check out the CAS website at www.calacademy.org.

Problems That Are Not "Problems"

Problem solving is what designers do. They use active prototyping, playing around with visual media, drawing out concepts in different formats, and many of the other tools I have been writing about.

But some problems are really more challenges of understanding and storytelling, than they are of fixing or designing. In the next chapter we will turn our attention to two very well developed approaches to idea mapping that help get a deeper understanding about things that you wouldn't necessarily think of as a "problem."

11. Storyboarding & Idea Mapping

How Innovators & Designers Work

Innovators and designers are people who want to see things come together in new ways that get results. Gathering information isn't sufficient. They want to understand connections and how things really work, and find ways to improve them. Storyboarding and idea mapping are two visualization strategies creative people use for designing. If you are interested in getting better results for your teams, students, or sales calls, there is no reason you can't use these tools as well. They are approaches that work very powerfully even if you are not experienced in them. This chapter is about showing how to apply these tools to your meetings, and get the breakthrough insights that they often support.

How Do Humans Make Sense of Things?

Storyboarding and idea mapping reflect two fundamental ways we make sense of things at the big picture level of thinking. The first is how we think about things moving over time. The second is thinking about how things are structured in space. Ultimately we want to combine these—since humans live in both time and space. Most of the time when we are learning about something new we focus on one of these and then the other.

Let me explain with a visual metaphor (imagine that!). On this page is a picture illustrating the project you want to lead as a boat or raft on a river. If you think about it, meetings are a lot like rivers. They have clear constraints—the banks of the river—that in the case of meetings are the boundaries created by circumstances on the one hand and leadership expectations on the other. They also have a lot of dynamics that need be experienced directly and responded to in the moment. These are like the water and weather.

VISUALIZING TIME AND SPACE

We live in a river of action and steer with maps of the territory. Storyboards help you see the time flow, and anticipate the stages in a process. Idea maps help you understand all the elements in a situation, how its organized, and what choices you have.

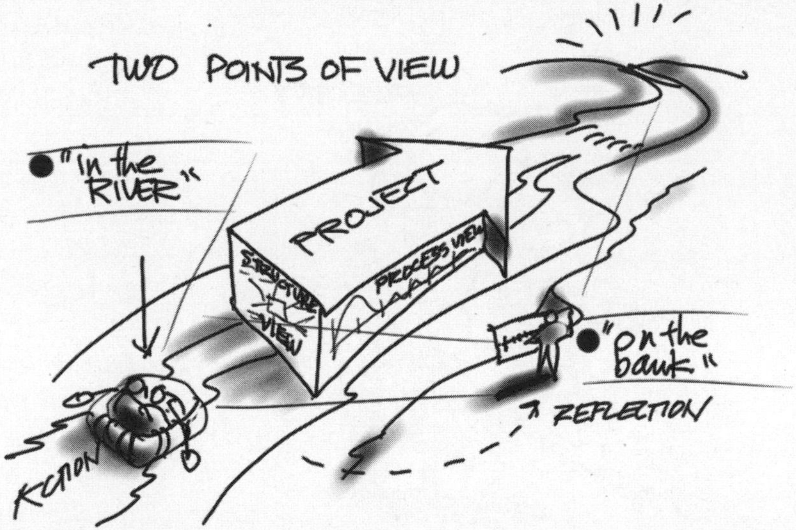

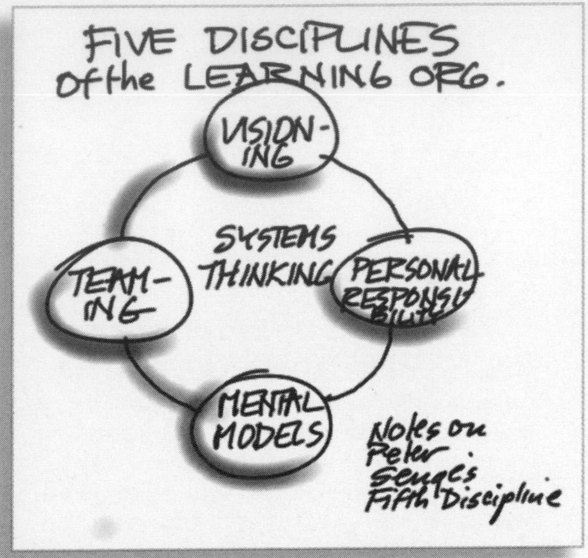

FIVE DISCIPLINES

Here is an idea map I sketched out of the five disciplines of a learning organization according to Peter Senge.

To navigate a river or a productive meeting you need to understand the whole journey from a time sequence point of view. Interestingly you get this perspective by pulling out and getting to an overlook, and using maps that show the different sections of the river. This is the storyboarding point of view of a person designing a presentation, meeting process, change process, or anything where understanding phases and stages is important.

On the river you need to remember all the elements involved to support your choices in the moment. The same is true during any kind of creative project or meeting. There are all the elements of a problem as we discussed in the previous chapter. This is the perspective we develop when we create idea maps, diagrams, and other visualizations that illustrate research, choices, organization, and connections. Groups often want to begin playing with these understandings before they begin thinking about how to put things together in action sequences. The activity of visualizing all the relationships is a way to think about whatever you are doing in a comprehensive way.

In a more general sense, these two views represent how we use geographic maps for any trip. Base maps illustrate the territory, Itineraries show specifically where we intend to travel. In action, these two kinds of understandings work together. In meetings peoples' mental model of the organization, marketplace, networks, and resources represent the base maps. The agenda is a kind of itinerary.

Maps and Itineraries in Organizational Thinking

I made an idea map illustrating Peter Senge's thinking when I first read *Fifth Discipline: The Art & Practice of the Learning Organization*. (See illustration here.) Later, in the narrative of the book, Senge describes many different paths, or journeys, through these same disciplines. Many of the mental models used in business and management have this map/itinerary feature, with the base map being a structure drawing and the stories about how to use it being a process. You might notice that the Learning Cycle model I'm using to structure this book has a similar design. Making these kinds of thinking oriented maps really helps the person who created the visual remember the information. Many teachers encourage students to take visual notes for this reason.

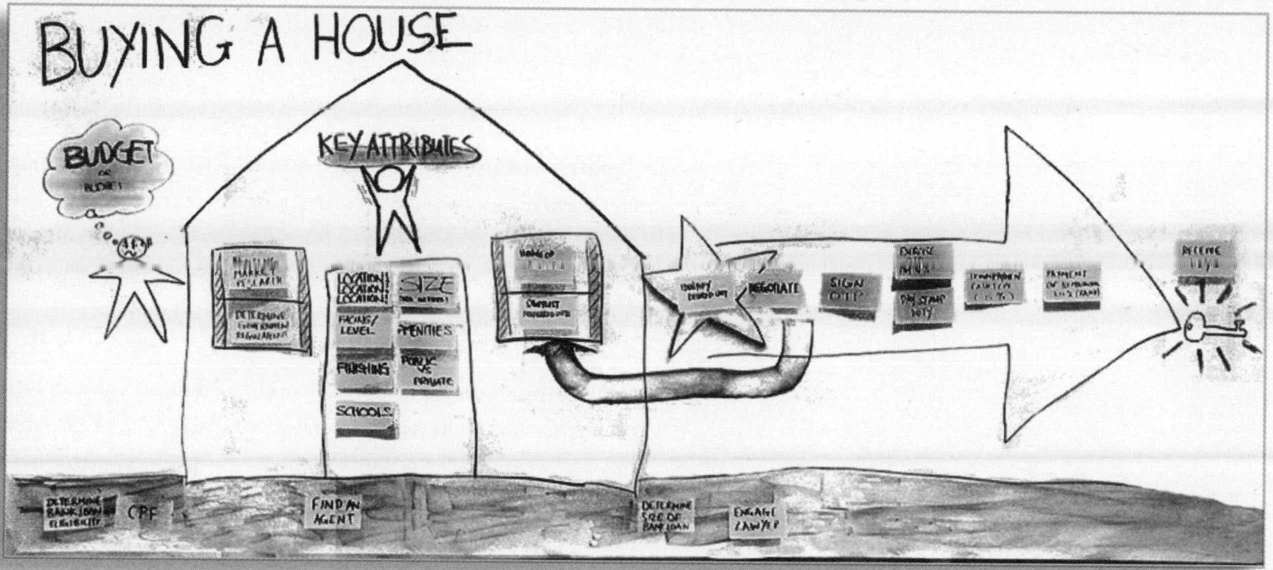

Here is a process map that emphasizes the time sequence more than the structure. It was created in a workshop on graphic facilitation for some young analysts and learning design staff in some of the ministries in Singapore. It illustrates the process of buying a house in Singapore, which is a daunting task if you are just getting into the market. The small group that created this only took about 40 minutes to think through the sequence with sticky notes and then create the illustration. You could see this as the itinerary of a house buyer through all the elements, each of which has a real-life location on a physical map.

Storyboarding Began with Disney

Walt Disney, the legendary creator of animated movies, is credited with formalizing storyboarding, a narrative, time-oriented perspective illustrating the sequence or "story." It has since become a primary tool for developing story ideas in any context, including training programs, strategy, sales processes, and many forms of communication media.

HOW TO STORYBOARD

1. Get large sticky notes or sheets of paper.
2. Brainstorm the elements in your story.
3. Play around with sequences that seem right.
4. Illustrate ideas that show what the step is about.

The basics of storyboarding are simple. They involve breaking information down into little vignettes, and arranging these in a narrative flow, looking at the big picture from beginning to end. In the process of making films the storyboards are sketches of each scene with simple captions pointing at the script. In organization work storyboard sequences can represent any kind of process, presentation, training program, or change process.

In organization work, storyboard sequences can represent any kind of process, presentation, training program, or change process.

I used storyboarding to think through a 10-minute presentation I made on Visual Meetings to a TEDxSoma conference the winter of 2010. The TED conferences (standing for Technology Education and Design) have become very popular with their format of short, well prepared presentations that are then shared via the Web. TED's motto is "Ideas Worth Spreading." They license other groups to organize mini-TED conferences, or TEDx events, and the concept has grown rapidly. Key to the events is having presenters prepare tightly designed talks with lots of visuals. I wanted mine to demonstrate how visual meetings are bringing about a revolution in meeting productivity.

You can see in my storyboard that I made simple little sketches of the examples I wanted to include, and some notes about the more general themes. I sketched these in my journal, but you could use either large sticky notes or regular notepaper taped with masking tape or artist's tape. When working with a group the idea is to work quickly, accept all ideas, cluster possibilities, and then use discussion and rearranging to come up with your final flow.

Pixar is one of the most successful movie producers in the world, with hit after hit following its first all digital animated film *Toy Story*. The extras included on their DVDs explain their process, which relies heavily on storyboarding. I worked on a symposium with the head of their internal Pixar University and he said that they work with the story for as long as it takes to arrive at a

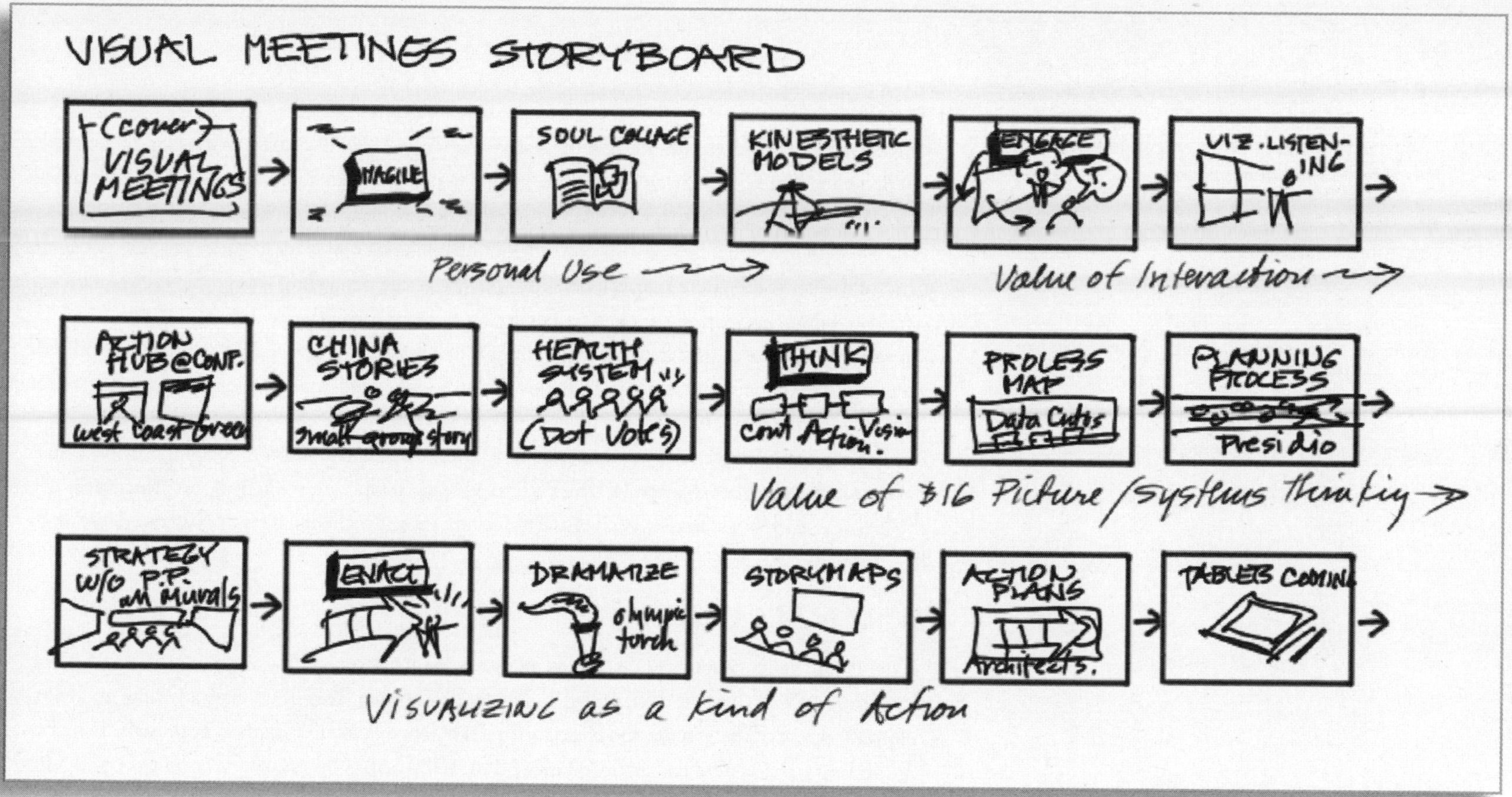

PRESENTATION STORYBOARD

This is one I made to prepare a 10-minute talk on Visual Meetings to the TEDxSOMA event (see text on previous page).

narrative they truly believe in. Only then do they go to digital renditions and production. It may take as long as a couple years in the storyboard phase.

For meetings you will probably want to work a little faster. I share the story only to underline the

IDEA MAPPING PROCESS

1. Hang a large sheet of paper and write the central idea in the middle of the paper.
2. Ask members of the group to identify something connected to that idea.
3. Create a branch and label it.
4. Ask "what is connected to this," and make those branches with labels.
5. When one branch seems to slow down, ask for another big branch and repeat the process.
6. Keep adding branches all around the central idea.

power of getting the story right. If your design challenge happens to be a workshop or a training program that needs to powerfully move a lot of people, then it will be well worth it to work through the story line so that the overarching themes are clear.

One of the projects where I experienced the power of storyboarding was with a General Electric subsidiary that was working to change its sales force from "box" salespeople to "consultative" salespeople. Because consultation with a client is much more of a process, with many steps and meetings over time, they needed a framework that would guide the design of this major training effort. The crucial meetings in that project involved working out the storyboard sequence of steps that a consultative sales process takes, and then shaping the training program around that narrative structure. In Chapter 21, The Path to Visual Competency, I include an illustration of the learning path you can take with visual meetings. It's a storyboard format illustrated in one big flow drawing.

What Is Mind Mapping?

When I lead visual meetings I often have people who are experiencing working this way for the first time say "Isn't this Mind Mapping™?" I invariably answer "yes," since diagramming and idea mapping is one of the foundation formats for The Grove's Group Graphics approach. Tony Buzan, an Englishman who has authored more than a 100 books on creativity, cognition, and Mind Mapping, has done more than anyone else to popularize this method. He is in fact credited with inventing the term. Mind maps explicitly branch all kinds of information around a central topic or theme, and include drawings, color, writing, connecting lines of all kinds—all aimed at creating a structural map to the territory of our thinking. They are the iconic kind of complex idea map. Buzan is convinced that this is the way the brain structures itself. (If you want to dig into this literature, look at the book and website references in Chapter 23.)

I used an idea map to think through the types of applications for visual meetings as a warm-up for writing and have included it here. You can see that in addition to the simple branching, I used the four steps of the learning cycle to guide my thinking. The elaborations on this format are really quite extensive as you start overlaying colors and other patterns.

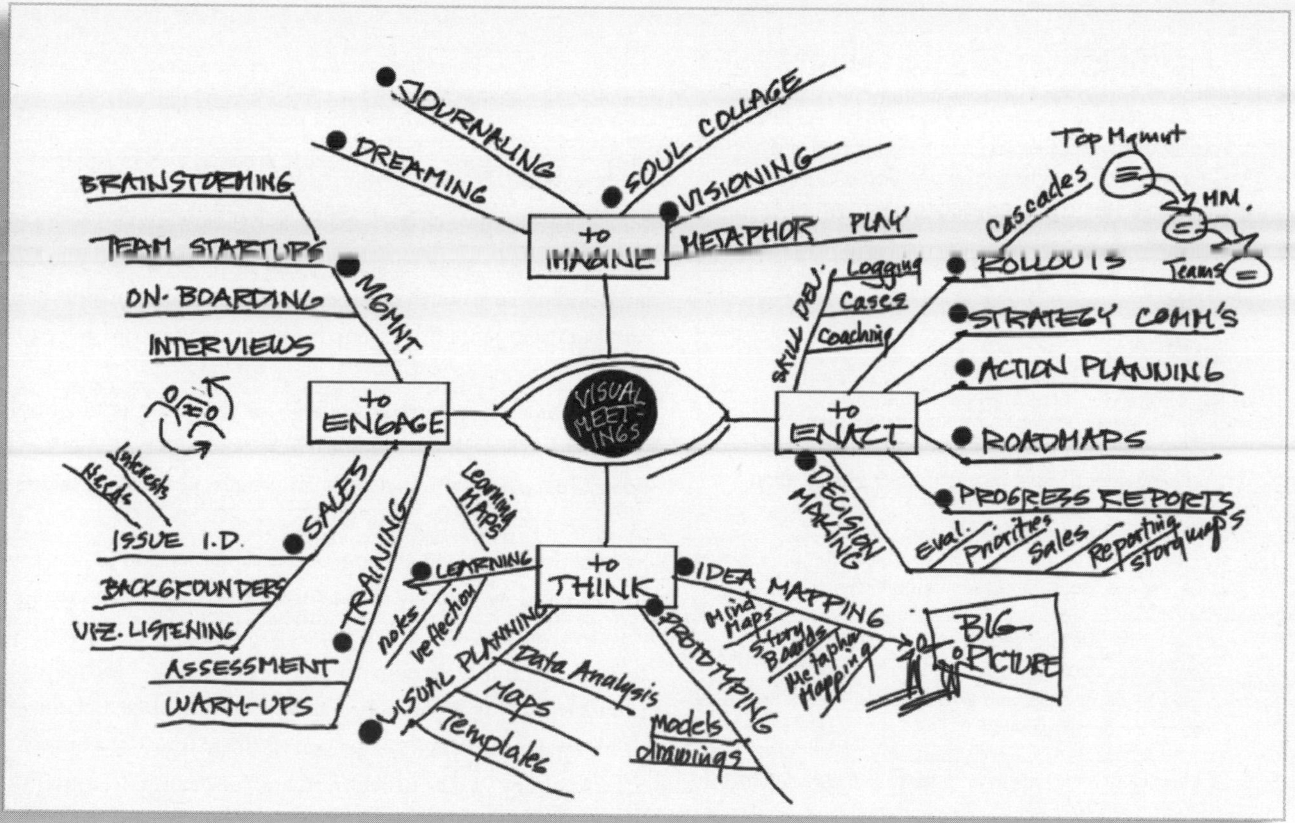

Mind Mapping is a very powerful tool for thinking things out personally, and having meetings with yourself. My writer wife uses it to brainstorm images she wants to combine into a poem. It has become popular enough that a number of software companies offer tools with names like Mind Jet that allow you to create these branching diagrams on your computer. One of the more advanced versions is called The Brain and allows a user to attach video, text, graphics, numbers to any node, and will adjust the entire diagram to center on whatever node you click on. As visual as these tools are, they aren't really designed for conducting meetings (although some do use the tools this way).

IDEA MAP FOR VISUAL MEETINGS

I created this idea map as way of brainstorming about what to include in this book.

MEETINGS WHERE YOU MIGHT USE IDEA MAPPING

Almost any kind of subject can be illustrated and explored with branching diagrams. Some of the topics that you might consider initially might be:

- ❑ Content that should be on a website
- ❑ Mapping your group's skills
- ❑ Mapping out client interests
- ❑ Exploring a complex concept or new phenomenon—such as knowledge management, quality improvement, social networking, or globalization
- ❑ Mapping the markets you serve
- ❑ Laying out ideas to include in a brochure
- ❑ Exploring "if-then" scenarios, with each branch being a possible development that could then lead to other developments that could then lead to other developments
- ❑ Identifying elements in an educational curriculum
- ❑ Identifying all the messages and media needed for a major sales presentation to a client

Using Idea Mapping with Groups

Idea mapping appreciated broadly, as creating pictures of how things relate and connect, is a very powerful way to work with groups if you understand some basic techniques. The application areas and dynamics are more complex than those surrounding visual listening with lists and clusters, but quite accessible by anyone with a whiteboard, big paper, sticky notes, and some markers.

At any point where a group knows a lot about something but hasn't really had a chance to put the information together would be a time you might ask them to create an idea map. In the simplest terms this is drawing a picture with a focus on all the elements involved and their connections.

Several things happen in the group during this kind of process. In the first place, it will begin somewhat slowly. People aren't sure what to add, or where to put it. If you are doing the writing just note the first idea down anywhere. That gets things started. The purpose of the process is to stimulate thinking, not completely organize it. Normally you would begin to identify and populate several big branches, and then find yourself circling back to earlier branches as your thinking develops. As you get out to the margins of a branch you may discover that items are also connected to other branches. Since any two-dimensional, flat display is a distortion of things that are alive and existing in physical space, you will find yourself creating dashed connecting lines and other devices to show those connections. You will also discover that it is possible to add little graphic ideographs and pictographs as icons on the display when you want to emphasize things.

Unlike sticky notes, which aren't organized when you generate them, the mind map channels thinking along logical streams of connection. Because it is visual and spatial, after you have a series of branches it is quite possible to jump around and think of more and more detail in distinctly nonlinear ways. The logical organization combined with the use of imagery, color, and form requires a group to use both sides of their brain. It's a both/and way of working.

Working with Metaphor Maps

In Chapter 8 on Group Graphics I wrote about what happens when you add a graphic metaphor to a chart and create a drawing that comes alive in everyone's imagination as they project their own experience into the viewing process. This is a kind of idea mapping that moves beyond explicit branches to a more image-based relationship. The looser connections really stretch everyone's thinking to fill in the white spaces, many aspects of which can't be explicitly diagrammed with branching formats. If you understand the metaphor it can be quite disciplined.

Looser connections (in metaphor maps) really stretch everyone's thinking to fill in the white spaces, many aspects of which can't be explicitly diagrammed with branching formats.

I was invited one year to run a workshop at Sematech in Austin, Texas. Sematech is a semiconductor association supported by the federal government that was created in the 1970s when overseas competition severely challenged the U. S. semiconductor industry. Semiconductor companies like Intel, Rockwell, Texas Instruments, National Semiconductor, and AMD all sent teams to Sematech's labs in Austin to work together and share their innovations across the industry. The challenge I was asked to address was the problem of managing the white space. While the formal organization charts were clear, the different cultures of the participating companies posed challenges in the informal aspects of their working together.

I chose to lead the group in some idea mapping about the nature of their work in the informal spaces. The process was quite simple. I began by asking everyone in the meeting to identify the most formative teaming experience in his or her life. They were things like being in band, the military, large families, food services, laboratories, and a group of ranchers. We created table

IDEA MAPPING WITH METAPHORS

A graphic metaphor is a picture framework that is not directly about the subject you are analyzing. In this case a ranch structure, like that pictured above, was used to draw out information about how Sematech, a large semiconductor R&D center, was organized.

groups of the clusters and asked each to create some flip charts answering the question "Sematech is like a _____." I asked them to draw a picture and label the parts. Twenty minutes later we had several dozen charts around the wall. Amid a great deal of laughter and good communication, we went around and people explained why they picked this or that metaphor.

I then asked if there was one they would like to explore in depth. They picked a "ranch" as their topic. I drew a big square frame on the wall and a horizontal horizon line. "What kind of soil does the ranch have?" I asked. "Chelate," someone said, and everyone laughed. Chelate is very hard clay, I happened to know. "What does the ranch raise?" I asked next. "Range animals," someone said. I drew some little cow-like figures. "Are there other kinds of animals?" I asked. "Yes, predators," someone answered. "What are they?" I asked. "Intel projects," the person said, and everyone howled. "Any others?" I asked, sensing this was a fruitful line of questioning. "Yes, rodents," someone said from the back. "What are they?" I asked, keeping straight ahead. "Consultants!" came the reply. There were more howls.

We kept this up for about 45 minutes and the group had a wonderful time exploring this metaphor in detail, talking about what they produced, how they got it to market, who the bosses were, the weather conditions, and all the other elements. I simply kept asking them to connect the metaphor back to the real world at Sematech, and kept my drawing loose. Even though I wasn't tightly connecting everything like I might on a diagram, the metaphor of the ranch embodied some inherent ideas about how things connect, and people were pointing at what they wanted to talk about through that window of understanding.

12. Visual Planning

Using Graphic Templates to See the Big Picture

Many of the meetings that organizations hold are focused on planning. Teams do action planning at the beginning of projects. Nonprofits create plans for grant proposals to foundations. Business functions create plans for their annual budgets and goals. Management teams plan strategy. Where idea mapping and storyboarding address creative processes, planning is what organizations do to get agreement and alignment in preparation for action.

Years of leading strategic visioning processes gave The Grove insight into the repeating kinds of visual strategies groups want to use in planning. We have evolved standard graphic templates and processes for different kinds of planning, beginning with strategy. We formalized the tools during the 1990s, when the Internet was exploding and businesses were head over heels trying to both take advantage of the new developments and cope with all the changes. This is the story of how these came to be is a case study about the value of visual planning.

HP Labs Looks for New Business Ideas

The concept of having graphic wall templates for planning grew from an engagement with Hewlett Packard Labs, which in the 1990s was in all likelihood the foremost business lab in the world, if attracting the very best engineering talent available and being considered one of the most desirable places to work is a criteria.

Joel Birnbaum was their inspired, entrepreneurial manager, whose background in different industries, including major sports, led him to take a fresh approach to getting the 12 different labs at HP to work together in the interests of the business. Historically the labs had the luxury of having many projects that were very edgy and almost pure science, with only slight nods toward eventual business application. The competitive edges in high tech, however, were increasingly in products that required cross-lab cooperation, and the larger business

MAKING SENSE OF SLIDES

Twelve separate slide presentations created an avalanche of information for the center and lab directors at HP. By capturing key elements systematically on a big wall I was able to give them a complete overview of lab activity.

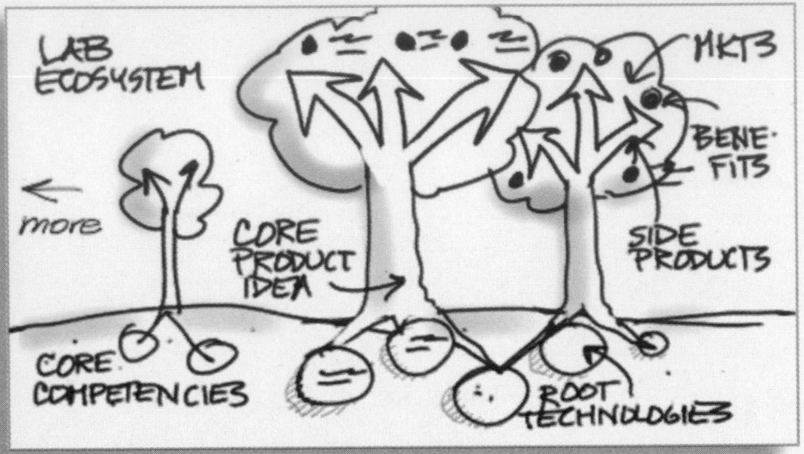

needed to be educated about what might be coming out of the labs in preparation for turning their inventions into major businesses. Getting these top scientists to connect the science and business opportunities was his goal. In this endeavor he enrolled an unusually creative HR manager, Barbara Waugh, and his director of strategic planning, Srinivas Sukumar, to propose an approach. They came up with the idea of enrolling a "keynote listener" who could listen the labs into seeing their interconnections. With coaching I got the job, and Joel's team responded to the idea of using visual listening to support cross-lab communications. The Grove's work went to a whole new level as a result.

AN ORCHARD OF TECHNOLOGY POSSIBILITIES

Imagine technology opportunities as an orchard, with the soil being core competencies, the roots being root technologies, the product concepts providing a trunk for branching product ideas, resulting in sales, and the fruit of marrying a technology possibility with a real market the crown of the trees.

Visualizing the Bristol Offsite

The complete story of this planning process is a book in itself. Let me skip to the part about how graphic templates came to figure prominently. It began at a major offsite in Bristol, England, where all 12 labs and their four center leaders assembled for a planning meeting to prepare for their annual business review by top management at HP. I was invited as the "keynote listener" during the meeting. They didn't want facilitation. These were the top brains at HP, after all. But they thought the graphics visualizing their ideas and reports might help.

It did. The first day I visually summarized a day of slide presentations, lab by lab, and gave them a chance to look at their current work on one wall (see illustration on the previous page). The next day they agreed to a suggestion I made to get creative and map out their technical ecosystem. Joel had responded to this idea in my initial talk with him and thought it was a good idea at the offsite. The visual I had in mind looked like the sketch on this page, except about five times as wide! I interviewed the group as a whole and encouraged participants to identify where they had full "trees" with all the parts connected. They caught on quickly and an hour later we had 16 different trees developed. I made them different sizes based on my listening how confidently people communicated their ideas.

I then asked the group to meet at their tables and come up with a flip chart of the five topics that would be the best use of their for time the rest of the meeting. When we posted the results from six tables, we had several right away that everyone agreed on.

Creating a Template for Strategic Planning

At this point I was way out on a limb, so to speak. They hadn't wanted a facilitator, but were responding, and I frankly hadn't thought this through ahead of time, assuming I would be simply recording. I knew they needed some guidance to do their small groups. So I counted again on their ability to be quick studies and sketched out the template shown on this page. They liked it. At the time I did have templates, but they were in my mind and I was using them to structure the blank paper. In this case with HP, it needed to be explicit.

Two hours later five groups came back with big charts, all hand drawn by these engineers. In their presentations it became clear that 3 or 4 of the ideas had real momentum, judging by how fully they were able to create their story.

Showing Off What Plotters Can Do

The group was so excited about the visual approach that they wanted to continue. I improvised again, based on what I'd found to be working in many years as a graphic facilitator. "Why don't you make your presentation to your management using big displays instead of slides?" I suggested. "You can show off your new plotter printers, and you can create a little planning theater

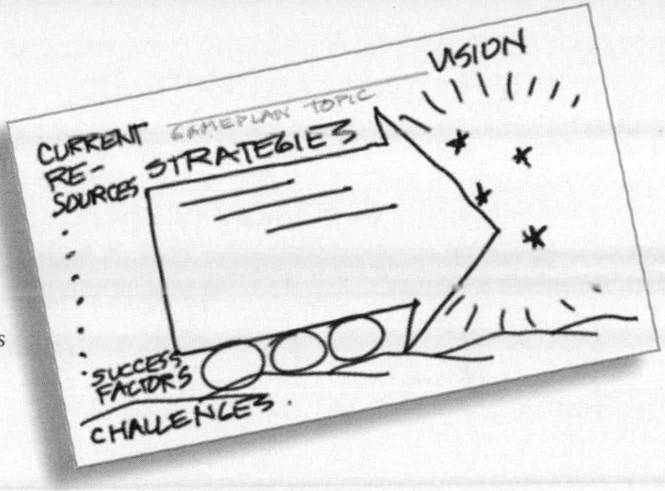

A GRAPHIC GAME PLAN

This template is The Grove's Graphic Gameplan, and was the first planning format I learned when getting involved with Group Graphics. The format involves characterizing the target, or vision, on the right, then the resources one has to work with on the left, and the strategies in an arrow in the middle. These move over a landscape of challenges, rolling along on wheels that are the success factors—behavioral agreements and operating principles.

BIG CHART PRESENTATIONS

HP LAB directors found that top management participation with big charts and a theater type presentation was three times what they had received in prior years using slide presentations. Three little theaters like this provided a panoramic look at the big business possibilities.

that will get much more interaction and engagement."

They liked the idea. They also liked constraining presentations to three graphics each. One would be a Context Map that contained all the information anyone should know to listen to the idea. The second would be a Vision Map of the potential benefits to HP in the business idea. The third would be a high-level Gameplan of how to begin working on the opportunity.

The teams used sticky notes to record top management reactions right on their big charts. They did in fact print them on their plotters, using graphics I hand drew for each idea, adding text and numbers on top in a draw program. Several big ideas came out of this process:

- Top management participation was three times normal.
- The process launched a new digital photography business based on new sensor technology.
- The Labs success with this process led many other divisions to get visual.
- I learned that graphic templates could be used to support important strategic planning activities with very smart people.

Allow the Rest of Us to Draw

At this same time Ed Claassen joined The Grove, leaving his job as director of the Training and Development function at SRI International in Palo Alto. He was an experienced consultant and a visual thinker, but not someone who liked to draw, or felt confident on blank paper at the time. "Why don't you make it so the rest of us can work in this big visual way?" he argued. The combination of the success at HP and Ed's insistence led us to articulate the Strategic Visioning Model and its basic templates. I was working with Rob Eskridge, a Grove associate who at the time had a robust strategic planning model with output documents we designed to be graphic. As these evolved into The Grove process we saw a way to provide planners the best of strategic planning tools, which tend to be analytical and historically oriented (since you can't be truly clear about anything except the past), and visioning, which aims to be compelling and inspirational about the future.

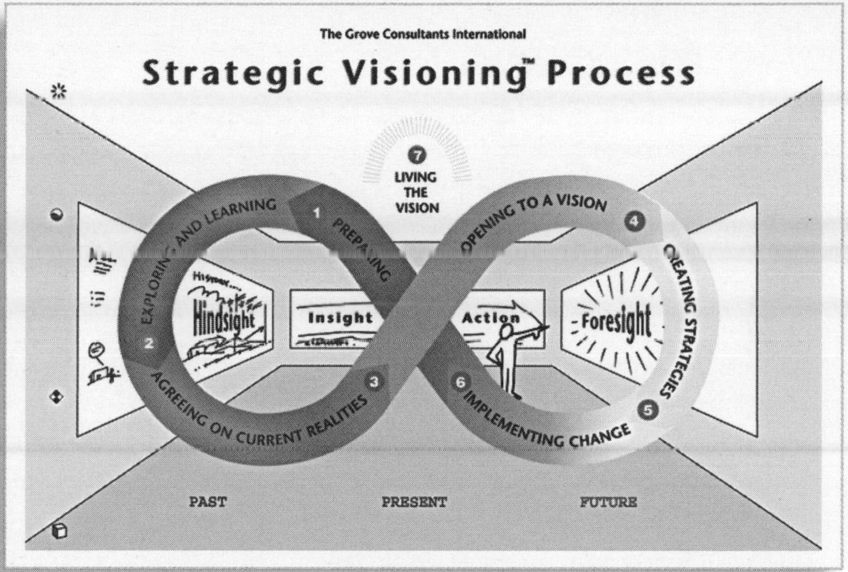

STRATEGIC VISIONING

The Grove's Strategic Visioning™ Model is a framework for sequencing Graphic Guide templates in a planning process. Visit www.grove.com for more information.

We also knew that organizations need to integrate a spectrum of thinking styles from people who are highly intuitive and visionary to people who are very hands-on and operational. We therefore illustrated the process as an ongoing loop of learning that integrates past and future into present action, and honors intuition, feeling, thinking, and sensing on the part of participants, illustrated by the little symbols on the left side of the model.

This book isn't meant to be a book on strategic planning, or an in-depth look at The Grove's Strategic Visioning (SV) process, but the success of this approach is very instructive in regard to using graphic templates for a wide variety of visual planning meetings.

Templates for Visual Planning

Following is an overview of the Graphic Guides® that have been most widely used for visual planning in The Grove's experience, treating each in a way that you can imagine using one of them in a meeting, or be inspired by their approach to improvise some of your own to get a

BENEFITS OF VISUAL PLANNING

- ❑ You look prepared.
- ❑ Templates provide a chance to clarify assumptions visibly.
- ❑ Writing down information acknowledges that it was heard.
- ❑ Template categories help guide discussion in appropriate ways.
- ❑ Charts can stay up the duration of a meeting and provide a panoramic reference when they are sequenced around the room.
- ❑ If you use sticky notes, templates function like game boards for flexible "what if" thinking.
- ❑ You can digitally photograph charts and help orient people, remember whatever work they did after the meeting.

similar result. Please appreciate that these are copyrighted templates, and can be reproduced by permission only. All are available through The Grove's store at www.grove.com.

Some of the kinds of planning that Graphic Guides® can be used for include:

- Team startup planning
- Annual business planning
- Strategic planning
- HR and talent management planning
- Marketing and sales strategy
- Organizational change

Templates for Orienting and Process Planning

Many of the tools discussed so far can be used by design teams who are preparing for a planning process. But a simple template we now call the Meeting Startup Guide has emerged as a standard. It came from working worldwide on a facilitation-training project for a large consumer goods company where the internal personnel organization wanted a simple, powerful toolkit for leading meetings. Our experience suggested there were four things that are most productive to get clear—the Outcomes, Agenda, Roles and Rules. These four categories spell OARRs, which becomes a memory device, if you think of a meeting as being like a river and your process as being like rowing a boat on it. All you need to do to succeed is "grab your OARRs." We built the metaphor into the template illustrated on the next page. In our experience this little tool goes viral—meaning people use it and tell others and it becomes a standard for starting meetings.

It is very productive to clarify your OARRs with or without visuals. It can be done simply at the start of any meeting. But it helps a lot to work out these agreements on paper or in a slide with the key stakeholders in a meeting. That way everyone is aligned going in.

Check over the list of benefits of templates on the preceding page. They apply especially to the Meeting Startup—River Rafting Graphic Guide. Having it up throughout the meeting does wonders for keeping people focused.

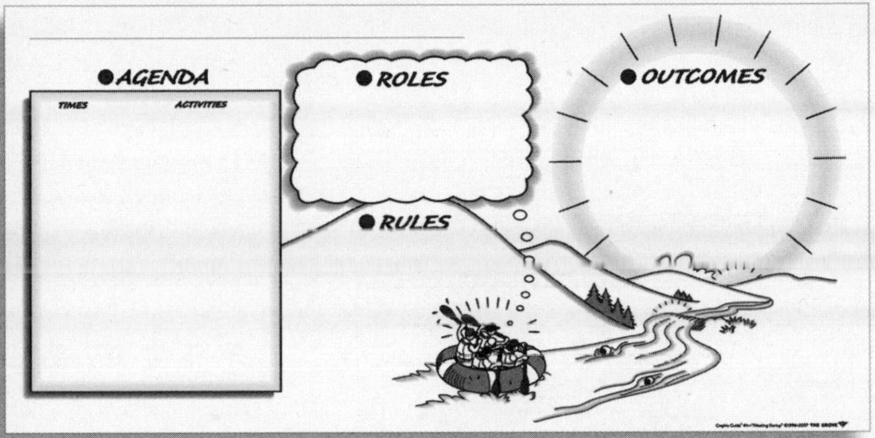

GROVE GRAPHIC GUIDES®

The Meeting Startup—River Rafting Graphic Guide features a simple tool for productive meetings—the OARRs process. This stands for:

- Outcomes
- Agenda
- Roles
- Rules

If you get these four things clear, then your meeting will be much more productive.

Templates for Developing Hindsight

Hindsight is about understanding your past and its lessons. A great beginning for any planning process is to tell the story of how you got to your current situation, and visualizing this story on a long chart. The structure for this process is a time line. If you remember the story about meetings being like a river, this is the long view of the whole flow, looking backward along your journey.

In doing graphic histories you can be simple or very elaborate depending on how you want to involve people. The process is mostly about the storytelling. Visualizing the story simply helps people feel acknowledged, and allows you to hop around, going forward and backward in time. Graphic histories help people see their bigger picture from the journey or process point of view I wrote about in the previous chapter on storyboarding.

At the Apple Leadership Experience, mentioned in the introduction to this book, we always related a story about the research Omar El Salway conducted years ago at the University of Southern California on how managers think about time. He reputedly instructed a control group of

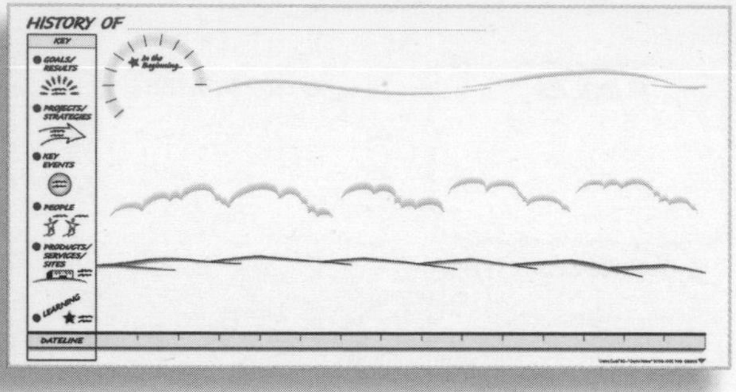

GRAPHIC HISTORY

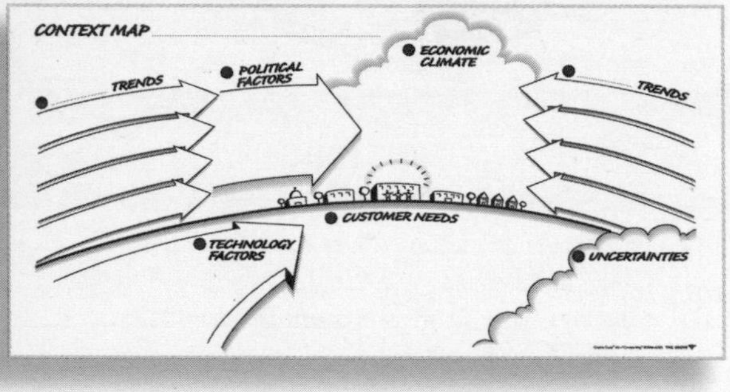

CONTEXT MAP

GRAPHIC GUIDES®

All Grove Graphic Guides and their accompanying Leader's Guides are available to order online in various sizes at www.grove.com. They are copyrighted so you cannot make multiple versions without permission. But you can be inspired by their designs to create your own templates for various uses.

15 to write their career histories and another 15 to write their career futures. On average the ones who wrote histories went backward 15 years. On average the future oriented group went forward 5 years. However, when they switched, the future group also reflected back 15 years. But surprisingly, the ones who did the past work first went forward 15 years! The experience of thinking in a bigger time frame stretched out their imagination. In strategy and visioning work it is especially effective to go backward to go forward because of this dynamic. I always think it's a bit like a softball pitcher winding up to power the ball across the plate.

Ways of Doing Graphic Histories

Here is how you can do graphic histories with minimal drawing required:

- **Group Graffiti Wall:** Put up a time line and then put out a basket of markers. Ask everyone to remember important events in the history of the organization, and create images and text on the time line all at once. The next 30 minutes or so will be a turmoil of talking and reflection and jostling. Then sit back and have people explain their drawings beginning at the beginning.

- **Sticky Notes for When You Joined:** Create a big time line with clear dates covering the length of time your story covers. Then have everyone put his or her name on a sticky note and paste it on the time line when he or she joined the organization. Begin with the people who came earliest and have them share what the organization was like when they joined, then ask the next cohort and the next, until everyone has had a chance to talk. Take simple notes as it goes along. Bear in mind people will almost always want to talk a lot longer than you planned. These kinds of stories are fascinating.

- **Collage History:** Use the process we used at Agilent Technology with the company's IT department and have everyone come to the planning meeting with artifacts from the history of whatever project you are looking at. These can be slides, brochures, logos, photos, and the like. Have people paste these up and then tell the story as a whole group.

- **Successes and Results Wall:** Ask people to use sticky notes and record key successes and special results the organization has achieved, perhaps using different color sticky notes. Start at the beginning and have people share these sticky notes and tell stories about the organizational dynamics surrounding those events. Take simple notes in and around the sticky notes.

- **History Storymaps:** One time at a large sales meeting the design team decided it didn't have time to go into an interactive history during the meeting. So we decided to have a small group create a 24-foot-long graphic history before the meeting, and then had it hanging in the room where everyone had breakfast. On everyone's nametag was a sticker with his or her name on it. Everyone was instructed to add his or her name to the chart when coming in for breakfast. We knew that conversation and storytelling would erupt around this visual and it did.

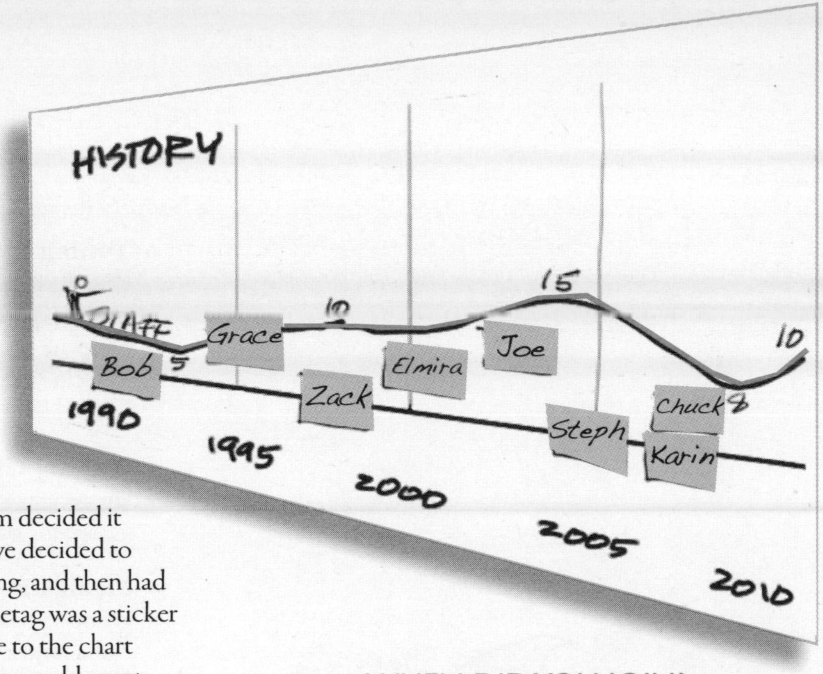

WHEN DID YOU JOIN?

A simple graph of number of staff or sales revenue, plus sticky notes of when people joined provides a great start for a history-telling session.

The Importance of Scanning the Environment

In planning, it always helps to spend some time looking at the larger environment of forces and factors that surround whatever group or organization is doing the planning. This is a perfect time to have a visual meeting, using large charts that illustrate the larger environment. These are called "context maps" or driving forces maps. There is good example of one on page 84. These context maps are really simple cluster displays without real precise connections. Many consultants will do environmental scanning on flip charts, creating pages and pages of lists until the meeting room is a real blizzard of data that is very hard to reference. Combining these lists into a template helps reduce the clutter, and stimulates people to think about the categories that are included and their relationships.

Some of the variations on this process that you might consider are the following:

- **Tuning the Categories:** What is relevant to discuss in your scan of the environment changes depending on what you are doing your planning about. It helps to have your meeting participants agree on what the big categories ought to be. The ones on the printed templates from The Grove are just starting places, and are the ones we find repeated enough to include them—but notice that even on the prepared template two of the trends areas are unlabeled.

- **Affinity Charts:** You can do context mapping using sticky notes and clustering them after everyone has generated the items. This is the more bottoms-up approach described in Chapter 7 on sticky notes.

- **Small Groups and Gallery Walks:** In a larger planning conference have many small groups quickly create context maps. Different groups will focus on different things, but overall most factors will get identified. Have people look over all the different maps in a big "gallery walk" looking for themes and then have people share what they see as agreed on forces and factors while someone creates a composite map. Having multiple groups identify similar things creates a lot of credibility. (See page 173 for more detail on this.)

- **Focused Small Groups:** A variant on this approach is to have different groups look at different aspects of the environment and report back. This might be a relevant way to do it when you want to concentrate pockets of expertise in the group.

- **Find the Missing Pieces:** Have a small team prepare a context map in advance of your planning meeting, and then challenge people to critique the map and identify what is missing. This can be helpful if the people participating need some guidance in thinking about things that they might not be aware of.

- **Reports from Field Interviews:** Have teams go out and interview customers and other people in the field and then report back using the Context Map template.

Situation Analysis

In the early days of strategic planning, an approach commonly called SWOT analysis (for Strengths, Weaknesses, Opportunities and Threats) was the whole of strategic planning. The assumption was that good strategic planning would look at internal strengths and weaknesses and then external opportunities and threats. A good strategy would build on the strengths, flip the energy bottled up in weaknesses, and catch threats when they were smaller problems. The Grove template is called the SPOT Matrix, substituting "problems" for weakness to make an acronym that suggests focus rather than aggression.

Some of the ways to work with a big SPOT matrix are:

- **Pre-work:** Have everyone come to a meeting with a small versions of the SPOT completed. The Grove provides PowerPoint versions that can be used if you don't want to use paper.
- **Small Groups:** Have breakout groups complete the SPOT charts themselves and bring them back and compare, creating a composite. The advantage of this approach is the agreements pop right out when they are on all the charts.
- **Ranking Items:** A more rigorous process involves numbering the different elements, and then asking people to pick the top one-third items, either with hand voting or dots. I described this process in Chapter 7. Having everyone agree on problems and weaknesses is very helpful in getting people ready to change by moving beyond denial.

Developing Vision and Foresight

Histories, context maps, and SPOT analysis all focus on the past and present and what we know about from our experience, reading, and colleagues. Visual meetings can also work to support people thinking about the future, and share what everyone imagines is possible. You will still

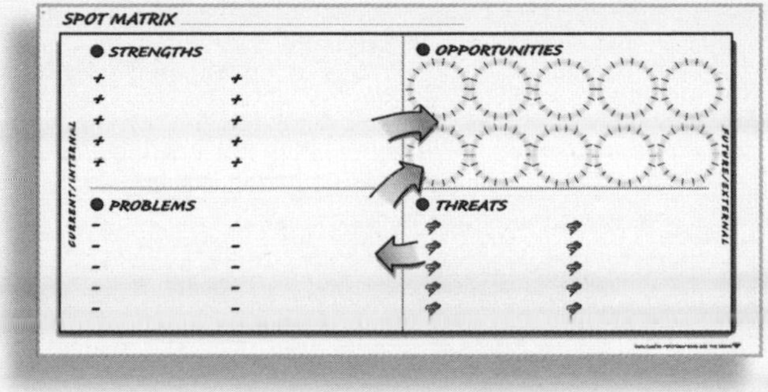

SPOT MATRIX`

A completed version of this kind of chart is included on page 92 as an example of using sticky dots after content is identified. This kind of analysis can be done entirely on flip charts, of course. If you do that, arrange the flip charts so everyone can make the comparisons suggested by the arrows. In most cases, even with this template, you will have to add a flip chart to the problems and opportunities areas.

GUIDED IMAGERY SESSION

1. Explain that you are leading a guided imagery session to warm up for visioning.
2. Explain that you will be asking very general questions and ask people to trust whatever images come to mind—suspending any judgment.
3. Have people then relax, close their eyes, and imagine that they are sitting somewhere where they like to reflect. Suggest they imagine this place by seeing, listening, feeling what it is like.
4. Then ask them to imagine a magazine they respect sitting in front of them and that their team or organization is being featured on the cover. You might say, *"Something important is being featured on the cover, what is it? Accept all ideas."*
5. Ask everyone to open the magazine and look at the cover story. Ask, "*What are the big headlines? They are featuring things you are very proud of having accomplished. There are special little sidebar features on different people and special projects. What is being featured?*"
6. When finished with questions like this, suggest people imagine themselves back in the room. Without talking, have everyone take notes of everything they imagined.
7. Share the results on a Cover Story Vision template, talking in the past tense.

be writing on charts, or scribing on a tablet, but the way in which you lead the process changes. Because moving to a future frame of mind is usually a significant shift, you probably need to plan some activities that will help people get in the right frame of mind.

The guided imagery session described here is a very effective way to begin. It involves asking very simple, general questions and letting people's own imaginations provide the answers and images. This provides a lead-in to an activity that many planners use to think about the future—having groups write a story from a future point of view. If you imagine that you or your team is being featured on the cover of a magazine that you really respect, you might also be able to imagine what that cover story would be saying about you. At The Grove we've create a Graphic Guide that supports this activity called the Cover Story Vision (see example on the next page).

The purpose of this kind of visioning is to get people into a future frame of mind. It's really meant to be something that opens the group up. There are some things from a leadership point of view that really help this activity work:

- Shift to a future time and talk in the past tense. Say something like, *"This story has already been written. You know what it said. Let's describe it."*
- Role-play talking in the past tense as if the future has already happened as a warm-up. Encourage everyone to think of it as an improvisation activity. Jump in yourself while holding a future focus, adding onto what people are saying.
- Lead the guided imagery activity suggested on the previous page.
- Coach the people who are planning on scribing on the chart to write down whatever people say and not filter or be judgmental.

RULES OF IMPROVISATION

A theater student explained to me that the rules for improvisational theater work well for facilitation, and especially for visioning. They are:

1. SIMPLE FRAMES: Suggest a theme or graphic framework like a template.
2. YES/AND: Accept whatever anyone says and build on it.
3. 100%: Do whatever you do with full commitment.

Focusing on Agreements

If you want to change your organization you will need to go beyond brainstorming visions, and really come to a shared agreement on what you are going to fight for together, and what steps you are going to take to begin heading in the new direction.

There is a lot of inertia in systems and a tendency for things to continue the way they have always worked. Systems do change when the whole is stressed in a way that it needs to resolve. In engineering stress of this sort is called structural tension and in humans is called creative tension or cognitive dissonance. Tension of this sort always seeks resolution, whether it is physical or psychic. If you dream of having a bigger home or sending your children to college and it is a strong dream, but your job and pocketbook can't afford this, you will experience structural tension. You will either lower your expectations, or you will work in every way possible to change your circumstances so you can afford what you want. Highly creative people have the capacity to keep themselves in this space of creative tension long enough that they coax extraordinary results from the physical resources they have to work with.

If a team or organization holds a very strong vision, and it is deep and compelling to the people involved, but current reality doesn't match, they will either give up on their vision or change current reality. The people who achieve breakthrough results are fierce about holding strong, positive visions and letting each day be a search for ways they can make progress. This kind of work is not planning in the sense of creating a blueprint and executing on it. It is stringing a strong

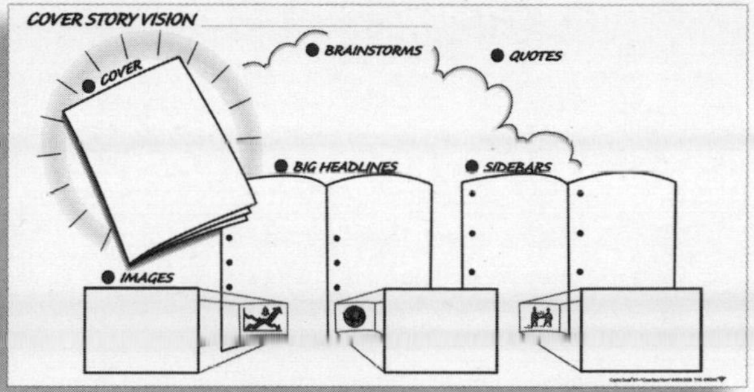

COVER STORY VISION

This is the most popular of a half dozen templates for use in the future oriented part of Strategic Visioning.

STRUCTURAL TENSION DRIVES CREATIVE ACTION

Humans resolve structural tension by either compromising on their visions or changing current reality (or not connecting the two). Creative people have an appetite for creative tension and hold their visions while exploring every way possible to change reality.

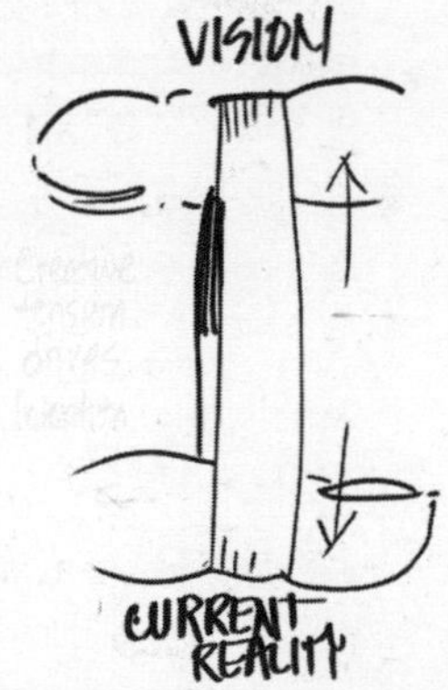

GETTING AGREEMENT ON VISION & BOLD STEPS

Use templates to get agreement by using them as a place to record commitments, rather than brainstorming. This is accomplished by:

1. Explaining the way systems change and the importance of having a vision that is truly compelling and reflects a real commitment to direction.
2. Asking pairs to reflect on whatever visioning you might have done to warm up, and record on sticky notes "individual vision ideas" that might be in the final vision.
3. Cluster the sticky notes in thematic groups.
4. When all the sticky notes are clustered pick one category and begin working the cluster using a flip chart. Ask for proposals about what a headline might be for that vision idea. Get wording that optimizes people talking about the key idea.
5. Record these suggestions, and ask for various talking points that would explain the headline.
6. When the group agrees on the best headline, write it on the chart, and then reflect the talking points out to the edges.
7. Repeat until vision ideas are agreed on. Repeat again for bold steps.

bow and having your commitment be the pull on the string. If a leadership group holds a strong intention and then improvises each day in search of fulfillment a system will change. Visualizing is a key way to both identify and strengthen this vision.

Getting real agreements on visions and bold steps will take a good 2 to 3 hours at best to get a good first draft. (See the sidebar for instructions.) It is then important for people to sleep on the ideas and come back again to double-check and perhaps create draft two. This kind of work is a waste of time if the vision you end up with isn't a real commitment. Once you have a good array of vision ideas identified, these can be combined into a vision statement, or illustrated eventually. This kind of work is not beginning level facilitation, and the charting doesn't do the work by itself. But if you are working with leaders who insist on having the important dialogue necessary to get shared agreement on a new direction, using a template like this as a commemoration device is very powerful. There is an example on the next page of a completed strategic vision.

Agreeing on Action Plans

Visual planning ends by circling back to the present and getting groups to agree on immediate action plans. That is also where we are in our learning process. Even though the next section in this book is all about moving to action, let's touch on it here, since doing action plans is a typical way to end an initial planning cycle. The Grove's Graphic Gameplan Graphic Guide, illustrated at the beginning of this chapter, is our tried and true way of doing this work. This template is designed around one of the most widespread metaphors used to think about planning —the journey. It reflects the "Where are we now, where do we want to go, how to we get there?" set of questions that guide any travel. What this template adds to these three basic things is a space for the territory through which the project will move—where challenges can be recorded. It also includes "wheels" on the vehicle, which are called "success factors" and can represent all the important things that are not tasks, like operational agreements, core values, and actions and behaviors that need to be embedded in the project. A team can fill out one of these in an hour or so and get a very good first draft of how they will go about moving to action.

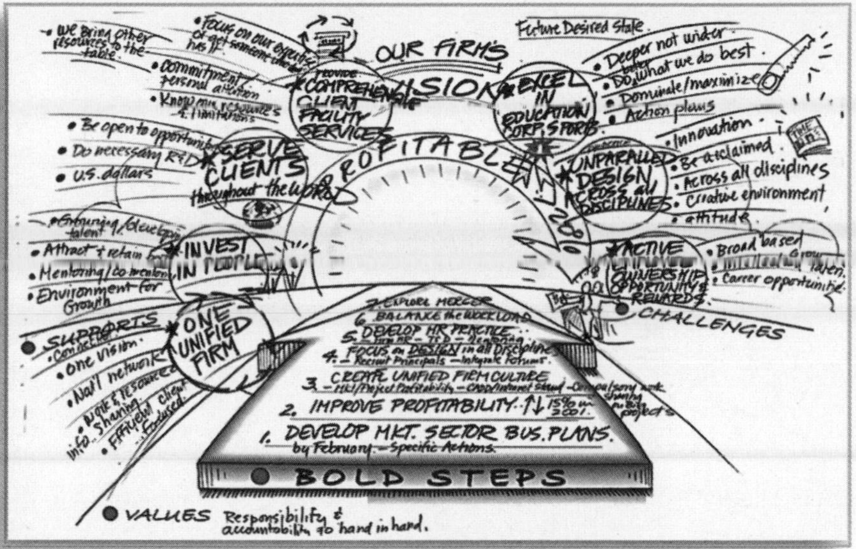

ARCHITECTURAL FIRM STRATEGIC VISION

Here is an example of a five-year vision of DLR Group that was reprinted just like this in large form and hung in a dozen offices around the country. Architectural firms are notoriously independent and collegial in their basic makeup, and it was a real achievement to get all the partners to align on these goals. This was the first one they did. Five years later they went through an identical process to generate a new vision, and five years after that another. The firm has grown steadily all during that time.

Designing Your Own Visual Planning Templates

The formats I have described here only begin to describe the full range of planning activities that benefit from having a simple graphic framework instead of a blank page. Designing simple templates like those described in Chapter 3 are well within anyone's ability to create. When you move into more specialized domains such as sales, marketing, strategy, leadership, and the many other subjects that have entire methodologies surrounding the practices and tools, it takes more experience to get templates that work time after time. This, I am admittedly biased in saying, is The Grove's value proposition.

The key success factor with templates is to ask yourself what the most important elements are that a group needs to focus on in a meeting, and then build these into the large worksheets. If you get the team involved in helping determine this, the templates will work even better.

Seeing the Really Big Picture

Beyond the use of single templates in a meeting is the kind of thinking that comes from using sequences of templates and creating entire environments that allow for truly panoramic thinking. One company I worked with had a very sophisticated kind of coin exchange technology that was a leading product in functionality. Because money exchange is such a universal activity, the product had application in more than a dozen different markets, with each market having a different

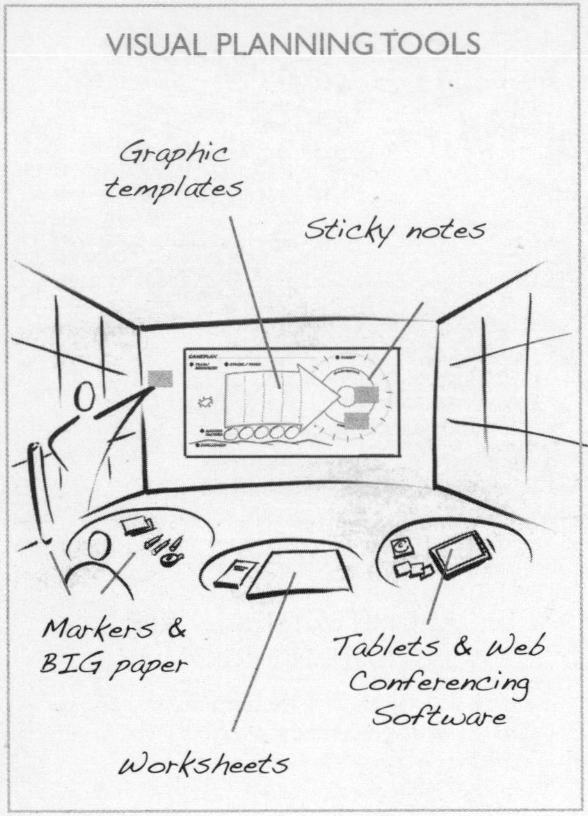

VISUAL PLANNING TOOLS

challenge in terms of how you would reach people, price, sell, and distribute the product. The top management wanted some guidance and analysis on which of all these markets had the best prospects. We decided to ask teams of middle managers to get involved in creating a series of charts for each market, and then gather in a special meeting to look at all of them and determine the most promising.

We decided that each team would create a Context Map of the market, a SPOT analysis of their company's position in relation to that market, and a Five Bold Steps chart illustrating a potential set of goals and initiatives to capture that market, with numbers sizes of the markets and revenue and expense estimates included. The day we gathered to share this work we had about 20 people in a very large room. Each group presented their three pieces of work in quick overviews. This took a while, but we ended up leaving all the Five Bold Steps charts up on the wall—all 12 of them. For about three hours we had the most engaged strategic discussion I have experienced in a work setting, because everyone could literally see what the opportunities and challenges were. I'd like to think it wasn't an accident that after a checked financial history, this division was profitable all four years I supported the management team visually.

This is what is possible with Visual Planning. With the prospect that large-scale digital walls and multi-displays appearing in our lifetimes, I suggest that this way of working has just gotten started.

13. Multiple Meetings & Gallery Walks

Making Sense of Things over Space & Time

Almost anything an organization does takes more than one meeting, and large gatherings are usually combinations of large and small group meetings. Somehow all this needs to come together and make sense. This is true in a sales situation, with multiple client meetings. It is true in a training design process, a planning process, a product development process, and any kind of learning and development process. In fact, I can think of very few things that ever happen in just one meeting.

This chapter is all about how you get people to see what is going on across the multiple meetings and scale of large conferences. In many ways, this is one of the strongest aspects of visual meetings, for without the practices I will be describing here, a large amount of what gets discussed and talked about gets forgotten, and that translates directly into waste and inefficiency. We'll start looking at how to orchestrate multiple face-to-face meetings. The following chapters will look at how you can digitally reproduce your charts and how you can work virtually with distributed teams.

Working with Breakout Groups

Let's start simply with the very common practice of using breakout groups to get maximum participation and input to a meeting process. Breakouts can be any size, from pairs to dozens of people meeting separately, usually charged with bringing back their ideas to a bigger group. We've already considered pair breakouts with sticky notes. For larger groups the most common practice is to

GALLERY WALKS

Each office in DLR Group, a large architecture & engineering firm, held meetings to look at their current environment, current situation, and visions. In a meeting to get alignment, the charts from the offices created a gallery that principals in the firm studied to find themes and patterns

INSTRUCTIONS FOR BREAKOUTS

1. Show everyone the template you are using and quickly explain the categories of information you are requesting.
2. Clearly announce the amount of time.
3. Encourage each group to pick a leader and a scribe.
4. Encourage the scribe to accept all ideas, and circle or mark the ones they think are best after writing things down (as opposed to filtering before writing).
5. Tell everyone you will use the 50% rule to make rounds and call time. (Alert people when 50% of their time is left, then when half of that or 25% is left, and maybe even once again when 50% of that time is gone. With this kind of warning, groups invariably complete the tasks on time.)
6. Tell people where to post the charts when they bring them back.

provide a flip chart for each breakout and have everyone bring back one to five or six flip charts and report. One would hope the results from breakout groups could be looked at together and inform a larger pattern of understanding, and not just be a tedious, reporting back process. Unfortunately, the flip chart approach is often painful.

When information is presented in small, uniform chunks the human brain cannot remember more than a half dozen or so at a time, so you can count on people glazing over at about the sixth or seventh bullet point chart or slide. When these number in the hundreds and charts in the dozens forget about having anything like real thinking going on. People will revert to moving the agendas they came in with.

Visual Meetings for Small Groups

Here are some of the ways you can improve on breakouts with visualization:

- **Flip Chart Templates:** Suggest a very simple framework for reporting back that will be consistent and focused. Listing top 4 or 5 items is very common. Another way is to provide a simple visual framework, such as a "T" bar graph if you are looking at pros and cons of something, or what worked and what could be improved in a process. Recently I asked small groups to identify potential markets for their organization on sticky notes and sort them into a grid with high and low potential, and easy and challenging on the two axes. This can be done either in physical breakout rooms or by bringing the flip charts to small group tables in a big room.

- **Graphic Guides:** The Grove's Graphic Guide templates are designed precisely to support breakout groups. They work wonderfully in groups of 5 to 12, and are big enough to provide for easy reporting back. The group carries just the one chart back into the room. It's amazing how this one shift creates a heightened sense of accomplishment.

- **Customized Large Templates:** Getting a group to focus in a short period of time is always challenging. If everyone walks into a breakout room and a large sheet is on the wall that has spaces for everything that needs discussing, chances of being productive are quite good. All you really need is a scribe who has decent handwriting. There is an example on this page of a template designed for a group that wanted to look at "What Bold Looked Like" in regard to their corporate vision.

- **Tabletop Templates:** Breakouts can happen at round or square tables in a large meeting room, without going to a separate location. In these cases it often works best to have a template that fits on the table with spaces to write. The same processes apply, but the logistics are a bit different.

- **Theme Teams:** In a meeting in Singapore an HR group summarized over 100 interviews with stakeholders on several dozen flip charts and then made presentation of all these. It was a forced march. But they then had five small groups meet to pull out themes for their vision and present these on one chart each.

- **Presentations and Skits:** Along with some instruction of what to bring back visually, have the breakout groups prepare special presentations that involve everyone and utilize the templates, if you are providing them. These kinds of assignments can range from the serious to the social. For breakout reports presenting visions or stories from the future, have everyone speak in the past tense, as though everything has already happened. This makes it come alive in a more compelling way.

- **Slide Templates:** In very large meetings where wall charts would be impossible to read, you can design a simple template in presentation software and ask small groups to report in a common format. During that process it is possible to have a graphic recorder synthesizing all the reports in a combined display.

CUSTOMIZED GRAPHIC TEMPLATE

When participants in an initial strategy session said that the results weren't bold enough, the design team created a special template to support small groups in the second meeting diving right in on this question.

TYPES OF BREAKOUT GROUPS

- ❑ **Dialogue groups,** for mutual understanding
- ❑ **Learning groups,** assigned a game or experience
- ❑ **Networking groups,** to allow people to get to know each other
- ❑ **Brainstorming groups,** to identify a range of ideas on any topic
- ❑ **Decision-making breakouts,** where caucuses decide what they will support in a negotiation
- ❑ **Proposal work groups,** to identify and shape an action suggestion
- ❑ **Prioritization groups,** to discuss and rank a series of options
- ❑ **Scenario planning,** where different groups have different assumptions and articulate a response
- ❑ **Visioning breakouts,** asking about potential futures
- ❑ **Action planning breakouts,** where teams are asked to prepare a draft for a Graphic Gameplan, for instance

Output Oriented Group Process

After many years of asking small groups to work on different kinds of assignments, I'm always amazed at how they are able to finish their work and produce a chart presentation even though I've given very little instruction on how to facilitate the groups. I've come to think of this as "output oriented group process." By defining the deliverable clearly, such as "bring this template back with your best ideas," I provide a clear goal. The groups deal with it.

Gallery Walks and Panoramic Display

Successfully getting small groups to work visually creates a challenge when everyone comes back into the main meeting room and wants to post their charts. This requires thinking through the staging much as the director of a play might. Your choices should be guided by what your goals are and what you want the big group to do with all the information. There is a wide range of potential purposes, varying primarily by how much pattern recognition and closure you would like to have. Check out the list of types of breakouts on this page and you can see that each has a different kind of result that could be used when getting back together.

The picture on the next page shows a company with small breakout group reports on the sides, and big theme chart about headlines from the future in the middle. The themes came from table groups after the breakout presentations.

Some of the possibilities following breakouts include:

- **Simple Acknowledgment:** The simplest goal would be to acknowledge everyone's work and have reports and rounds of applause.

- **Flip Chart Array of Top Items:** Constrain the groups to report on a select number of items and then arrange to have all the flip charts posted where they can be scanned for agreements.

- **Call-Out Clustering:** You can let the small groups reference their charts, but gather the suggestions across a range of groups by having people call out an item, and then getting related suggestions posted at the same time. This process involves making a large new cluster map of the combined small group responses.

- **Gallery Walks:** You can have small groups post their templates in hallways, foyers, or around a big meeting room, and then instruct everyone to circulate around and read the charts, hunting for common themes and good ideas. The instructions can be precise or general, all aiming at getting everyone to read all the charts. When finished, everyone returns to the big room and shares what they discovered.

- **Digital Capture:** In a very large gathering, where participants would have trouble seeing big charts you might use to combine small group reports, the alternative is to record suggestions on a computer and project the items on several large screens. This approach is

COMING BACK FROM BREAKOUT GROUPS

Staging the big sessions when small groups return with their charts creates a very energized surrounding for town-hall-style meetings. Here is a picture of DLR Group principals looking at the vision themes arising from their various offices. The big chart in the middle is a cluster format created from the reflections of the large group after gallery walks.

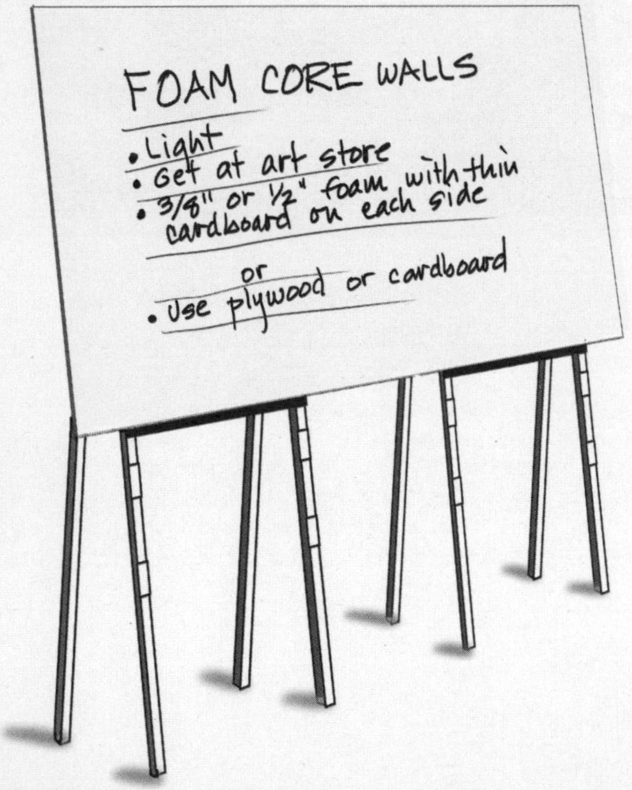

not as supportive of seeing visual patterns in the data, but does acknowledge all the input in important sessions.

FOAM CORE WALLS
• Light
• Get at art store
• 3/8" or 1/2" foam with thin cardboard on each side
or
• Use plywood or cardboard

Staging Techniques for Working with Big Paper

Most designers of meeting rooms assume that if people are working visually, it will be by projecting slides on a screen in big rooms, or working on whiteboards or blackboards in smaller rooms. Even then the assumption that people will be meeting with slides is clearly evident with the central placement of screens. This has resulted in quite a bit of creativity on the part of those of us who want to work visually in an interactive way, using large displays. The issue is getting wall space, and then confronting the challenge of hanging the big paper with tape. In spite of the many seeming obstacles, there are solutions for all of them. I want to go through a number of the technical details by indicating the problem and the solution.

Challenges and Solutions for Working BIG

- **No Smooth Walls:** The most flexible approach is to create your own walls from large sheets of smooth material, like the foam core poster boards available in art stores, or plywood, or fiberboard. Rest these large 4' by 8' panels on a pair of same-size easels. All hotels and conference centers have easels that have little prongs for resting displays. Just make sure you get two that are the same for each panel. It is also possible to use rolling white boards or portable display walls (See www.neuland.biz for portable folding walls.)
- **Can't Tape on the Wallpaper:** Many hotels have prohibitions against taping to what they consider sensitive wall surfaces. If you don't have portable walls, then you need to get inventive. I use special, white artists' tape. One advantage of large rolls of paper is their ability to span 10 to 15 feet without support. You can often tape to moldings, picture frames, or

windows and not hurt anything.

- **Moving Charts and Walls:** You need to plan ahead for where the breakout charts will be posted, and how they will move if they have to during a big meeting. It helps to have a team dedicated to this. Foam core walls are very light and can be moved by one person. Plywood and whiteboards probably need two people to move them around. Moving large charts is also a two-person job.

- **Panoramic Scanning:** In cultures that read left to right try and have the large charts in that order as they are created during a meeting. For breakouts this isn't so important. It is critical to imagine how you want people to see the charts. If you need to reference them during the plenary meeting, or do any sticky dot ranking or voting, then they need to be toward the front. If they are to be used for a gallery walk only, then they can be posted many different places. If you can help people see and scan the sweep of their thinking, the more potential there will be for finding new patterns of meaning. The way to test your thinking is to walk to the most remote part of the room and imagine being one of the participants who is sitting there. Does your planned arrangement work for them?

- **Inconsistent Chart Titles:** Often breakout groups will not title their charts big enough or consistently enough to allow for scanning when they are all assembled. Some ways of achieving this gracefully are to:

    - ❑ Title the charts in advance when they are posted in the breakout rooms
    - ❑ Title the charts during the rounds when you are calling out the time
    - ❑ Add large titles after the charts come back into the main meeting room

- **Lighting:** Many conference room designers assume meetings will use slides and arrange the lighting so that the front of the room can be dimmed. If you are working with templates

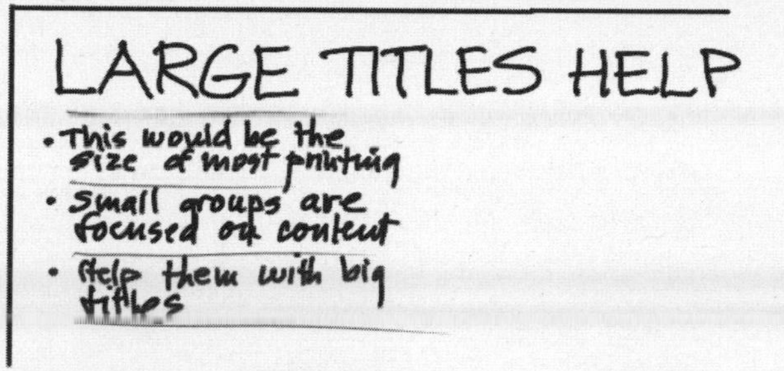
LARGE TITLES HELP
• This would be the size of most printing
• Small groups are focused on content
• Help them with big titles

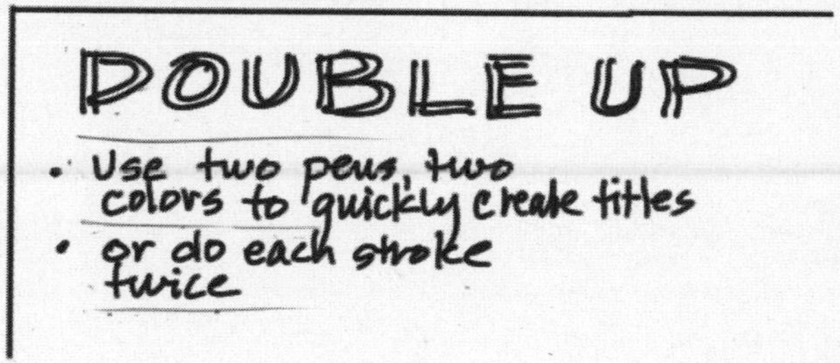
DOUBLE UP
• Use two pens, two colors to quickly create titles
• or do each stroke twice

Part of creating a strong meeting container involves having leadership agreeing on constraints and advocating that people stay within them. But containers are essentially open. Filling every space in your meeting with pre-scripted activity does not result in engagement and creativity. Having spaces for interaction and improvisation within constraints does.

and charts you will want the opposite. I've come to accept that I need to see the room in advance or have a client send pictures, and then actually check how the lighting is set. There are so many variations I can't outline them all here, but some of my favorite work-arounds are the following:

- ❑ Ask the hotel or conference center for floodlights
- ❑ Arrange for slide shows to happen off to the side
- ❑ Orient the front of the room to a long side wall, and keep projections going toward the narrow wall.
- ❑ Put the charts opposite windows if possible

Creating Containers for Dialogue

The underlying design objective in any small group or large group meeting that you want to be interactive and innovative, is to create a strong container for the dialogue. "Container" is a metaphor for the features of the agenda, ground rules, and other conceptual structures that provide boundaries for the experience, and the room itself. If people in your meeting are confused about purposes and objectives, confused about the agenda itself, or confused about roles and ground rules, then they will spend energy on those things and this will take away from the dialogue. If they can't find bathrooms and navigate physically this will also take energy away from your meeting. This is why the OARRs practice I described in Chapter 12 on Visual Planning is so important. Part of creating a strong meeting container involves having leadership agreeing on constraints and advocating that people stay within them. But containers are essentially open. Filling every space in your meeting with pre-scripted activity does not result in engagement and creativity. Having spaces for interaction and improvisation within constraints does.

TYPICAL SEATING DESIGNS

What if I want the meeting to be creative and unconstrained?" you may be wondering. Interestingly, there is a direct relation between freedom and constraint. One kind of freedom comes from having no controls in place—an open, free-for-all of a playground. Long breaks, special open space times, and sessions that have almost no structure provide this kind of freedom. But there is another kind of freedom that is the flexibility and performance that comes from having and mastering constraints. This is the freedom of a skilled jazz musician, sports team, or dancing troupe. It uses the efficiency gained from *not* having to worry about structure to fuel creativity. To support this kind of freedom you need your containers to be very clear and explainable.

Having the physical environment support your desired meeting outcomes is part of this discipline. On this spread is a map of the typical choices you will have in setting up tables. They each make it easy and hard to do certain things.

- **Rows:** The straight seats make it easy to focus on a screen, difficult to interact. This is sometimes called Theater Style. If people are used to being in school in this configuration they will feel like

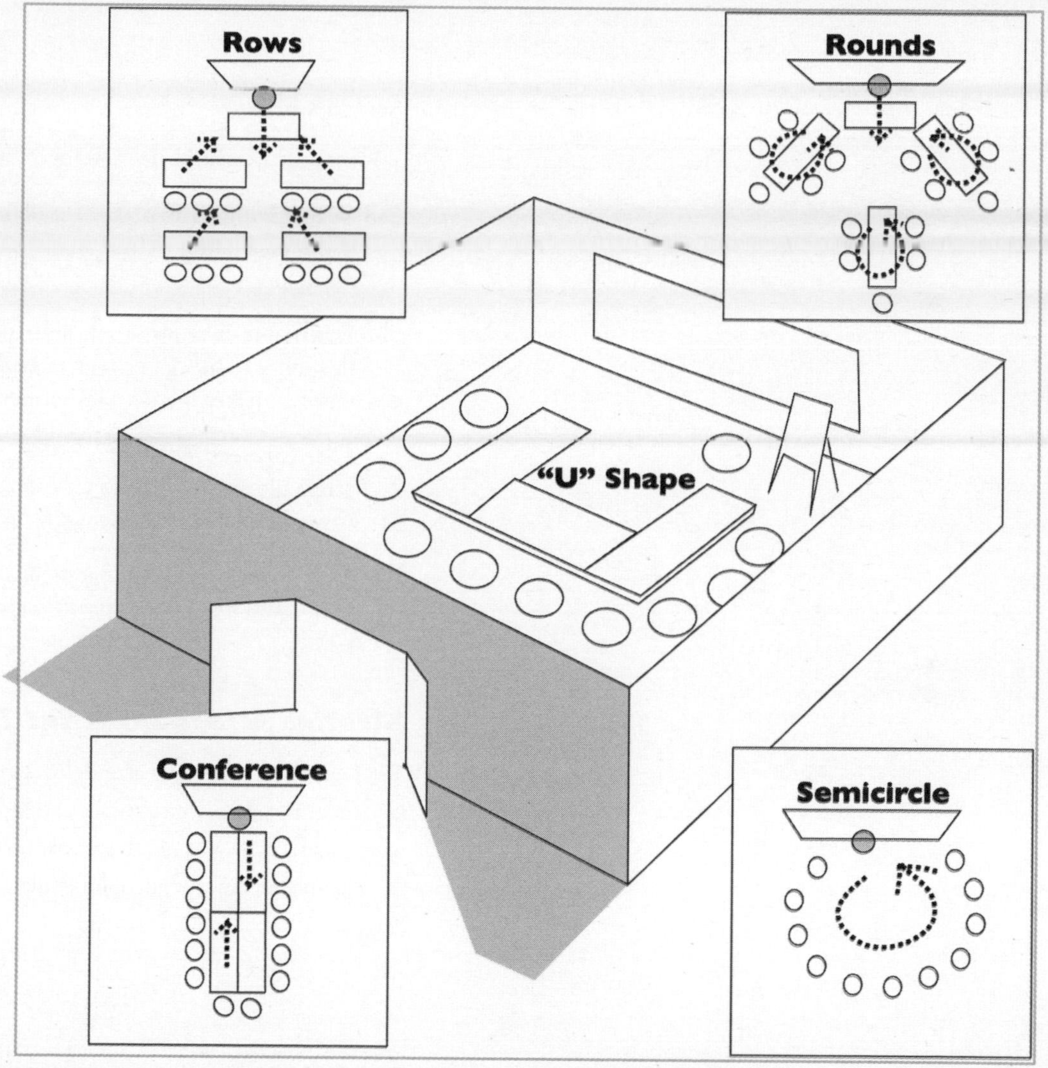

they are in school. If you want to break out of this feeling choose another arrangement.

- **Semicircle:** This makes it much easier to see everyone and interact. This is perfect for dialogue. Having a chart on one side allows the group to cocreate big pictures of what they are talking about.
- **Rounds:** Seating people in small groups around a round or square table provides the flexibility to move between table discussion and large group discussion. This is a typical workshop arrangement sometimes called cafe style seating.
- **Conference Tables:** Many boardrooms have a built-in, large conference table. This setup allows everyone to see each other well, and have a smaller chart or screen at the narrow end. This arrangement is more formal.
- **"U" Shape:** This arrangement allows for everyone to see each other and see the large charts and work on a table. It's a great format for workshops, team meetings, and planning sessions.

Meeting across Space and Time

The next two chapters deal with how to reproduce charts so you can use them between face-to-face meetings, and how to work with graphics in virtual environments. For large organizations, many teams now work in this distributed fashion. If you don't, then skip these chapters and read the ones about supporting taking ideas to action.

14. Digital Capture

Extending Your Meeting with Visual Documentation

Imagine being finished with the meeting you planned. It was most likely just one part of a larger team process or project where follow-through will be essential to getting results. In this time of digital photography and electronic mail, many people expect to see reproductions the next day so they can follow through immediately on whatever things were decided.

Creating a Work Flow

Working visually invites taking your imagery and special charts and evolving them into ever more useful arrangements and presentations. You need to learn to manage versions of plans and get more input. If you are at teacher you want to reinforce the lessons and special presentations. In a sales situation you want to demonstrate your attention to your clients by timely follow-up. If you are a consultant you want to add value to whatever was created in the meeting. Rapidly reproducing the large displays and moving them into other media facilitates these results. People need to remember what they have committed to do, and when. Scan the checklist here on the value of follow-through to remind yourself of why this is so important.

Investing in a Good Camera

Digital photography is well established as a way to bring almost any visual imagery into a form that can be used and processed on computers and sent through e-mail. It has put flexibility into the hands of anyone doing visual meetings if you take a little time to learn the basics. This guide isn't meant to be a tutorial on digital photography, but it contains some of the things you should consider at a basic level.

VALUE OF MEETING FOLLOW-THROUGH

- ❑ **Remembering Commitments:** People are overloaded with information. Feeding back commitments and action plans is essential.
- ❑ **Deepening Retention:** Photographed charts received a few days after an event invite review and a deepening of what everyone retains from a meeting.
- ❑ **Support Briefing:** Well-designed reports can make it easy for meeting participants to brief others about what happened.
- ❑ **Providing a Reference for Subsequent Meetings:** Visual reports allow teams to literally pick up where they left off.
- ❑ **Creating a Tangible Result:** Managers like to see results from resources and time spent on group process. Documentation of substance is almost always welcome.

DIGITAL PHOTOGRAPHY TIPS

- ❑ Take pictures as you go along, before you move displays if possible, or get an assistant to help.
- ❑ When shooting, hold your breath and brace your arms to hold steady.
- ❑ Remember to number your charts.
- ❑ Larger cameras with telephoto lenses can help in shooting charts across tables.
- ❑ Set your camera for fluorescent lighting if that is what your room uses.

Learn How to Shoot

Any point-and-shoot camera above four megapixel resolution will work well for reproducing charts. Most are well above that now. The flashes on these standard cameras are also strong enough to take eight-foot-wide pictures without additional lighting. The more professional cameras will, of course, give you great ability to work in low light, and greater resolution, but they require a bit more learning.

The key to good pictures with any camera is holding the camera steady. A tripod isn't necessary, but is recommended. Set your camera to automatic flash, then point and shoot, holding as steady as possible. Now let's look at what to do once you have the digital images.

Processing and Using Your Photos

- **Transferring to Computer:** There are two ways to get your images into a computer. One is to use a cable. The other is to use a memory card reader that fits into a slot in the side of a laptop. It acts like a miniature hard disc.

- **Photo Processing:** Most photo-editing software gives you some ability to edit and adjust your pictures to isolate charts, get rid of background wall space, people, and windows, or turn the background white. There are special programs that do this automatically. Photoshop by Adobe is the preferred tool for professionals. It gives you the most flexibility and allows you to erase and rearrange things if need be. In any photo program, save your photos in different sizes for different purposes.

- **Hard Copy Reproduction:** If you want to print an 11" x 17" or A3-size copy of your chart (a size that is proportionate to the charts from the meeting room), you will want to save the chart photos at 144 dots per inch resolution or higher. If saved in a TIFF format, the images will not degrade with use as JPEGs can. Page-layout software allows you to make frames, captions, and titles for the images. A collection of 11" x 17" spiral-bound pages makes a wonderful report, and retains the panoramic feeling of the charts in the meeting room. If your organization doesn't have the reproduction capabilities there are many kinds of digital reproduction convenience stores that will print out any size of material from your digital photographs, including very large wall charts.

THIS LOOKS JUST LIKE IT DID IN THE MEETING!

- **Slide Presentations:** An easy way to create a fast report is to drop the pictures into a slide presentation. These kinds of programs are great for making quick annotations and including pictures you have taken of the group as it is working. You need to save your pictures at 10" wide or smaller, and as lower resolution JPEGs (96 dpi for Macs and 72 dpi for PCs), or your presentation file will get too large. For readability I've found that eight feet of chart is very readable on a slide in PowerPoint or Keynote presentation software. You can also save a copy as a PDF for easy e-mailing.

- **Website Posting**: As you will see on the next page, websites are an emerging, flexible way to provide feedback after meetings. For your chart pictures JPEG and TIFF files at low resolution are required for quick online viewing. You need to check the size you intend to post and then save in that size. If you intend to have a small version that can be enlarged, you will need to save two sizes of the photo. If you recorded a long history chart or context map you might not want to have it broken into sections. You can save several sizes online with links that allow people to look at a larger view or print a big copy.

These basic choices have many options. Let's zoom in a bit on several of these and see what they are for print and online communications.

PRINT REPORT FORMATS

HAND COPIED CHARTS: Redraft by hand if you are in a hurry and want to neaten it up.

SIMPLE DIGITAL PRINTS: Sometimes printing an 11" x 17" version in full color is enough.

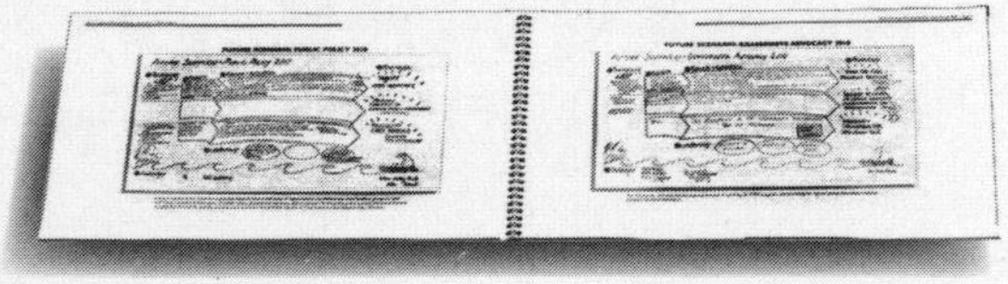

ANNOTATED REPORT: Add page titles and captions to create a meeting chronology.

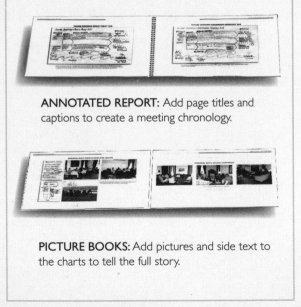

PICTURE BOOKS: Add pictures and side text to the charts to tell the full story.

Support Group Memory with Printed Reports

Getting images of key charts back to everyone is critical to keeping links between meetings and having people remember what they agreed on. Some of the most useful ways of doing this are illustrated to the left here. If you reproduce an eight-foot-long chart on an 11" x 17" format, and then hold it up in front of you to read, you will be looking at an image that is almost exactly the same size as the chart looked if you were sitting in the meeting room. Add some photos for context and it is possible to create an image that directly links back to people's experience. This greatly improves the retention from meetings. If you take a chart and convert it to text, many who get the report will have trouble linking directly back to the meeting.

While these reproduced graphic images mean a great deal to the people who saw them created that is not so true of people who weren't at the meeting. If you need to connect with additional people, you might want to write up the results in a more conventional way and print those text versions on facing pages. This way you get the best of both text-based and graphic representation.

Using Online Capabilities

The Internet is evolving quickly and the tools are becoming simpler and simpler for posting all kinds of material in e-mail, company websites, blogs, social networking pages, and special team rooms. Digital capture is making utilization of all these communication channels a very important one if you want to have productive processes that link over time and space.

Here are some of the options that are already available for quick online communication.

- **E-mail Simple JPEGs:** Process the photos and save them in a low-resolution format to e-mail to participants. This is good for overnight documentation.

- **Combine charts in a PDF document:** Adobe Software's widespread Acrobat program allows you to combine photos into one PDF document that can be compressed into a very manageable file.

- **E-mail Annotated Slides:** Create 8" x 10" JPEGs in a slide-presentation program that has captions and post for download or e-mail to participants. This is almost as fast as sending individual slides, but it may create a big file that some people could have trouble accessing. Presentation programs allow saving as a PDF as well.

- **Post in an Online Site:** Post the slides individually on a project website or one of the public photo sites. On a dedicated website create a small version of the chart, say 3" x 4" wide, and a larger version that may be 16" wide. Then link the two with a button that says, "To see a larger view."

- **Send Downloadable Print Files:** Send very large files (over 10MB) via a web service that allows you send large files, and then e-mail a password to your client or meeting sponsors.

- **Reference in a Web Meeting:** Use presentation software to review what happened at an earlier meeting by uploading to web conference software, or share applications during the session to use whatever software you used to author the report.

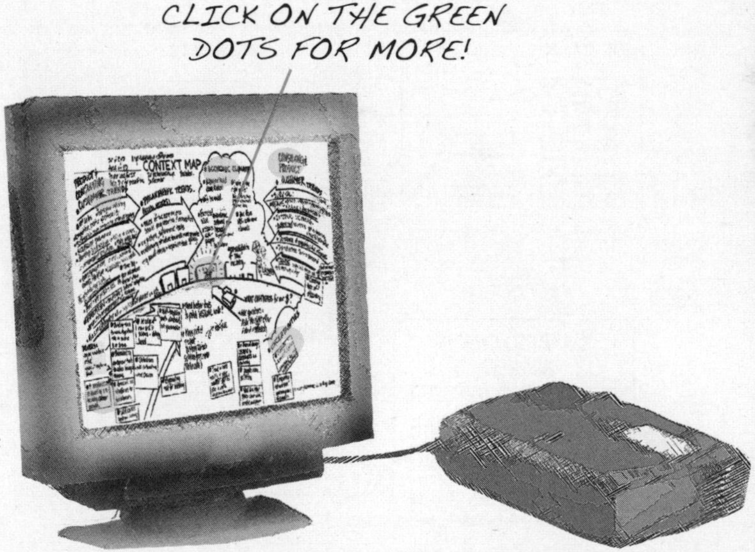
CLICK ON THE GREEN
DOTS FOR MORE!
CONTEXT MAP

Link to Additional Data

If you are using an online system to communicate, format your charts so they can be divided into easily readable sections. One advantage to online reference is the prospect of linking the charts to backup materials that can provide more information. With a bit of processing, it is possible to cut up a chart and make parts of it "hot," where clicking on these parts will take

DRILL DOWN ARCHITECTURE

I used a simple diagram to illustrate the basic way that a team website might use visual data from a meeting.

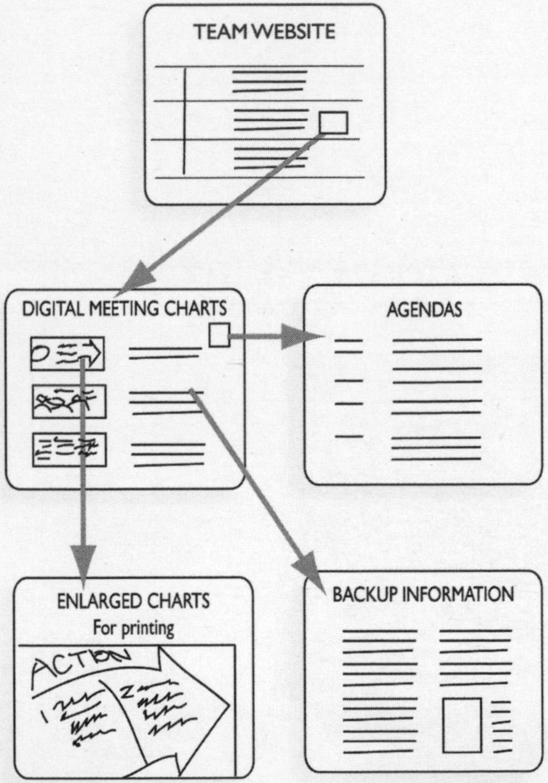

you to more elaborate information. This is worth doing if you have created a dense framework or map that will become a shared reference for a whole group of people. Several visual practitioners have gone the additional step of using rollovers that pop the information up right on top of the image. These kinds of effects are increasingly possible with widely available software.

I've illustrated to the left here how electronic documentation might link on a team website. This kind of functionality is available on many of the off-the-shelf social networking frameworks and blog websites if you don't have an organization Intranet and webmasters who can help you post material. It does take time to do all this, but having the material in visual form is part of what supports productivity and group memory over time. The interior illustrations show the two sizes of digital photo that you would need to save and then post. The bigger ones usually appear in a separate window.

15. Visualizing at a Distance
Using Tablets in Web Meetings

Teams are increasingly using teleconferencing and web conferencing to save travel time and costs. Some are seeing the bulk of their teamwork done virtually, with only occasional face-to-face meetings. Many sales teams never have face to face meetings since they are distributed over wide geographies. I remember flying East one time sitting next to a salesperson from a high tech firm. I asked about how they organized their sales teams and this person said that they worked almost entirely by web and teleconference. "Why are you traveling?" I asked. "I have to meet people in person to have a relationship. As their manager there is no substitute for showing up."

Another colleague insists that teams don't need to have any face time to be effective. She lives in California and has very trusted colleagues in England that she has never met. I believe this is increasingly possible, especially with Internet telephony and video, making the costs of distance communications affordable.

LET'S FILL OUT THIS
ACTION PLAN TEMPLATE.
ANY SUGGESTIONS FOR
THE TARGET?
GAMEPLAN
GAMEPLAN

Most of the people I know would still say that knowing people personally helps a great deal, and that investment in occasional, well-designed, get-togethers makes a big difference. I believe face time is especially important in cross-cultural teams of any sort, where people make very different use of business English and life experiences produce very different metaphors for understanding collaborative work. As work becomes more virtual, the importance of having well-run meetings will increase, in both face-to-face and virtual settings. As stressful as online work can be if you are just learning to work this way, there is good news. Solutions are increasingly available.

SIMPLE WHITEBOARD TEMPLATES

MAPS
Check, type, or stamp

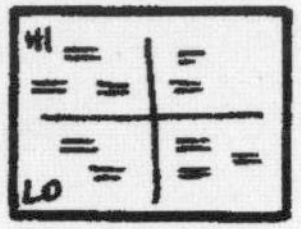

4-BOX GRIDS
Type data and sort or fill in categories

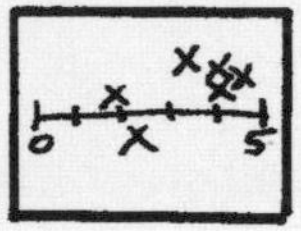

CONFIDENCE INDEX
Check 1 through 5

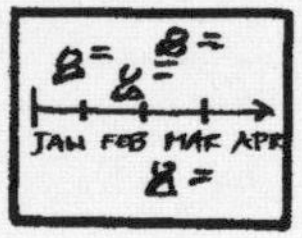

TIME LINES
Type info, add pictures

Visualization Increases Involvement

In online meetings of any kind, keeping people involved is a huge challenge that active visualization addresses directly, for all the reasons described in the section on engagement. Leaders of virtual meetings without graphics have to work hard to mirror back what people say, call on people, conduct go-arounds where everyone speaks, and keep participants involved. Multitasking is still a steady feature.

I facilitated a meeting recently using a web conference tool that showed when people had their screens active and when they had switched to another screen. During the meeting about 25% of the people did not have the web conferencing screen as the primary screen. The only way to get more engagement under these conditions is to have the meeting itself be compelling enough to command attention. This requires a good bit more planning and discipline than that required for a face-to-face meeting. The time is shorter in which to get things accomplished, and you have many fewer clues as to how people are actually responding.

Working with Web Conferencing Software

Most large organizations now support one form of web conferencing software or another. All of them have some form of whiteboard function and ability to import slide presentations and other documents for viewing. The slides and documents can be as visual as you want to make them, of course. What the conferencing software provides is an additional ability to circle things, point at things, draw arrows, and type text over the images. Some allow participants to have cursors personalized with their names for pointing at information. With some practice you can get quite interactive visually with just this much activity.

BENEFITS OF RECORDING ONLINE

Active recording brings the same benefits to virtual meetings that it does to face-to-face ones. Graphic facilitation helps in specific ways:

- ❑ Immediate visual feedback keeps people involved, provided it doesn't graphically interrupt the verbal flow.
- ❑ Precharted templates sent in advance can focus teleconferences and web conferences.
- ❑ Graphic agendas help with the increased organization required for online work.
- ❑ Graphics allow for summaries of decisions and suggested actions.
- ❑ Active recording provides an engaging documentation of work completed.

A great way to begin with a group that doesn't know itself well is to have all the participants send in digital pictures of themselves so you can create a little virtual seating chart. Then have a go-around where everyone shares an introduction and provides some information that is relevant to working together.

If your whiteboard functions allow for participants to enter text, or make check marks and simple graphics, there are ways to use simple templates like the ones illustrated on the previous page. One of my colleagues loves to have people brainstorm information with the text tools and then sort them into a simple four-box model she draws on the spot. Of course there are cursor wars, but that's part of the fun, and the group is very engaged. Time lines work just as well for this kind of interaction if people have name stamps they can show when they joined a project or organization. Participants can add key events as they review the stories of their work.

In my experience the whiteboard functions on web conferencing software are too crude for doing anything like real-time graphic recording where a lot of printing and drawing is required. The menus for changing colors and line widths aren't designed for real-time use. But there are now drawing programs like Autodesk's Sketchbook Pro or Microsoft's Windows Journal for the tablet that are wonderfully flexible for doing live recording on a tablet. This requires stepping up to using other applications than those provided by web conferencing software and learning to use a tablet.

Almost all web conferencing software will have a function called "application sharing" that allows everyone to see your desktop if you are made the presenter. When you have that function clicked, then any application you have open will show to everyone else. All you have to do is have a sketching program open and you will have a full line of tools to work with—pens, pencils, airbrush, brushes, erasers, and highlighters.

Using Computer Tablets

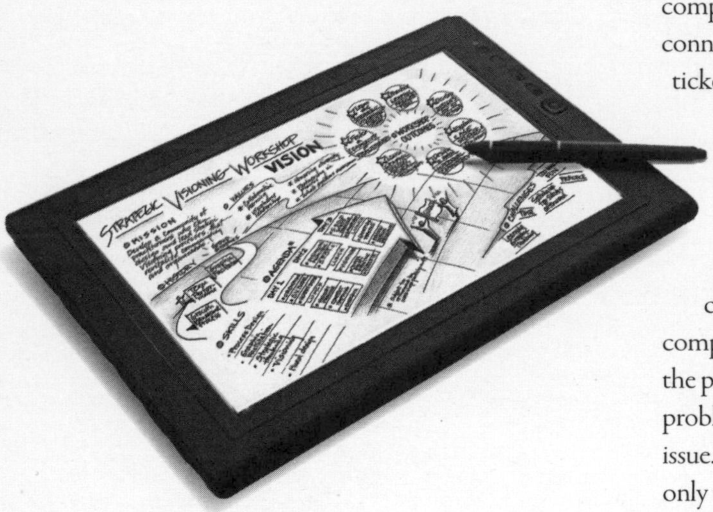

Tablet personal computers or tablets connected with your computer work in application sharing mode as long as you mirror your screens or have the tablet screen as the main one. Tablet computers cost about the same as regular computers, as do the special designer tablets that you connect to your computer. This kind of investment is worth it if you consider the cost of plane tickets and other expenses for travel. The time investment to learn these tools is probably more of a consideration. The detail and refinement possible on the tablet makes it well worth the investment if you live a world of virtual meetings.

There are some challenges in using sketching software in application sharing mode. Most of the web conferences have a window that allows everyone to see who is on line and see chat, and possibly respond to questions or polls. These windows, if open on a participant computer, will cover up part of the display. They can be minimized, but that requires having all the participants know how to do this. If your team is used to working virtually this is usually no problem. If you are running a meeting that is a new experience for people, then it might be an issue. Do a workaround to make sure that the working area you use in the sketchbook program is only using the two-thirds of the space that would not be covered up by the chat window.

This book is not intended to be comprehensive about all the details of working virtually, but to provide an overview of what is possible with visual meetings should you need to learn. Nor am I able here to cover all the details about learning to use the web conferencing software, tablets, and your own computer. What I do want to communicate is that whatever tools you end up choosing, be prepared to learn them inside and out so technical issues don't get in the way. In the beginning you will probably need to have someone support you technically if you want to work this way.

Working without Sketching Software

The Grove now provides its line of Graphic Guides in PowerPoint formats that can be used online in application sharing mode without a tablet. This doesn't allow for graphic recording, but does allow someone familiar with PowerPoint to use typing to reflect what people are saying and agreeing to. Any templates you would invent yourself can also be used in this fashion. The main challenge to this way of working is learning to use software as quickly as people like to interact. Doing anything graphically usually takes a lot longer than people would have patience for in a live meeting. In very large meetings recording what people say in text in a word processing program is an alternative to recording on big paper. This is providing the visual feedback that tells people they have been heard, but in text form only. Some people call this function being a "techretary." It requires being a fast typist.

Taking graphic notes on a tablet like one does on paper is still the best support for group thinking activity. Erasing and changing information slowly doesn't disrupt people's memory theaters.

All during the 1990s I worked with The Institute of the Future in Palo Alto on a project called the Groupware Users Project. It involved four dozen large organizations, all of which were trying to assess the impact of different kinds of group-oriented software on their operations. These were companies like P&G, Bechtel, HP, the World Bank, and government agencies. We had our two annual client meetings in state-of-the-art groupware facilities at Apple, Microsoft, MIT, and University of Arizona and tried almost every kind of tool then being invented. This included video conferencing, audiographics, shared whiteboards, web conferencing, teleconferencing, collaborative drawing, and team rooms. In face-to-face meetings we would project the computers and use different kinds of recording software. As a lead facilitator for these events, I tried almost all these kinds of equipment at one time or another and came to some conclusions.

When people are trying to understand something complicated, each person gathers the information and displays it in his or her own mind or in notes in what I came to think of as their memory theater. I found that if I recorded a chart in one part of a room, and then moved it, people would still gesture toward the space where the information was originally recorded when they referenced it. I came to realize that these memory spaces need to be stable if you want to think about relationships and patterns in data. If the information moves around and constantly changes its relative positioning, then participants can't create the internal constructs that allow for the second-level pattern finding. Any of the various kinds of software that keep changing the display when you add new information are destabilize this internal structure. They are good for capture, but not for group analysis and pattern finding. This is why I think that taking graphic notes on a tablet like we do on paper is still the best support for group thinking activity. Erasing and changing information slowly doesn't disrupt people's memory theaters so much.

Visual Teleconferences

If you are primarily working with teleconferences in your meetings, you can still work visually by providing discussion documents that support the thinking the group needs to do. These may be maps, diagrams, models, lists, or even a written proposal. If pages and paragraphs are numbered, and titles and areas on the drawing are clearly designated, then the group can begin to work visually by referencing the source document. Many smaller work groups use teleconferencing and e-mail together, sending documents back and forth in real time during the meeting. This way of working is very common for agenda planning meetings.

IV. Graphics for Enacting Plans

Visuals for Teams, Projects, & Getting Results

IV: Graphics for Enacting Plans

In this section you will learn how to use visual meetings to support action and the kinds of meetings related to team performance, decision making, project management, training, innovation, and change processes. These are all the types of meetings that are integral to getting results and being truly productive.

Chapter 16: Supporting Team Performance Overview of the stages of a team process and the types of meetings that support implementation and high performance.

Chapter 17: Decision-Making Meetings Overview of types of decision systems; keys to building a decision funnel visually; best visual practices for getting agreement.

Chapter 18: Project Management Meetings Aligning a team with roadmap graphics; working with project management software; importance of feedback and checkins.

Chapter 19: Facilitating Innovation & Change Inventing new business models; supporting organization change; P&G Innovation Workshop; using Grove Storymaps to support change.

Chapter 20: Training & Workshops Using visuals in learning-oriented workshops; discovery-based learning maps; graphical presenter interfaces.

16. Supporting Team Performance
Visualizing Goals, Roles, & Action Plans

Moving from thinking to action is a shift from looking at systems and structures conceptually to coordinating actions over time. It begins when decisions are made to apply resources to plans and ideas, and moves through project organization and implementation and sometimes to high performance. Highly productive organizations also invest in learning and development so that experiences benefit future projects. There is a lot you can do to support everyone in this process with visual meetings. It starts with using visualization for decision making and commitment, then involves graphics for action planning and project management, and eventually using visualization to support innovation and learning—the high-performance results organizations would love to have from meetings.

WE BETTER LOOK
AT A TRAIL MAP!

Facilitators, project managers, team leaders, sales teams, change managers, and development professionals all face the challenge of anticipating and managing processes over time. As a way of getting into this material, we will begin by looking at a general level at a map of the process that any group or team goes through, and what the predictable phases and stages are. Then we will take a closer look at how the different kinds of visual meetings support this natural process. Subsequent chapters explore each step in a little more depth.

What Is a Team?

A team is any group that has to cooperate to get things done. There are many work groups that are called teams, but are actually collections of individual contributors with a manager. This kind of work is important in call centers, customer service, and even teaching. But visual meetings are most important with groups that have to collaborate to get things done, like production teams, change teams, sales teams on large accounts, and professional teams like medical staff, designers, and agency directors. Why? Because teams that need to cooperate need to share a common idea of who needs to do what when, and that is helped enormously by visual tools.

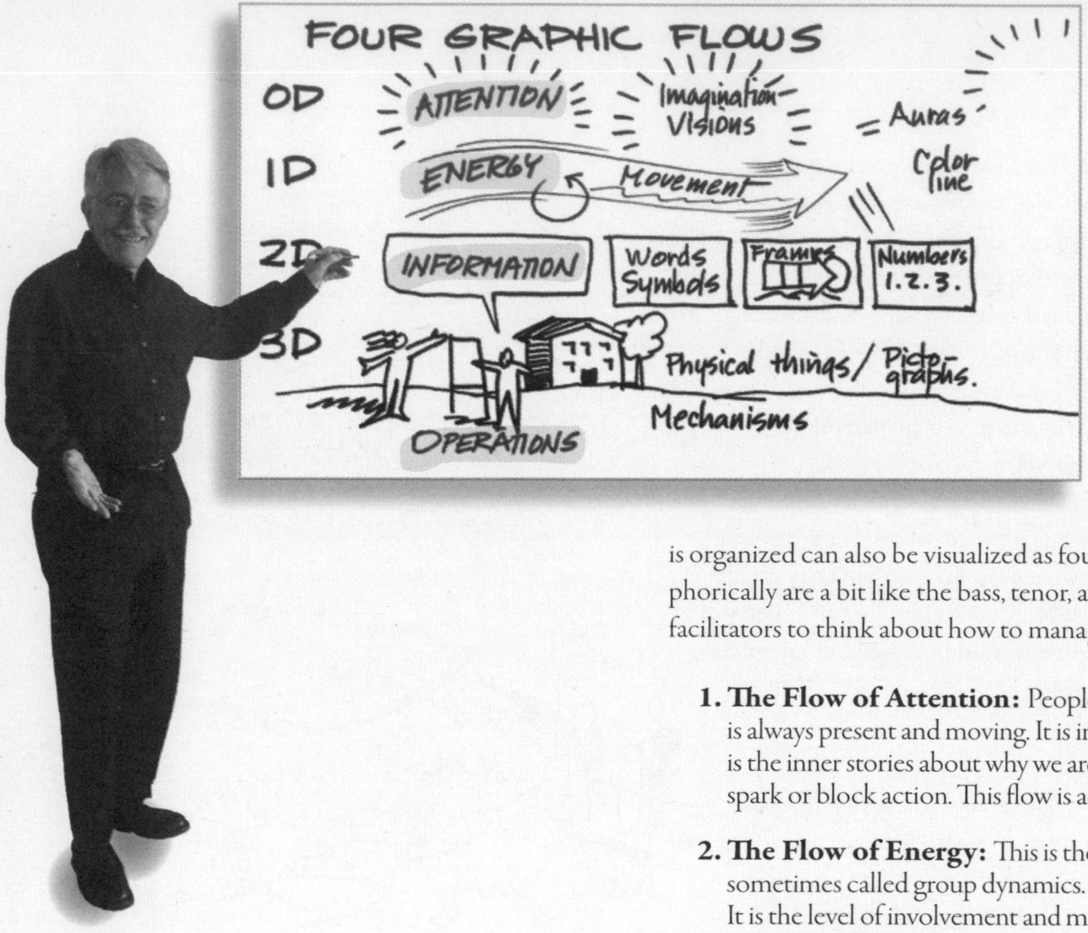

The Key to Team Performance Is Managing Four Flows

All through this book I have been arguing that the way things move is more important than the way they appear. The key to enacting ideas is to take this perspective and see everything as movement over time, and begin looking at how each element plays its part.

The four stages of learning around which this book is organized can also be visualized as four flows of activity that operate over time, and metaphorically are a bit like the bass, tenor, alto, and soprano levels in music. The Grove teaches facilitators to think about how to manage each of these.

1. **The Flow of Attention:** People's consciousness and awareness about what is going on is always present and moving. It is intangible but an essential part of team performance. It is the inner stories about why we are doing things and what we intend to accomplish that spark or block action. This flow is addressed through imagination and awareness.

2. **The Flow of Energy:** This is the emotional, and social flow in a meeting or process sometimes called group dynamics. Connecting at this level is what engagement is all about. It is the level of involvement and motivation. Part of this is the pacing, rhythm, and intensity of interaction. You experience this flow directly through feelings.

3. **The Flow of Information:** This is the flow of thinking and communications—about ideas, research, and analysis that represent, interpret, and symbolize everything we work

with. In an information society more and more work is happening on this level. Thinking, as we have seen throughout this book, is not static, but a dynamic process of exploring, finding patterns, connecting to meaning.

4. **The Flow of Operations:** Purpose, motivation, and ideas need traction in real operations, and tangible resources and mechanisms to accomplish much. Enactment involves connecting the top line of aspiration with the bottom line of financial results. The flow of decision making, project management, organization change, and innovation all require deep understanding of this level.

The four flows of activity in a meeting are the four levels that Arthur Young describes in his Theory of Process. His work has been very helpful in distinguishing them clearly, and graphically! He used spatial geometry to describe his ideas, freeing up from having all the meaning carried in words.

These four flows of activity in a meeting are the four levels that Arthur Young describes in his Theory of Process, and his work has been very helpful in distinguishing them clearly, and graphically! He used spatial geometry to describe his ideas, freeing up from having all the meaning carried in words. I've translated these into words you can remember as the AEIO, or the vowels, of graphic facilitation. The "U" is you! How you manage each one is translated in your own style.

Cartoonists know about this. They illustrate physical reality, the bottom line, operational side of life with three-dimensional (3-D) drawings. Pictures of real physical things cast shadows, have shape and contour, and have details we can see. Cartoonists reproduce thinking with two-dimensional (2-D) conceptual drawings, talk balloons, thought balloons, diagrams, and words—all symbolic representations. They indicate movement and feeling with color and action lines that are one-dimensional (1-D). Finally, they illustrate the imaginary part of life by pointing at it with auras of light and halos indicating that these have no dimension (0-D) and are completely imaginary. Recording information with this discipline helps groups sort out the levels they are talking about. This system also maps onto our natural human orientation to see concrete reality as down and three-dimensional and imaginary realities as up and unconstrained.

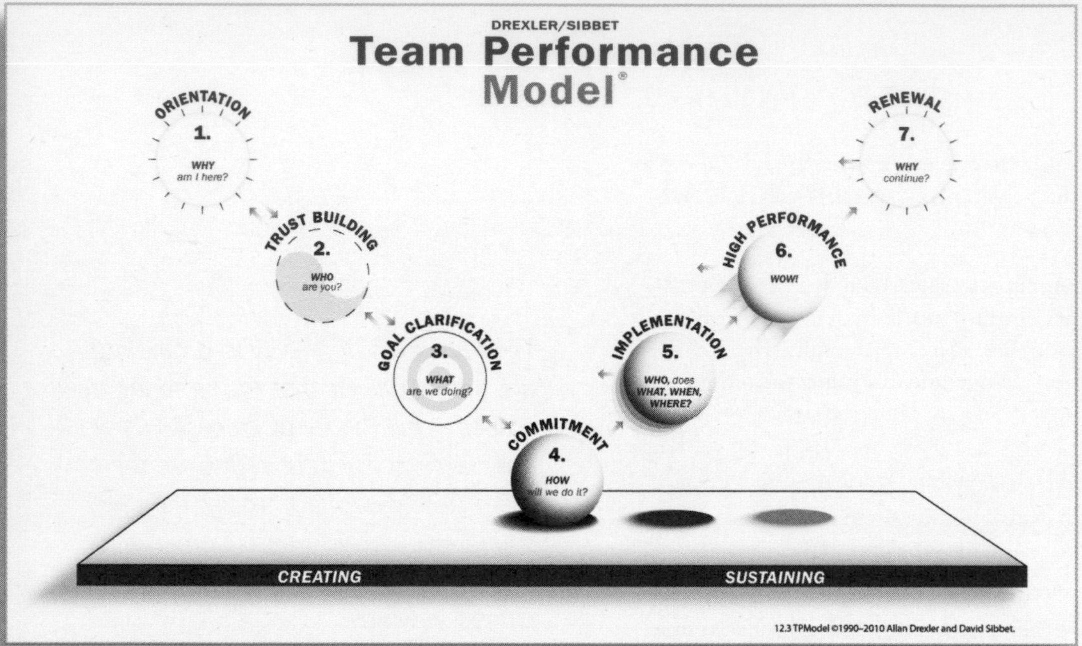

THE DREXLER/SIBBET TEAM PERFORMANCE MODEL®

In teaching Team Performance, Allan Drexler and I have created a visual model that helps people imagine the big picture of what is involved in getting people to cooperate over time. It's now widely used in organizations to talk about both the stages of creating a team and the stages involved in sustaining performance, what we are calling "enactment" here.

Seeing Team Process in Four Flows

If you can imagine the four flows I just described as running behind the illustration of the Drexler/Sibbet Team Performance Model® (TPM) shown here, then you will begin to appreciate why it is drawn as a "V" shape and not in a simple, linear sequence. It is a product of Alan and I evolving his Gibb, Drexler, Weisbord model (discussed in Chapter 4) with Process Theory.

Young argues that all processes move from having no constraint in the beginning, when they are merely potential and a sense of purpose, to having lots of constraint at the point you assign a budget or allocate real people resources to a project. This is the Stage 4 of Commitment to Direction in the TPM. Enactment is the process of overcoming these constraints and regaining the freedom of high performance—the kind that comes through mastery of constraint. This is not a book on Team Performance (see Chapter 23 for references to the *Team Leader Guide)*, but the framework helps to understand where visualization is effective.

You might notice that the initial sections of this book support the initial stages of team process as illustrated in this model. Imagining addresses *WHY* you are reading about visual meetings. Engaging addresses the trust-building aspects of letting people know *WHO* everyone is. The thinking section addresses the issues around *WHAT* goals and other information you need to understand and clarify. The next chapter on decision making directly addresses *HOW* you will make decisions, and get commitments. When commitments are made, then implementation can begin. The TPM is another way to understand the learning cycle visually, seeing it as a journey from the freedom of our imagination to the constraints of real-world resources, only to return to freedom through mastery of the enactment stages of implementation, high performance, and renewal.

You may wonder why the model then "bounces" off the bottom platform during the right side enactment or sustaining stages. The reason the graphics move off the bottom line is due to the fact that when things start being implemented, timing comes into the picture, and timing is a bit uncertain, in that it is affected by all four of the flows, some of which aren't predictable.

What this map makes clear is one way to integrate the four flows in action, a default way if you want to use a computer analogy. But you have to look at the little arrows that point backward and forward to understand that in the reality of team process, individuals will be at different places in their awareness and focus, and the group as a whole will move in different directions, cycling back to address things they missed. Like the Group Graphic Keyboard Model illustrated earlier, it is organized with the foundational elements on the left and the more complex elements on the right, and like the Keyboard, the foundation elements recur in the later stages. Thus the TPM becomes a mental keyboard for making many observations about team process.

Thinking about Teams In Action

Recently our Grove staff finished setting its goals for the year and had a lot of agreement about our primary objectives. But our challenge is in the realm of coordinating action over time, and balancing competing demands, not so much around the goals themselves. During initial planning we felt good about our level of agreement. When we put up a Roadmap with a time line built in, and began actually setting specific milestones for the specific initiatives, the conversation took on a whole different level of specificity and traction. We had moved to enactment.

Visual Meetings & Team Performance

I took the TPM and used it as a framework to look at the types of meetings people conduct and realized that the repeating ones can be understood as supporting the different stages teams need to go through. At the most general level, strategy formation, team building itself, and planning are supported by orientations, team formation meetings, and project planning meetings. The early sections of this book are loaded with tools for these kinds of meetings, some of which are indicated here.

The enactment stages, shown on the next page, are supported by decision making meetings, progress and project reviews, creative innovation sessions or labs, and finally development activities. In today's digital environment all of these are also supported by the online world, conference calls, and web conferences.

VISUAL MEETINGS OPPORTUNITIES MAP

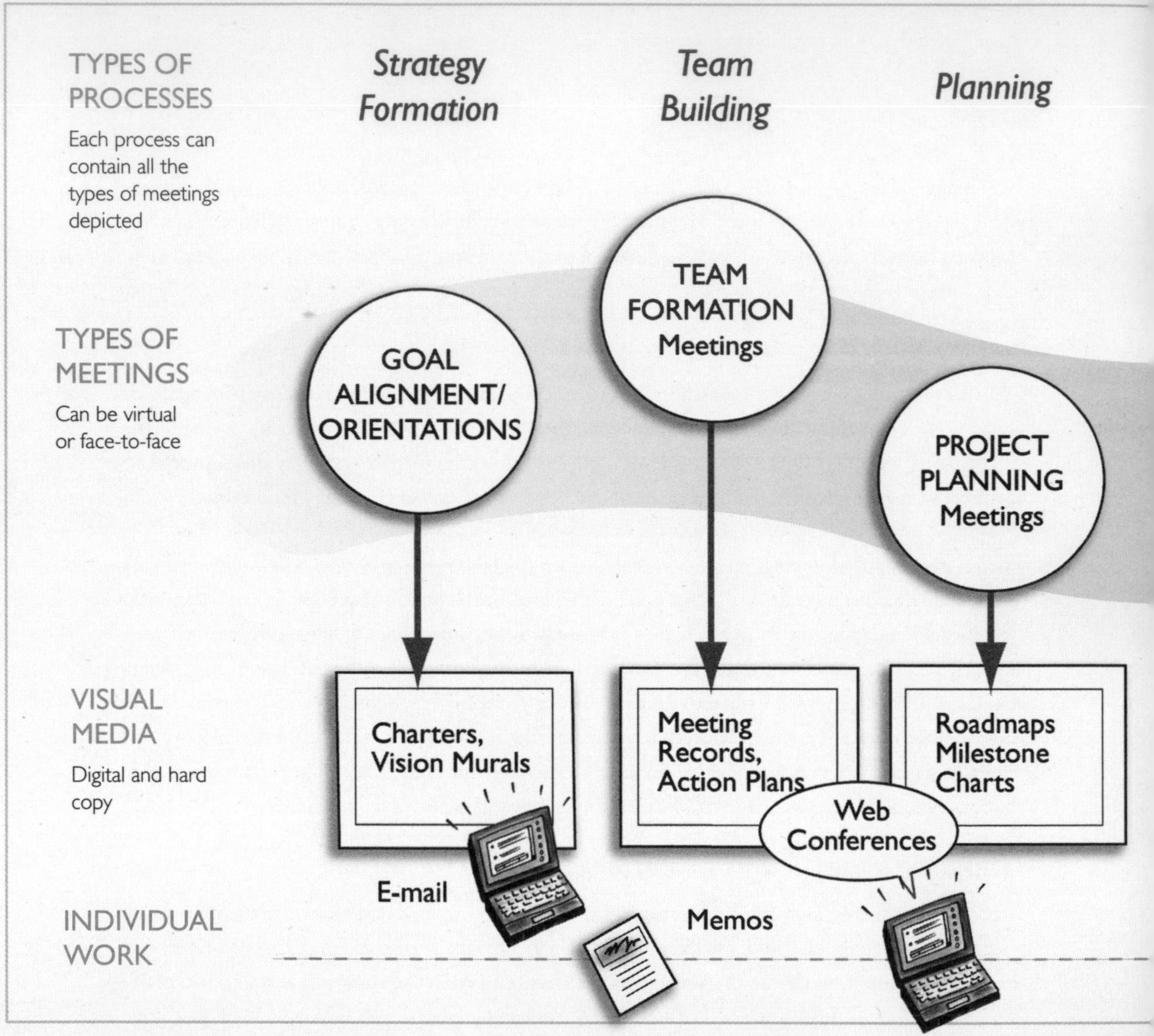

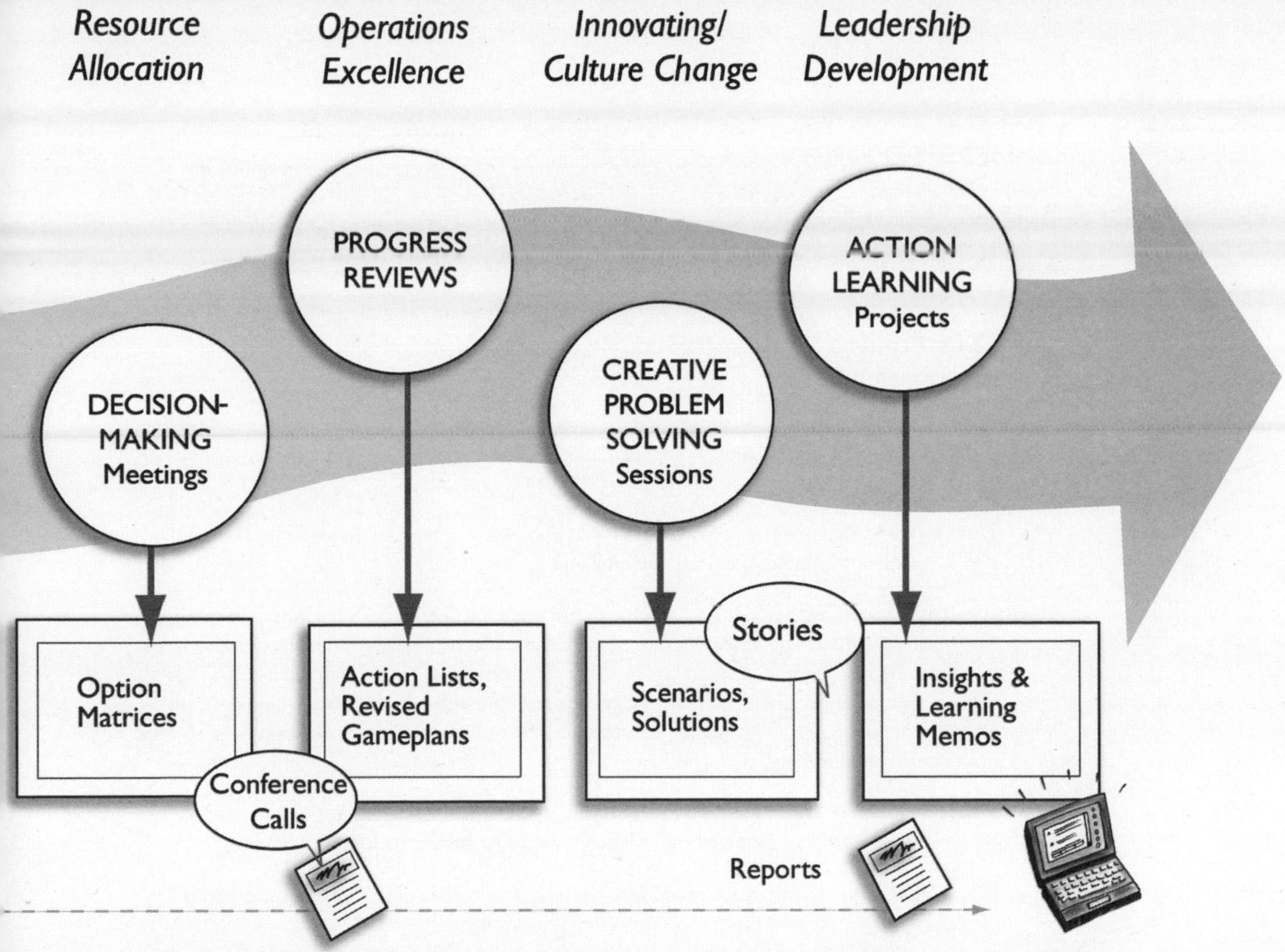

This process map illustrates the kinds of visuals that most often support the kinds of meetings shown in the circles. One of the things you will appreciate as you begin to think about organizational processes, is how the more focused ones nest inside the more comprehensive ones. You can have a large-scale planning process, for instance, that will have all these kinds of meetings included. This can be true for an operations excellence campaign as well. Or you can focus in and do planning with just one or two of these types of meetings. This is the flexibility of keyboard type models of this sort.

Team Best Practices

Some of the tried and true visual meeting practices for teams that are included in this book in various places are the following:

- **Team Charters:** Get all the team's purposes and objectives as defined by sponsors in a visible format. This is your team charter.
- **Team Profiles:** Spend some time charting out all the skills and resources people are bringing to the team.
- **Goal Clarification:** Creating a specific target for the team's activities is invaluable. It is a central feature in the Graphic Gameplan. Some of the sticky note processes described earlier work well for this.
- **Decision Making:** The next chapter looks at how to create a decision funnel visually and work through the steps toward closure and agreement.
- **Action Planning:** Creating a Graphic Gameplan, Roadmap, or equivalent will provide the guide to action that a team needs to stay aligned. Doing this together and doing it visually will greatly improve the chances that everyone shares a common picture of what is happening. Having one person do the planning might seem more efficient in terms of getting the plan written, but will encounter problems in implementation if everyone doesn't understand or agree with it.
- **Project Check-Ins:** A critical practice for good teaming is having regular progress reviews. Using visual game plans and action lists is an essential productivity tool.
- **Case Studies:** An organization dedicated to high performance teams will support people taking time to review past projects. Doing graphic case studies of projects and processes creates a wonderful environment for everyone to see and share what they learned.

17. Decision-Making Meetings

Aligning on Agreements & Getting Commitments

Meetings reach the pinch point or turn when decisions need to be made. Orienting and engaging a group and even getting it to think through its ideas all come to a head when people have to agree and make commitments. Visual meetings are a real help if you follow some of the simple guidelines outlined in this chapter. The process is the following:

1. Be clear about what decision process you want to use before heading into that part of the meeting. (Use the illustration of Decision-Making Processes shown here to discuss choices with your meeting sponsor.)
2. Make a "decision funnel"—a chart of steps you will take to bring closure.
3. Make the decision and commemorate it graphically.
4. Lead a confidence check.
5. Document and communicate the decisions after the meetings in e-mail.

We'll go through these step-by-step and see how visuals can help.

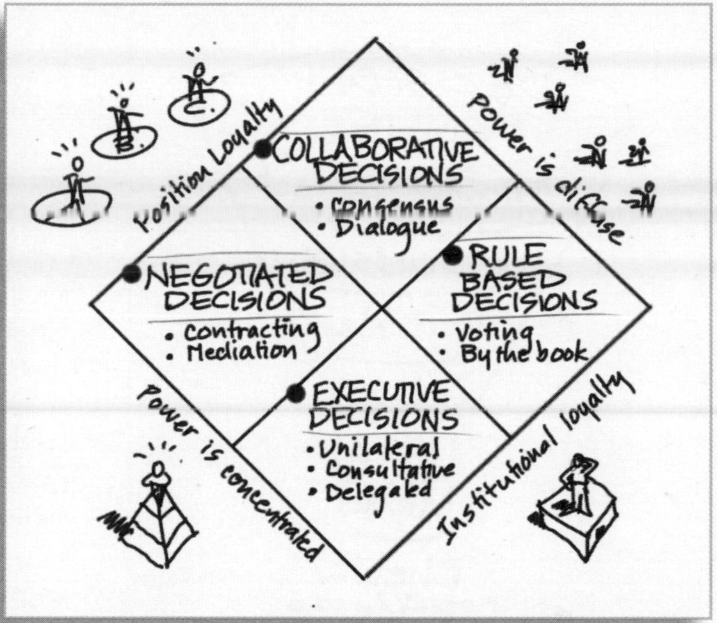

TYPES OF DECISION-MAKING PROCESSES

How power is distributed and what people are loyal to are two powerful determinants of which type of decision will be needed to be effective. The four decision-making approaches shown here tend to work best if conditions are as described on the grid.

Be Clear about Decision Choices

In teaching facilitators how to lead decision processes I surveyed the literature on the field and created this integrated illustration of the different decision choices. I often sketch this out to coach clients on the choices they have heading into the decision part of a meeting. The four quadrants are created by looking at how power is distributed and where people have loyalty. If your group has diffuse power, as in a parent/teacher association, or a cross-organization gathering or conference, and people are more loyal to their own interests and positions than to an institution, then collaborative decision making is in order. However, if institutional loyalty is high, as in a military organization, sports team, or tight knit company, and power is relatively concentrated—

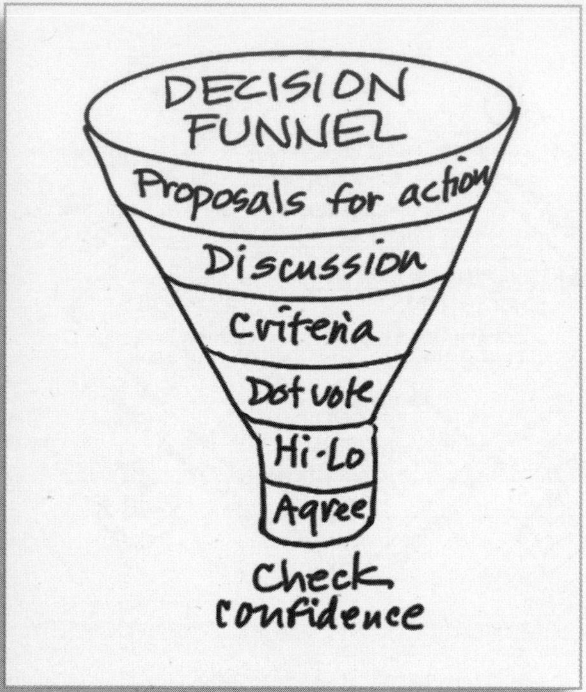

DECISION
FUNNEL

Suggest a series of steps that get meeting participants to see their agreements a bit at a time.

say in a management team—then you can use executive decision making.

Negotiations and rule-based decision making complement these.

Each approach has its variations. This isn't a book on decision making, but on visual meetings and how they can support decision making. Providing a visual framework is a big start, and people can use this model to talk over what they mean by each of the different choices and get clear on which to use.

Combinations are possible, of course. A common one arises when a team is having a short meeting, and needs to take a decision and move to action quickly. The team leader may well be the one the organization holds responsible, who has the power to decide what the team will do, but wants to have input and be as collaborative as possible. During the startup of the meeting you can get an agreement to work by consensus as much as possible during the short time, but if at the end of that time an agreement is not reached, then the team leader will decide by executive decision.

Creating Decision Funnels

The art of decision making in a consensus-oriented meeting involves moving people toward agreement in a series of steps rather than all at once, and creating a path to commitment that lets people see how much they agree as they go along. People in sales are trained to make trial closes with a customer. This means asking easy questions to which a customer will respond with an agreement. The questions move steadily toward the big question, of whether or not the customer will buy a product or service. By the time they get there a whole pattern of agreement has been established. The same strategy works in a meeting.

Here are some of the best practices that combine into a decision funnel. Each is supported by chart work.

1. **Making Proposals for Action:** This involves asking people to write their choices on sticky notes or call them out while you write them on a big chart, usually in a list format.
2. **Developing Criteria for a Good Choice:** This is usually a list of criteria
3. **Discussion:** As people advocate for this or that proposal, take notes in the margins of the chart near the item indicated so the attention of the group shows up graphically as items with more writing.
4. **Dot Voting:** Hand out dots, usually one-third the number on the total list of items, and have everyone place them on the chart near the item they prefer. (This supports social interaction around choices.)
5. **Multi Voting:** Number all the items and ask people to make a "hot list" of their one-third favorite items. Then record the votes with raised hands. (This avoids any "follow the leader" voting.)
6. **Hi-Lo:** Make a chart with "High" at the top and "Low" at the bottom and ask people to sort the sticky notes. If you add a second axis—"Easy" and "More Difficult"—you get another sorting out.
7. **Leadership Advocacy:** Invite team leaders or other people to indicate their interests to precipitate the group to decision.
8. **Ask for Agreements:** Ask the group to call out what it thinks the agreement is. When you hear it, then check if that is really a total agreement. Ask, "*Is there anyone who can't live with this agreement? —Going once, going twice, going three times.*" Providing this kind of space is critical to get everyone on board.
9. **Sleep on It:** Do a draft one day and come back and check the next.
10. **Confidence Check:** See the steps-at-a-glance practice here for instructions.

CONFIDENCE CHECK

1. Begin at the point where a group has reached agreement on something—like a goal for the year, or a set of target goals on an action plan, or a design for a training.
2. Draw out a line and mark off 10 tick marks from 0 to 10 along the line.
3. Ask each person to rate how confident they are that the decision they made was a good one, with 10 being completely confident and 0 as having no confidence.
4. Have everyone call out their number and make "x" marks at the appropriate tick.
5. The result will be a graphic picture of confidence.
6. Have persons who provided the lower ratings talk about what would need to happen to make them fully confident.
7. Appreciate that bringing out these kinds of concerns will strengthen the commitment to the decision and translate directly in more effective implementation.

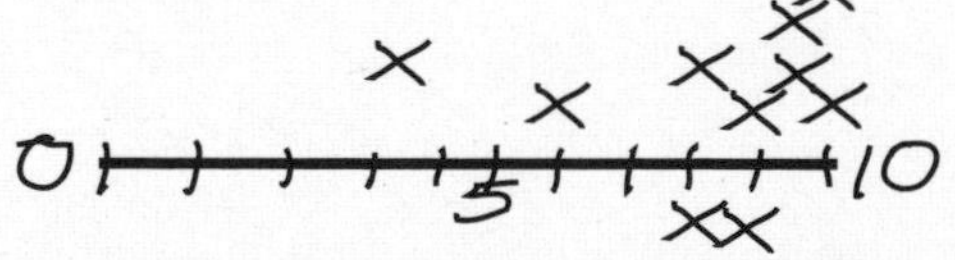

You can repeat the discussion periods, cycle back for more proposals, and dot vote again. If you need to have consensus on a decision, then be prepared to spend the time. During decision making it helps to go slow, then go fast during implementation.

Assign Owners and Communicate the Decision

Once a decision is made a way to graphically anchor it is to write it on a master template like a vision or a strategic plan. At the decision point in meetings it helps to shift from the practice of recording whatever people say, to recording only the agreements. You need to make this shift clear to the group, but your modeling this shift graphically helps everyone see it and support it. The final step is making sure that the decisions have people assigned to follow through on them. Sometimes this isn't possible right in the meeting, but when it is, then write those people's names on the chart.

Another way to commemorate the decision is to have everyone sign the decision chart themselves, and then go a final step and have everyone get in front and take a group picture. If you send out copies of the chart and the picture after the meeting it works to reinforce the agreement. Commitment is so essential to implementing anything that it really works to spend extra care in your agreement-making process.

Good project managers and team leaders would in addition take the agreements and decision, write them up in a formal memo of some sort, and send that out after the meeting as well.

18. Project Management Meetings
Mapping Progress with Pictures

Industrial Light & Magic, a division of Lucasfilm, is well-known for pioneering computer graphic visual effects. One day I received a call inviting me to facilitate a debrief of one of the movies they had just completed. It had been a challenge and they wanted all the different functions to share their learning so the next movie would benefit. We invented a template, shown here, that was the focus of the meeting and successfully guided a group of nearly 35 people in having a robust, two-hour dialogue about everything they learned. This kind of project review meeting is invaluable during the enactment stages of projects.

While I was there I had a chance to tour, and was struck by another visual tool that was central to how they managed the day-to-day operations at ILM. It consisted of a large display in a hallway near their studios. It had colored cards for every single project and which shoot was happening on what day. The cards contained some basic information about the project and the type of shoot, and was visually mapped against which studio it would be using. The wall showed the total utilization of the facilities at a glance. Projects logged in and out of the big wall almost like a time-card system. I was affirmed in the power of big, analog displays seeing it here in the center of the digital revolution!

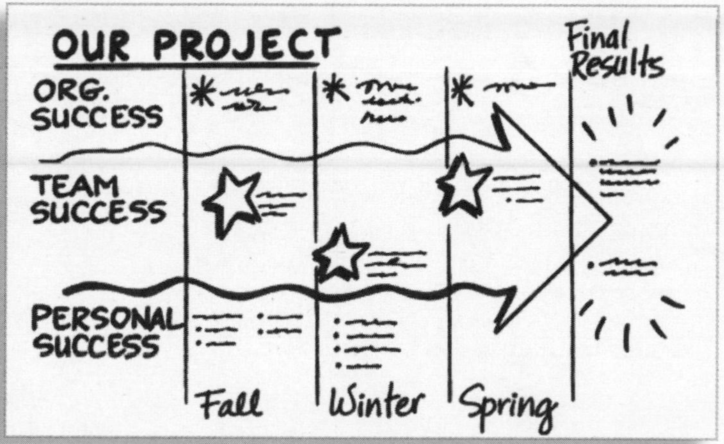

PROJECT DEBRIEFING CHART

This template was invented to draw out all the learning from completion of a major film.

Visuals for Project Review

When projects launch after key commitments and decision are made, visual meetings play a role in three general areas:

1. **Group Action Planning:** This involves getting the team to collaborate in articulating how it intends to go about conducting the project or program, and putting those agreements on a time line. The Graphic Gameplan and Roadmap templates described earlier in this book are both examples of these kinds of visuals.

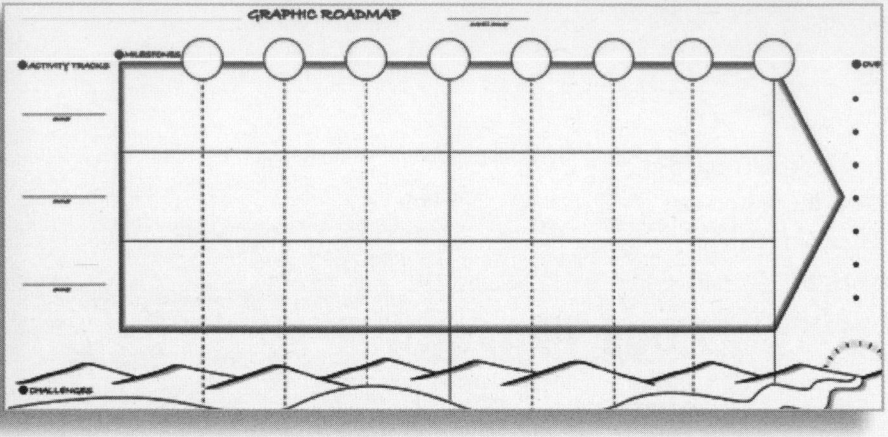

2. **Graphic Progress Reports:** Once a project plan is developed, you can illustrate it in a form that can be sent out periodically with progress notes.

3. **Project Review and Problem Solving:** Projects need touch-ins frequently to keep everything on course and aligned, and to solve problems.

GRAPHIC ROADMAPS

When you ask a project team to map its tasks against time this will drop everyone into an action mode that feels quite different than more general planning. This is an image of The Grove's Graphic Guide® for roadmapping.

Making Roadmaps

Mapping activities against a calendar directly involves a group in a simulation of what implementation will be like, and actually begins the action in many cases. A Roadmap visualizes the streams of activities that logically go together and need leaders. It also illustrates the goals and milestones. Once you have this framework then the activities are added with sticky notes.

I worked with a group of HR managers in Singapore who had developed a vision and strategy for talent management in Asia. The company is European, but is growing rapidly in Asia, and believes that its success will depend on recruiting Asians to key positions and having them begin to lead operations in that part of the world. It is very important to have each country in the region implement the strategy in a way that is specific to that country's constraints. They decided to develop graphic Roadmaps for each country as the first step in enacting their plan.

Once the framework illustrated here was drawn, the China team was quite able to use sticky notes and collaborate in mapping out a plan of action. The four members all stood around the chart and made suggestions, argued for changes, and in about an hour had a first draft of a pretty comprehensive plan.

Some organizations have project management software that they use to develop specific plans. However, if you use a visual meeting to collaborate in generating the content, then there will be more ownership when the formal version emerges. If a team leader or project manager does this alone on special software he or she then has to spend a good bit of time convincing everyone of the merits of the plan, or fall back on a "trust me" mode of operating.

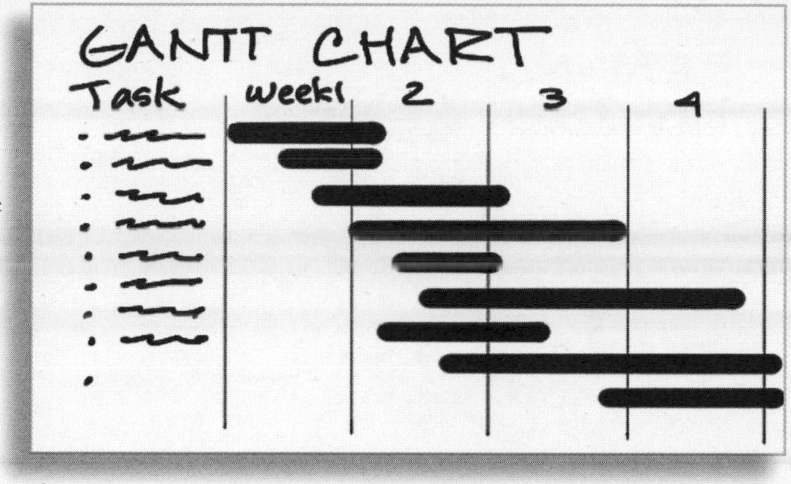

GANTT CHART

Gantt charts plot tasks showing start and stop times, and are standard project management tools.

Visuals for Showing Progress

A standard graphic format for project management is what is called the Gantt Chart, which is a kind of road map without the metaphor being so obvious. It is a simple matrix that shows task over time, with starting and stopping points, and sometimes other information. These are standard charts in project management software. They look like the illustration on this page. These kinds of charts are very helpful for detailing everything that needs to take place, and can be overwhelming to look at if you aren't the project manager. But they can be used to show progress by making a copy and highlighting the work completed, or doing that in whatever software program you might be using.

In addition to their big wall showing studio utilization, Industrial Light & Magic had a project coordinator. In her office was a smaller Gantt type chart, with color bars for each of the five or six predictable phases of their projects. These were illustrated on a magnet board that showed two months worth of work, phase by phase. She could pick one, two, or three of the different phase magnets and show how long it would take. The board was updated weekly, and took a lot of time to maintain, but provided everyone a complete picture of where everything is at a glance.

At The Grove our design group has a large laminated matrix and uses dry erase markers to

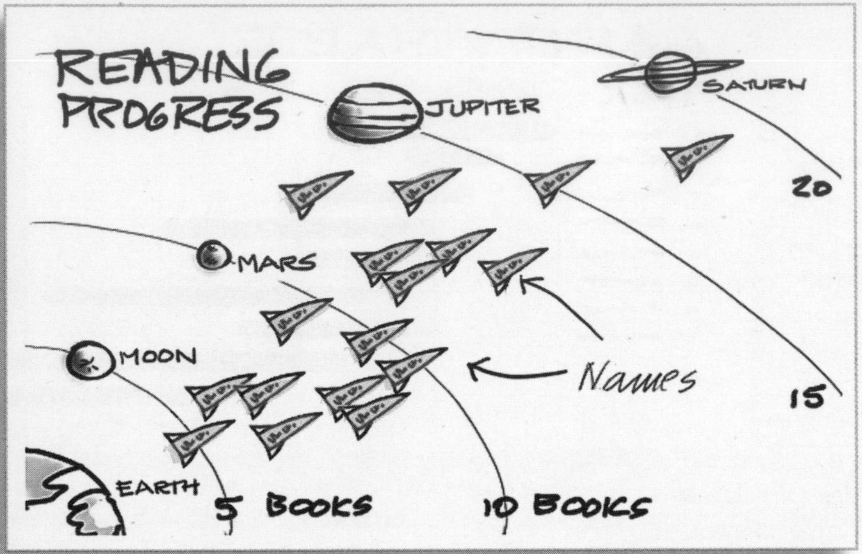

PROGRESS CHART

Feedback on progress is a great motivator. This chart was used in my sixth grade classroom to encourage all of us to read books.

indicate every project and what is due on each date. The chart is made in week-wide strips so it can be rotated to keep up-to-date.

Thermometers and Dashboards

Campaigns use visuals to show progress with different kinds of thermometers and dials that fill in as progress is made. I remember in grammar school when my sixth grade teacher put up a solar system on the bulletin board, and each student had a spaceship that could advance to the outer reaches depending on how many books they read. I was completely engaged in watching the progress of these ships and was determined to get as far as Saturn! (I made it!)

Visual Problem Solving in Total Quality Management

The use of visuals for problem solving is described in Chapter 10. I want to add here a story from Procter & Gamble that underlines the importance of visuals in quality improvement, one of the areas where problem solving is integral to the process. In the 1980s P&G made a very large investment in total quality management (TQM) processes, as did many other organizations. These ideas were credited with the success of Japanese companies growing so rapidly in the 1970s. They were enacting the ideas of the American statistician Edward Demming, credited as the father of the quality movement. He believed that if you came to look at processes as a whole, rather than functionally, you could improve them. P&G wanted to follow up their training about the general principles of TQM with a practical course on the tools of quality improvement, which would support team problem solving about process improvement problems in an ongoing way. I worked with the internal team to go over the content for the course and realized that 80% of the strategies for doing team problem solving were visualization strategies! Here are some I remember:

- **Frequency Checklists:** Simply count the frequency of different problems and tick them on your chart.
- **Scattergrams:** Take an independent variable and plot occurrences against a dependent variable, like geyser eruption duration against wait time for the next occurrence.
- **Pareto Charts:** Visually arrange the frequency of occurrences of a problem to show which have the greatest frequency , and plot the percentage of each one. This gives rise to the 80/20 idea that 20% of the items cause 80% of the problems.
- **Cause and Effect or Fishbone Diagrams:** I described these earlier, but they involve putting the problem in the head of the fish and identifying the "bones" that contribute to the problem.
- **Histograms:** Illustrate the frequency of different events arranged over some standard, non-overlapping intervals.
- **Flow Chart**: Create an end-to-end visual of a process showing each step of the process and the different choice points, represented by diamonds.
- **Control Charts:** Plot statistical variations in the performance of a process against a mean. Incidents outside the limits become targets for problem solving.

TQM practice can involve a lot of measurement and statistics, but these don't come alive until they are visualized and teams can see the patterns end-to-end in a process. The P&G people I worked with explained that metaphorically Demming was asking people to stop looking at the ballgame through a knothole in the

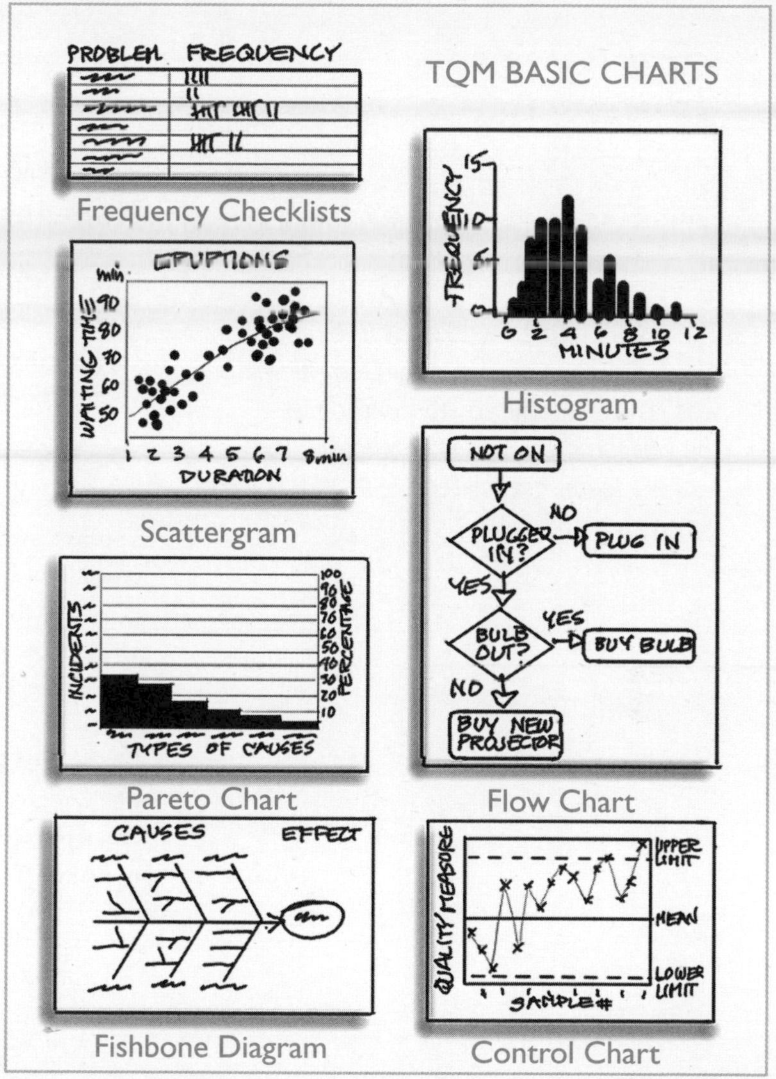

TQM BASIC CHARTS
Frequency Checklists
Histogram
Scattergram
Pareto Chart
Flow Chart
Fishbone Diagram
Control Chart

outfield fence, and instead look at the game as a complete process. Getting groups to analyze and visualize what they were doing was the heart of the approach!

If you are interested in TQM, search on the Web under that term and look at the images connected. The movement has evolved and branched into things like Six Sigma and Balanced Scorecard practices. Visual models illustrate each approach. I take this as buttressing my argument that systems thinking and visual thinking are almost the same thing.

The P&G people I worked with explained that metaphorically Demming was asking people to stop looking at the ballgame through a knothole in the outfield fence, and instead look at the game as a complete process.

The Importance of Feedback

Feedback about progress is one of the most important ways to help a group self-adjust during a project. I've been part of numerous attempts to create graphic dashboards for businesses that could show how things are going at a glance. The most successful are simple, and often not so graphic as they are consistent and visual as a single report where the numbers are always in the same places. Adding some framing boards and nice titling to the different measures adds to the accessibility of these kinds of tools.

On the less complex end a simple action matrix with tasks and names and a weekly review of progress goes a long way toward making teams productive. This kind of visualization is not about pictographs and ideographs, but about numbers and other indications of progress one can measure.

19. Facilitating Innovation & Change

Playing with Prototypes

The most challenging kind of enactment is getting a whole system to move to a new level of functioning. This might be a desire to become more innovative or to become more efficient or change the basic business model. Years of working as an organization consultant have convinced me that people do not change by having new information presented to them. People need to feel in their guts that the current situation is not right and needs to change. This felt sense of urgency and what some call seeing a "burning platform" is an emotional thing. If a group has not experienced the need to change, they won't. This is why successful companies get in such trouble when new technologies come along. The old success habits are too deeply rooted.

I'm convinced it is necessary to have hands-on, immersive experiences if you want truly new thinking to emerge in a group. This is why playing with prototypes and simulations has become so popular when conducting innovation. Let's start by looking at the change challenge in general.

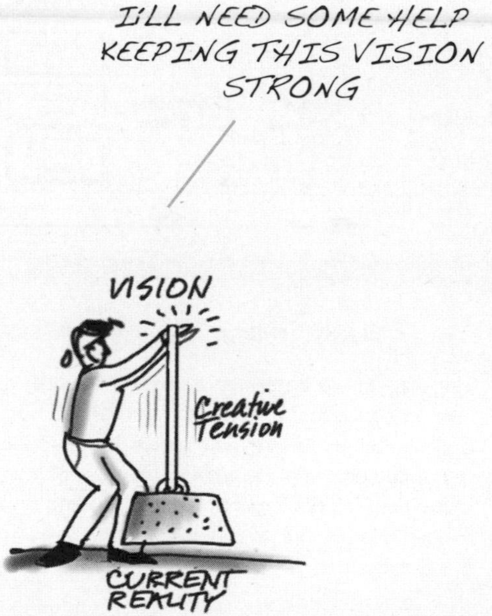
I'LL NEED SOME HELP KEEPING THIS VISION STRONG
VISION
Creative Tension
CURRENT REALITY

We Need a New Business Model!

After the economic meltdown in 2008 many organizations have been thrown into a full reconsideration of their traditional ways of working. I got a call about a 30-year-old organization that provided organizational support to nonprofits. It had been very successful teaching cross-cultural communications, board/staff relations, leadership, strategy, talent management and many other things in addition to providing services in these areas. But its "business model" wasn't working anymore, meaning that it wasn't making ends meet in its traditional ways. The board had hired a new director with a history of turning around nonprofits and needed to engage the whole system in reinventing itself.

We had several telephone and web conferences to design the planning process we would go through, understanding that it needed to be, in truth, a process of organizational change.

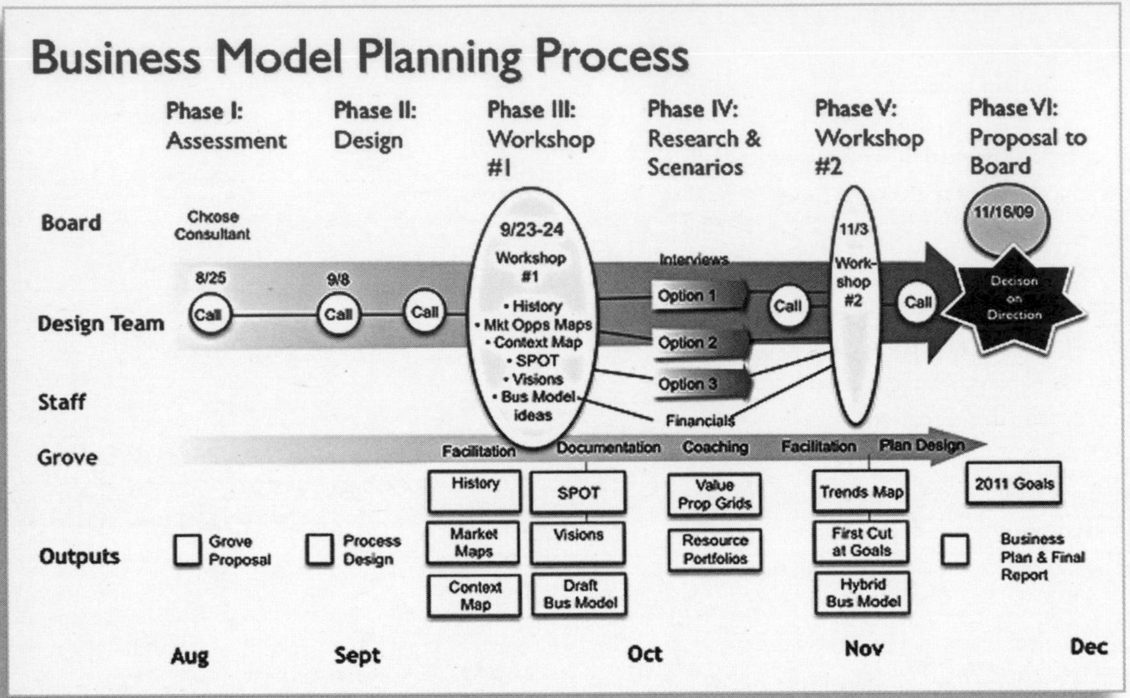

CHANGE PROCESS MAP

This diagram illustrates a four-month-long planning process aimed at organization change. The circles indicate meetings. The rectangles are output documents, and the arrows are projects. The calls were web conferences where I worked on a tablet computer to sketch out ideas and record the conversations.

We used visualization strategically throughout the process. The chart shown here illustrates at a big picture level the process and all the outputs. Creating it collaboratively was critical in getting the internal design team to agree on the process we would follow. You can see that many of the outputs referred to are names of templates and formats that have been described in this book.

New Experiences Change Minds

Drawing out ideas is a kind of construction activity that has feeling attached. When a group has to coconstruct an image, as the Vancouver department did when I asked them to draw a picture of their city as a vehicle, the people doing it have a new experience. It's different than just listening to information. When an operations group put sticky notes on parts of the procurement process that were broken and then discussed the patterns they discovered, they were engaging emotionally as well as intellectually. When I made the one-wall picture of the supply chain for a top management task force and they saw the 35 conflicting projects all competing for attention and resources, they experienced the problem rather than just thinking about it.

With the nonprofit organization I knew that the board and staff needed to deeply engage with their internal stories about how they worked, deconstruct them, and have a chance to cocreate new ones. Having them working graphically was a central strategy. Here were the things we did that had a very engaging effect.

- **Organizational History:** We told the story of the organization over a 16-foot graphic chart, and posted when people joined and told all the stories of how the organization came to be what it was. Many of the newer people had never taken the time to see where their different values and strategies were anchored.
- **Context Mapping:** We had all the board and staff, together generate a map of the driving forces of change. We worked this several times to really connect with the case for change.
- **Market Analysis:** Small groups used sticky notes on a simple four-box model to identify promising opportunities for services and product revenue.
- **SPOT Analysis:** The staff had done a lot of research about strengths, weaknesses, opportunities and threats, across all their functions. We visualized this into a chart on which they could look at these factors as a whole system.
- **Visioning:** We had the entire organization work in small groups with collage and Cover Story Vision templates to create a new story for the organization.
- **Business Model Canvas:** We used a Business Model Canvas for mapping out just what they were offering, to whom, how much they would charge for services, how much profit they expected to make, what supports were needed, what technologies, and so on. See side story for more details.
- **Strategic Goals Mapping:** In the context of the business model planning, the board met and agreed on its implementation goals for the following year.

BUSINESS MODEL CANVAS

This template is from a book on business modeling called *Business Model Generation*. (See Chapter 23 for details.) The book was a collaboration between some 460 resources in Europe and around the world collaborating online. One of the core authors was quite influenced by The Grove's graphic approaches and the book is a wonderful example of how visualization strategies apply to business modeling.

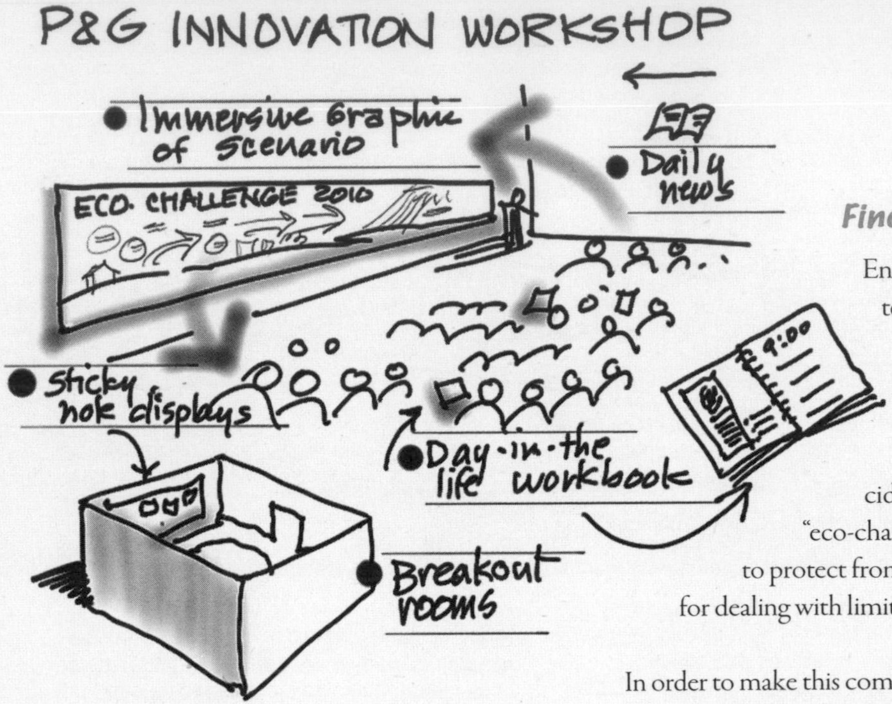

Finding Innovative Business Ideas

Enactment does not have to be about organization change at a systems level. It can focus on stimulating innovation. One of the most interesting innovation sessions I ever led was for a group in Procter & Gamble charged with developing new product ideas. It is an excellent example of how visual meetings can immerse people in a subject so completely it almost becomes real. In this case we decided to use a scenario approach and imagine that the whole world was "eco-challenged," with everyone having to wear special clothes and cosmetics to protect from holes in the ozone, special things to detect toxins in food, strategies for dealing with limited energy supplies and the like.

In order to make this come alive we designed a process that involved three parts. An initial weekend fully immersed everyone in the simulation. During the week small task groups brainstormed new product ideas. A final weekend brought all these ideas together, showcasing the best. A key tool we used to support the process was a "Day in the Life" workbook that had pages for each segment of a day. Paragraphs and illustrations described the eco-challenged situation people were facing when getting up, when eating breakfast, when going to work or day care. We left a lot of space to record ideas of how people were responding and what kind of products they were using to cope.

The entire event began with the whole group creating an enormous mural of what the eco-challenged world looked like. We seeded the event with some assumptions and a few descriptions, but the dialogue made it come alive. I recorded while 60 people improvised. Then each morning we published a newspaper with stories about the world the participants were imagining.

The small groups were encouraged to work with sticky notes and other visual media, and come back on the next weekend with presentations of their best ideas. They came back with workbooks full and large displays that eventually created a gallery of possibilities ringing a big conference room.

The workshop generated so many new ideas that the internal ventures group was occupied for a long time just working from this resource!

If "point of view is worth 80 IQ points" as Alan Kay says, then getting people to play with new perspectives through the mediums of drawing, simulation, scenarios, and model making is how people change. This is the way the design firms hired by the California Academy of Sciences worked to reinvent the twenty-first-century natural history museum. This is what Autodesk encourages in its designers. It is how IDEO, the Silicon Valley design firm works. This is what The Grove organizes when clients want to get to breakthrough ideas. Humans need to tell stories, make models, and explore things in simulation before taking really big steps toward change.

Using Big Picture Graphics to Support Change

If you have done a good job engaging stakeholders and thinking through the new ideas that need to be implemented, you then face the challenge of getting the wider organization to accept the new ideas. This will most certainly require leadership communicating and supporting the change with decisions and actions that communicate their seriousness. At The Grove we have developed a methodology to support this kind of communication we have branded as Storymapping®. The process involves making large graphic displays ranging from 8 to 24 feet long and

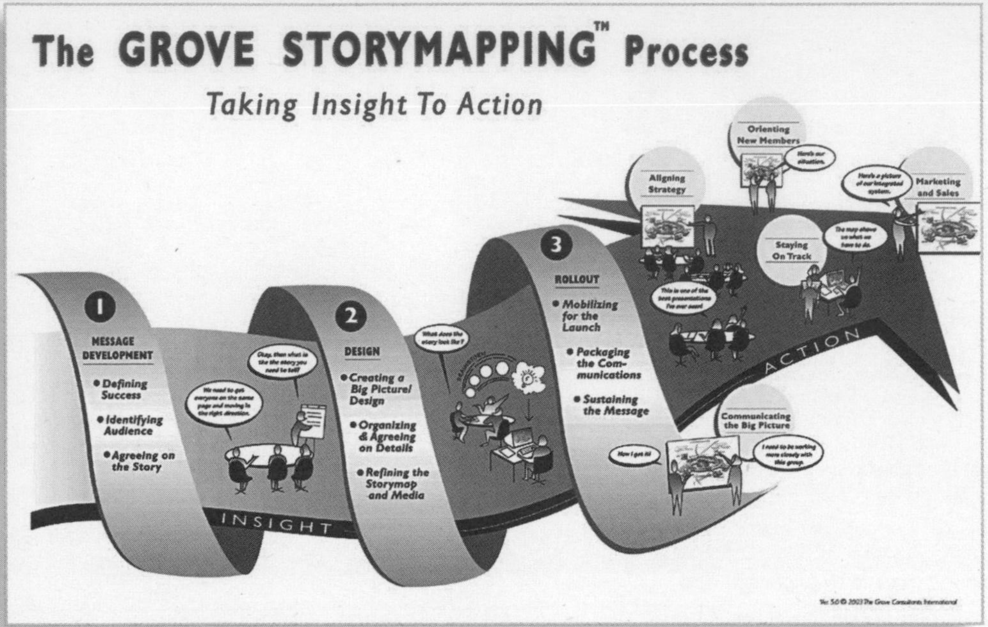

STORYMAPPING PROCESS

Here is a Storymap about Storymaps! The big arrow is the Insight to Action process of the client. The spiral is the Storymapping Process that wraps around, clarifying message, design, and rollout plans. The benefits are shown on the far right.

3 to 4 feet high that support anyone telling a story about the content on the map. Our assumption is that leaders showing up and telling the story is a key part of what leads the change, not the graphic itself. Having all the key information in one place helps. It also helps to get leadership away from slides and directly engaging people. Working from a large display does this, because a person can improvise, work forward and backward, and all the information stays up so people can really soak it in. If a small version is made available after the communication people will remember a huge amount of what has been communicated.

These kinds of story murals look a bit like idea maps designed for team learning, and can be used that way, but they are really designed for presentation.

Organizations Using Storymaps Successfully

Some examples of organizations that have achieved great results this way include:

- National Semiconductor shared its turnaround vision worldwide in the early 1990s, and in four years achieved 95% vision recognition throughout the company.
- Hewlett Packard Labs shared potential new business ideas to top management using plotter-generated murals instead of slides.
- Raley's top management shared its history, vision of the future, and strategy of their grocery store chain store with managers.

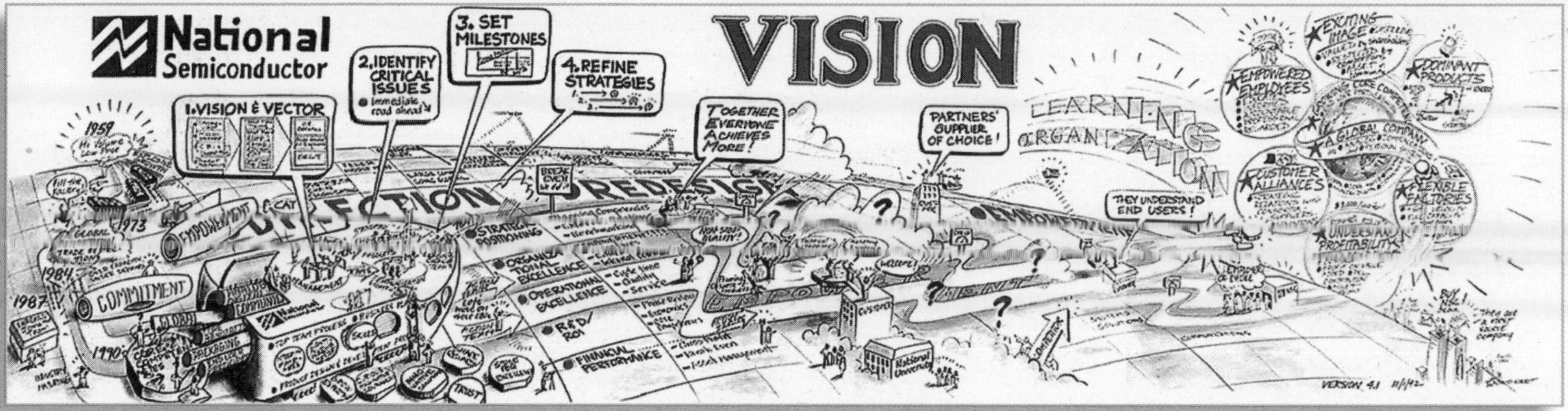

- Save the Redwoods League shared its vision, strategies, and goals with all its stakeholders in three different 5-year planning processes.
- VISA corporation orients all new employees with a large graphic history (updated three times so far).
- Adobe Systems created a graphic history of Adobe and Macromedia when the two organizations merged.
- The RE-AMP collaborative illustrated how its system works to the 120 environmentally oriented non-government organizations and 15 foundations at its annual meeting in the upper midwest. They also used large charts to map progress toward their goal of cleaning up global warming pollutants in the energy industry.
- Nike communicated its visions for its Treasury function, and then later for its IT function using large Storymaps.
- National Academy Foundation designed large Storymaps to illustrate its process of establishing high school learning academies.

NATIONAL SEMICONDUCTOR VISION MAP

During Gil Amelio's turnaround of National Semiconductor in 1993–1994, I illustrated their vision for change as this large Storymap. Every top executive could tell this story, using this mural as a backdrop. It shows the overall vision to the far right, the history to the left, leading to the unassembled spaceship represented current realities. Critical business issues lie in front of the ship. Key values are the windows. Marketing messages are in the talk balloons. The top of the spaceship illustrates the new organization. The way forward has question marks intentionally, because Amelio wanted to enroll the rest of the organization in redesign. This vision got 95% recognition in employee surveys by 1994.

USE BIG PICTURE COMMUNICATION FOR

- ❑ Orienting to histories and culture of an organization.
- ❑ Communicating the need for change.
- ❑ Understanding driving forces in an industry.
- ❑ Understanding customer needs.
- ❑ Sharing new visions and strategies.
- ❑ Sharing implementation plans.
- ❑ Communicating new process designs.

- Otis Spunkmeyer communicates its history, vision, and strategy for growing its successful fresh baked goods business to its organization systemwide.
- Juniper Networks process owners designed a large chart that illustrated the aligned goals and implementation schedule for a big enterprise data project.
- The San Francisco Film Society used a large Storymap as a centerfold for its five-year business plan focused on growing this very successful, full-service film arts organization.

20. Training & Workshops

Leveraging Action Learning

During the 1990s I worked with a team to design a facilitation training program that ran worldwide within a huge consumer goods company. It focused on how to lead meetings, teams, and organization change in one three-day program. We organized the course around the Team Performance framework, explaining that teams are really the molecules of an organization, and meetings are mostly about supporting them getting results. Organization change was the work of creating an environment where the teams could thrive.

All the HR personnel and IT staff in this company eventually went through the program in Europe, North America, and Asia Pacific. We succeeded in creating a program that within a couple years was conducted completely by internal staff and continues in an evolved way today. Visualization played a central part. An unexpected dividend is having this visual way of working migrating to many of the other programs this company conducted. The process was a great example of training trainers through experiential action learning.

SUPPORTING WORKSHOPS WITH VISUALS

Here is a picture of a facilitation mastery workshop where we used large person outlines for introductions, journals for note taking, and digital cameras for documenting.

Using Visuals in Learning-Oriented Workshops

Here is a list of the ways you can use visuals integrally in a training workshop. Many of these examples have already been explained:

- **Outcomes & Agenda Charts:** The OARRs chart (standing for Outcomes, Agenda, Roles, and Rules) came from the worldwide facilitation training project. Use it as a standard way to orient people to any meeting, training, or workshop.
- **Introductions Chart:** Have groups create a seating chart using sticky notes and sharing information that would be useful in the training.
- **Models and Frameworks:** Use large posters of the key models that integrate the

learning experiences. Most training has a framework of some sort that can be visualized in large format and stay up as an orientation graphic throughout.

- **Content Presentation Murals:** Use murals to present major content instead of slides. If the information is up persistently in a murals participants can return to the key ideas again and again until they really soak in.
- **Activity Instructions:** Create flip chart agendas for each small group activity, listing desired outcomes and guidelines.
- **Coaching Feedback:** Have small groups record "What Worked?" and "I Wish" feedback on flip charts or cards following their assignments. If trainers provide written feedback to individuals they observe this is also very helpful.
- **Visual Workbooks and Manuals:** If graphics are used to explain and supplement text in training manuals participants can remember more of the material.
- **Worksheets:** For individual activities create small templates and worksheets that training participants can use to summarize their learning, work through plans and application ideas, and share best practices.

English is a widespread cross-cultural language, but its use puts all non-native speakers in a handicapped position. Slide presentations often go too quickly. Working with interactive graphics and presentation murals creates a different energy and level of engagement

Graphics Work Cross Culturally

I've led training workshops all over the world that involve different cultures, usually working with business English but sometimes with translators. I've received continuous feedback that people with language challenges are so appreciative of the visual approach. It allows them to read as well as listen. Comparison of the two channels leads to much more comprehension. English is a widespread cross-cultural language, but its use puts all non-native speakers in a handicapped position. Slide presentations often go too quickly. Working with interactive graphics and presentation murals creates a different energy and level of engagement, as I have explained many times in this book. Scan back through with this thought in mind and see where you can pick up ideas for training.

Working with Discovery-Based Learning Maps

One way to work with groups in a learning situation is to create a graphic map of the information people need to learn, purposely creating a big framework where pieces of the information need to be linked together. Then assign small groups to figure out different things using the map as a base of information. The U.S. Department of Education retained The Grove and the Institute for the Future in 2000 to create a map of Education Technology (shown here) that could be used with school boards, teachers, and educational organizations.

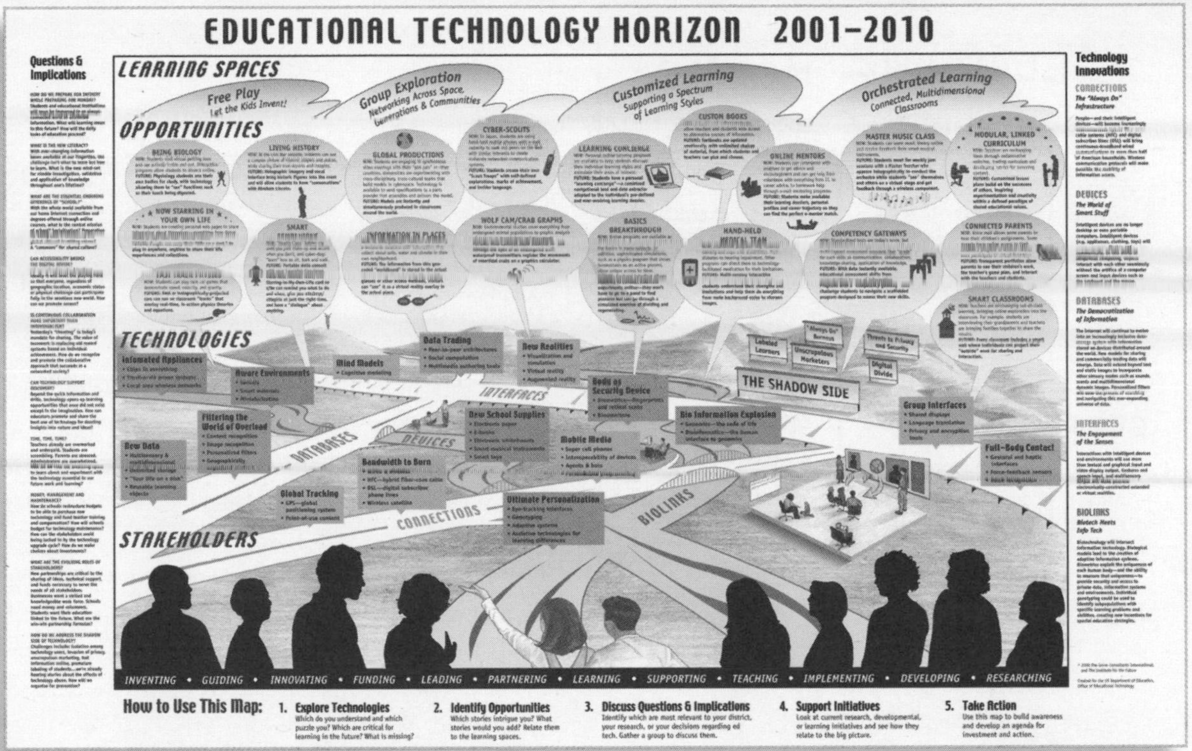

ED TECH HORIZON MAP

This is an example of a map designed for group-oriented, self-guided discovery learning. It supported five learning activities shown along the bottom of the map.

It's far too detailed to read in this format, but the overall design is instructive about how to create maps designed for discovery-based learning. This example would be one designed to let people understand a field of knowledge and applications. It doesn't proscribe anything, but simply juxtaposes a lot of relevant information. In this case a landscape of educational technologies is

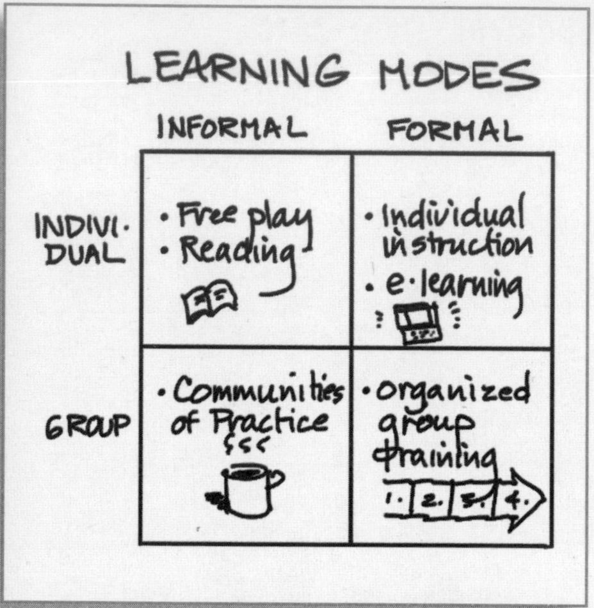

IRL LEARNING MODES

Xerox had an Institute for Research on Learning (IRL) that did direct research with how people learn in business. They observed there were four main modes, illustrated here as a combination of individual, group, formal, and informal learning. IRL is no longer in existence but its work has continued through WestEd, a federal research lab, and Communities of Practice networks.

shown as a helter-skelter of roadways underneath opportunities for application as talk balloons. Our original design was much neater, but a National Science Foundation focus group said that showing the technology landscape as a neatly organized environment would be completely inaccurate. The emerging world of educational technology is chaotic and dynamic! So we complied. The right border explains in text what each of the five categories of technology contains.

Above this landscape is an array of 20 talk balloons, each containing a small vision of what could be done with the technologies. Each balloon has one story of something that is actually going on and one that is speculative, in bold face type. These were identified in a special design workshop with a team of educational thought leaders who knew the subject intimately.

These ideas are loosely grouped under the four categories along the top of the chart, indicating four different ways people learn as described by the Institute for Research on Learning, a Xerox think tank that has been absorbed into WestEd, a national nonprofit educational research and development organization. They had a nice model for the four types of education that we adapted. We called the four "Free Play," "Group Exploration," "Customized Learning," and "Orchestrated Learning."

The left side of the chart is a list of the challenges involved. We devised five different exercises people could do with the map and explain those along the bottom. Because none of this information is linked and connected, it creates a puzzle environment that is a wonderful stimulus to group discussion.

I first heard about this kind of visual method when creating some maps of this sort for National Semiconductor's vision implementation. I worked with a colleague who had been trained in the process. She shared a map that Volvo created to train its salespeople in a new car. It had an explosion drawing of the sort you might see in the instructions to building a model boat or car, but none of the parts were labeled. The names were all around the border instead. The sales teams would need to link all the names with all the parts using their map. By the end of an hour of work everyone knew the new model car intimately.

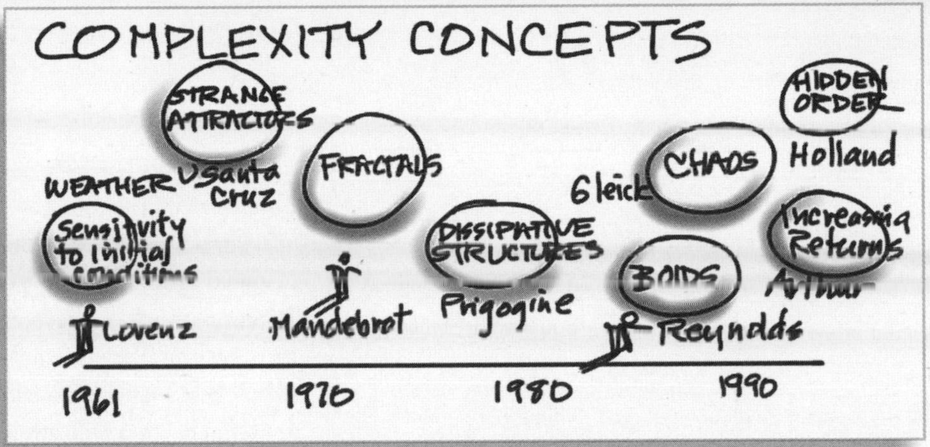

Graphical Presenter Interfaces

When computers began to use graphical user interfaces the Internet exploded. Presenters and teachers can use the same technique with graphic murals. I first heard about this from a colleague who described a presenter at Hallmark Cards who would come on stage with two chairs and clothesline strung between them. On the line he clipped some 20 different card images, each with a story behind it about the company and how it did its business. One of the cards said "stop talking now." He would then ask people to pick a card and off he would go, in whatever direction was picked. He would walk off the stage and stop if anyone picked the "stop talking" card.

INTERACTIVE PRESENTATION MURAL

Living systems science, or what is sometimes called the science of complexity, uses visualization extensively in its research. I used this simple mural to support an interactive Q&A presentation on the subject. People could "click" on a topic and I would summarize what the concept was about.

I was so impressed with this idea that I decided to use it to explain complexity theory to The Institute for the Future staff. This was in the late 1990s when research on living systems was just becoming known, and a whole range of books were coming out on the subject. James Gleick's *Chaos: Making a New Science and Complexity* was published in 1987 and became an international bestseller. In 1992 Michael Waldrop wrote *Complexity, The Emerging Science at the Edge of Order and Chaos* and featured the Santa Fe Institute, an organization dedicated to applying living systems theory to organizations. I was enormously excited about this, especially when I realized when reading Gleick that 80% of the advances in this new science were coming from using computer visualization of chaotic processes and finding visual order in them.

I created a mural that showed a time line from the first experiments in 1961, when Edward Lorenz studied weather patterns with quadratic equations, up through the mid-1990s. I drew little people all along the time line with a circle and label indicating their big idea. It included things like Benoît Mandelbrot and the idea of fractals (the phenomenon of complexity being similar at any degree of magnification in living systems), U.C. Santa Cruz and its work on strange attractors (the consistent visual patterns created when mapping unpredictable phenomena like dripping water faucets), and Craig Reynolds and his "Boids" artificial life program (found that bird flight could be simulated with only three simple rules—1. match speeds, 2. leave a little room, 3. head toward the center of the flock).

We put up this chart during a brown bag lunch and asked people to pick what they wanted to hear about. The session took off like a rocket and was a lot of fun. This format invites people to explore the whole range of ideas, puzzling about them and then jumping in. It simulates how we informally explore any new topic, and is new and different.

V. Seeing It All Come Together

Tools for the Seriously Hooked

V. Seeing It All Come Together

Tools for the Seriously Hooked

This section is about taking visual meetings to the next level and learning to work this way as a normal practice. These next chapters will give you a sense of what I think is possible as this way of working evolves, and why it is such an exciting and important development at this time.

Chapter 21: The Path to Visual Competency Shows the useful stages in learning to develop proficiency as a visual practitioner; how to learn from the groups you lead.

Chapter 22: The Future Is Visible Now Overview of where I think this work is going, and the potential of combining this highly analog way of working with the new digital revolution.

Chapter 23: Resources & Networks Reference material on different books, guides, networks, and supplies that you can use to further your own study of this subject.

21. The Path to Visual Competency

Learning from the Groups You Lead

I often feel that writing about visualizing as an interactive medium is a bit like writing about talking. Visualization is a language with almost as much range as spoken language, and can be learned and used widely in that same way, as you have probably concluded reading this book. I no longer think of drawing and communicating with pictures as something separate and special, but a regular part of the give and take of any group trying to make sense out of their organizations and work. And the uses have migrated into everyday life as well. My journal is like a friend that I can talk with and to and learn from, mirroring back my thinking in *both* writing and drawing.

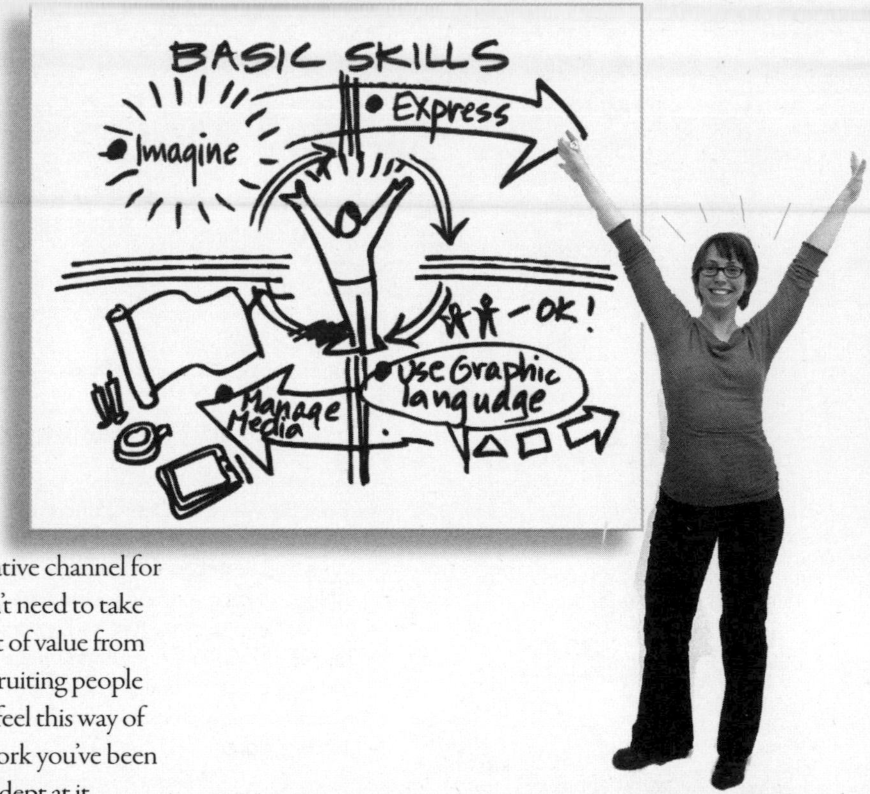

Competency Development Continuum

In The Grove's facilitation training, we use a competency development continuum I co-developed with Suzanne Bailey when we were working together to train teachers in California to work this way. The progression was inspired by the same Theory of Process that inspired the Group Graphics® Keyboard and the Drexler/Sibbet Team Performance Model®. It suggests that you have a lot of degrees of freedom in the simple early stages, and that these become foundations for the more complex skills. The "turn" in the process is learning to record anything that is thrown at you in a meeting in an appropriate format. Mastering this opens a doorway to being a visual facilitator, a visual process designer, and eventually a creative channel for group expression that is quite exciting. You don't need to take on this kind of development in order to get a lot of value from visual meetings, especially if you get good at recruiting people to help you. But you may be among those who feel this way of working is the integration of left and right brain work you've been looking for, and worth the dedicated effort to become adept at it.

Let's invite her to jam. She looks ready!

GRAPHIC SKILLS CONTINUUM

FOUR FLOWS

ATTENTION

ENERGY

INFORMATION

OPERATIONS

I CAN DO THIS!

1. WORK WITH INNER IMAGERY

❑ Imagine succeeding

❑ Record your dreams

❑ Meditate

❑ Imagine pictures in clouds and scribbles

❑ Listen for imagery in people's speech

❑ Practice active imagination about personal plans

❑ Free associate

BEST PRACTICES

This listing of best practices is organized on the Four Flows model (see Chapter 16) so that the fundamental ones are on the left, building to the right. The first three on this page will help you unlock your connection with working visually, and provide enough structure to apply most of what is in this book. The ones on the next page are the kinds of practices you might want to consider if you want to work visually as a primary way of leading groups.

2. PRACTICE FREE EXPRESSION

❑ Keep meeting notes in a blank sketch book

❑ Keep a personal visual journal

❑ Doodle

❑ Diagram your own ideas in branching idea maps

❑ Create quick sketches and gesture drawings

❑ Use colored pencils and creative media

❑ Play around with really big drawings

❑ Play Pictionary

❑ Work on large display paper

3. CREATE PRESENTATION CHARTS

❑ Prechart agendas, welcome signs, theme posters, checklists, and models

❑ Practice block lettering and titling

❑ Learn a dozen or so simple seed shapes/icons

❑ Use color chalk pastels

❑ Trace cartoons and sketches to develop spacing and design

❑ Study the Group Graphics® Keyboard to learn display formats

4. RECORD VISUALLY

- ❑ Interview one other person and record it visually
- ❑ Record presentations from television, videos, or talk radio
- ❑ Practice being conscious about using different display formats
- ❑ Record a staff meeting
- ❑ Work with a facilitator to record a whole-day meeting
- ❑ Learn to check with people for accuracy and ask for feedback

5. FACILITATE VISUALLY

- ❑ Practice introducing activities as a facilitator and shifting to recording as the group gets going
- ❑ Both lead a group and visually record as you go
- ❑ Facilitate a team startup process or a planning meeting by yourself
- ❑ Use graphic templates for small group work
- ❑ Follow through with reproduction of displays and reports

6. DESIGN VISUAL PROCESSES

- ❑ Lead an agenda-design meeting and make suggestions about graphic processes
- ❑ Use large process maps and Storymaps® for change efforts
- ❑ Help groups explore visual metaphors and the deep structures of thinking
- ❑ Become aware of the role of archetypes and culturally embedded imagery

7. TEACH OTHERS

- ❑ Lead cocreative drawing sessions with colleagues
- ❑ Lead teams of facilitators and recorders in support of large meetings
- ❑ Teach learners to channel group energy intuitively
- ❑ Lead workshops on visual meetings and graphic facilitation

These best practices come from over 38 years of teaching people graphic facilitation and leading visual meetings all over the world. They are by no means exhaustive, so add some of your own. The continuum does represent an increase in complexity and challenge left to right. Remember that in keyboard models the ones on the left nest into the ones on the right—so 4 through 7 involve all four flows.

Playing "What's Next"

Most of us who survived traditional schooling have a healthy sense that there is a right and wrong way to do things. Of course there are standards of excellence, and some results that are more valued than others, but with a methodology that is as flexible and broadly applicable as visual meetings this impulse to get it right may stand in your way.

I like to do my best with a group, planning and implementing whatever I think will be of value, and then be in total acceptance of whatever happens when the meeting actually starts.

I prefer another framework as a facilitator. I like to do my best with a group, planning and implementing whatever I think will be of value, and then be in total acceptance of whatever happens when the meeting actually starts. Acceptance means looking for what was created without being heavily judgmental, and concentrating on where that activity leaves the group and you. There is always something that can be done next, and that is where I choose to focus. Having this "yes/and" orientation is a key to good improvisation, and a key to facilitating groups where you want high participation and innovation. So consider putting your "right/wrong" sensibility in a drawer while you are learning to lead visual meetings, and try some things. Then learn like crazy in regard to what happened, and what can happen next.

I remember working with a very skilled strategy consultant early in my career in a meeting with a big Canadian conglomerate. We were trying to get the CEOs of the various business units to begin to think of themselves as a learning community, and start engaging across their very different businesses. This was a stretch for them. And it was a challenge for us. My colleague had been their strategy consultant for a number of years and knew them well. His style was to introduce ideas and frameworks and then get them to wrestle with them. He generally had a well-developed presentation with slides for these times. On a pivotal evening he had prepared a special showing of a video he had created depicting team and communication processes that could become shared language. We finally gathered after dinner, having had a bit of libation, and in a generally good mood. My colleague started the show, and soon realized all the slides were mixed for some reason. He stopped and began to try and correct it. The projector then malfunctioned. He was a fellow with a good sense of humor and kept up a little patter during this, but basically the whole design broke down and he couldn't use the show. Seeing him mess up like this, however, broke the group open. The jibes and laughter were hilarious, and the dialogue went to a whole new level of depth as they actually engaged without any media at all.

I've seen this happen again and again, where the breakdowns and times when the agenda skids out of control become times of true engagement and progress. Getting it "right" with a group is actually overrated as a strategy if your aim is empowerment and facilitating the emergence of leadership. Try things, do different things, do unusual things, and learn from whatever you did about what works and what you can do differently next time.

Getting Feedback from Groups

If you can get in the habit of evaluating what you do in a way that supports real learning, your progress will begin to accelerate, for groups you work with are the very best teachers of what they did or didn't get out of what you tried. It's as simple as putting up a flip chart and asked people to share "What Worked?" and "What Could Be Improved?" Turn the pens over to someone else if you really want to listen.

One of the toughest facilitation challenges I ever had was taking over as scoutmaster of my oldest son's scout troop when he was in high school. I followed a scoutmaster who they had not respected. The scouts had gotten in the habit of resisting anything and everything any authority figure suggested. I felt completely handicapped. I realized they mostly wanted me as a driver for

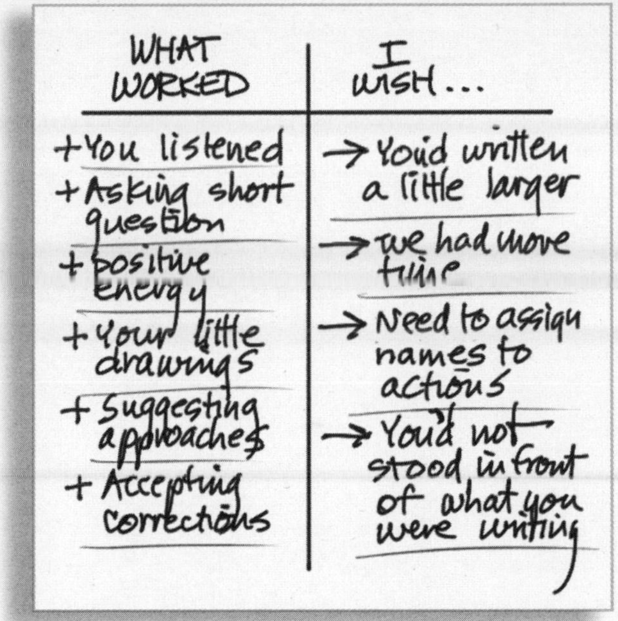

WHAT WORKED/I WISH

The simple activity of getting a group to spend 5 or 10 minutes reflecting at the end of a meeting will greatly improve its functioning over time, and your learning.

their campouts, which were a chance to get away from everything that was bugging them. So I took them camping. We had our first overnight out on the California coast near Point Reyes. We had an 8-mile hike going in—plenty long enough to magnify any problems with pack adjustment, shoes, and water. Several of the scouts suffered a bit as a result of not being prepared.

In the next meeting I made one simple suggestion that actually worked. I said, "These are your campouts. I really don't care how they go, but I would think you'd want to make sure they were as fun and useful as possible. Write down on this chart what you want to repeat next time, and what you want to change." I turned over the pens, and sat back. I watched the troop train itself over the next three campouts. They had several members who knew a lot about scouting from their older brothers and could teach the others.

I did do one additional thing. I promised to take them for a week in the High Sierras in the summer if they really learned to camp. That offer was a big fat carrot that got them very serious about learning what they needed to know. We ended up going and had an amazing time, for many the first time in the high mountains. They all went to college and various places and the next summer came back and asked if I would do it again. I did. That group of boys has been camping in the mountains every year since, well into their adulthood.

I think most groups have many more resources than are generally recognized, and these can be accessed to help you improve what you are doing if you provide groups the tools and your confidence.

22. The Future is Visible Now!

Seeds of a Real Revolution in Meetings

Science fiction author Neal Stephenson wrote in *Snowcrash*, an iconic novel about virtual reality, that "the future is here now, it's just not evenly distributed." If you look at what we consider breakthrough technological developments, like the helicopter, Internet, or computer chips, they all have long histories of developments that foreshadowed their breakthrough into everyday use.

Visualization has a long and rich history. Most of the ideas I've shared have been used by architects, designers, teachers, and engineers in one form or another for centuries. In fact, my claim that graphic language is natural and built into our very gestures and bodies argues for re-accessing what is indeed a very old way of communicating.

We Live in an Information Age

What is new is the explosion of electronic media and the emergence of a society based on the creation and sharing of information in ever-increasing volumes. Digital tools amplify and transform communications in ways that we are only beginning to discover. But I believe the future is already here, and can be discerned. I don't pretend to predict how these seeds will grow, but they all will in some form. Let us end our exploration of visual meetings by reflecting on five developments that I think will be revolutionary in regard to how meetings are run in the future:

1. **Multitouch Walls and Tablets**
2. **Video**
3. **Object Oriented Design Tools**
4. **Collaboration Software**
5. **3-D and Virtual Environments**

AN ANALOG-DIGITAL WORLD

Here I am digitally photographing a video image showing on my personal computer of hand-drawn charts and templates. These different worlds amplify each other if you explore the connections.

BIG VIZ AT TED

At the 2008 TED conference I recorded the entire event on a Wacom Cintiq tablet hooked to a Big Viz multitouch wall collaboratively created by Autodesk and Perceptive Pixel. The small drawings are of each presenter, and the large drawings were those linked to their presentation—accessible by touching the little picture.

Multitouch Walls and Tablets

The TED conference is an annual gathering of the best and brightest in technology, entertainment, and design and has become quite a phenomenon. Its motto is "Ideas worth sharing," and the business model is to charge a lot for the conferences, and then post the 50-plus 18-minute presentations made at the conference on the Web for free. They have figured out how to replicate this gathering in TEDx conferences, licensed to use the format and engage in a similar spreading of good ideas.

Tom Wujec, an Autodesk Fellow deeply involved in visualizing in this new medium, organized a Big Viz demonstration of a large multitouch wall in one of the simulcast rooms at the 2008 event. I and another visualizer from Autodesk drew pages representing key concepts in the presentations, about eight per presentation it turned out. All of our work would immediately link to a small portrait of the presenter that was prepared ahead of time showing on the Big Viz wall. A person approaching this wall would see the row of stamp-sized portraits and could touch any one, to have it zoom up into the center of the display, along with all the drawings we were making. These could then be resized, rotated, grouped, and saved in any combination you like with the sweep of the hand. It was like a gigantic iPhone.

A popular movie called *Minority Report* illustrated this concept of the multitouch wall. Smart phones and tablets are now bringing this technology to popular culture. The wall we worked on cost well over $100,000 to program and create. It was about 3.5 feet by 12 feet in size and the software was actually created for the event. These kinds of walls are now used on television to report on politics, weather, and other things, but are heading toward the traditional conference room, and will eventually provide a window into organizational databases.

Large multitouch walls could transform the way planning and meetings are conducted in large organizations. Will they be popularly available? There are several indications that variations might be. The iPad from Apple and new Slate from HP have this multitouch technology embedded, where pinching and gesturing at items on the screen moves and resizes them. Because computer screens can be projected, these kinds of interfaces will be available for large groups as well as small ones. I am already using tablets to do graphic facilitation remotely with clients. The Canadian company that makes Smart Boards™ has developed a whiteboard surface that is touch sensitive, with the image handled by projection rather than a touch screen.

There are many technologies heading into this space, for all the same reasons I argue for big picture graphics in the beginning of this book. The only real difference here is the medium of representation, not the content. The visual experience is still superior with regular paper, but the capture, storage, manipulability, and sharing functions of the digital medium will compel its growth, I believe.

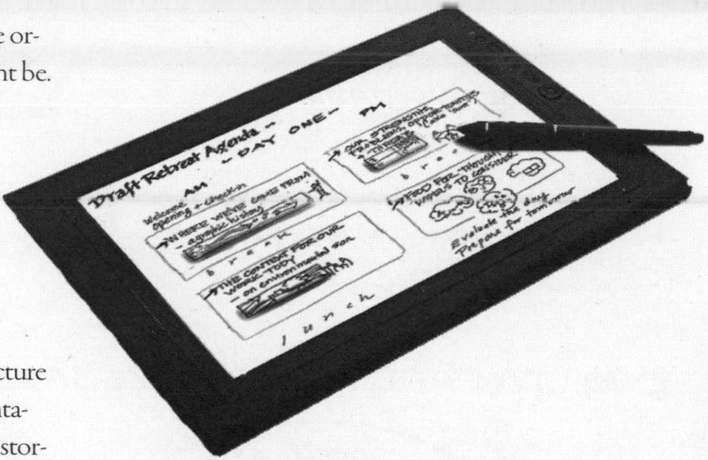

REMOTE AGENDA DESIGN

Here is an actual copy of an agenda design sketched out on a tablet being used in a web conference with a Grove client. As people talked, I erased and upgraded the ideas until we all agreed.

Video Is Becoming a Common Language

For digital natives, those kids born after the cell phone became common, using video is almost as natural as making a call on the telephone. Most point-and-shoot digital cameras will record video. Skype video's quality is good enough for many to use at small meetings. At the high end, video systems are emerging that make it seem like remote participants are right across the table. With more and more teams located in different places, and with travel budgets shrinking, video will allow remote attendees to participate. A foreshadowing of what is possible occurred in a meeting at Autodesk that we held about sustainable design. The content is confidential, but the process we used involved a central group in San Rafael using large-scale wall graphics, and two satellite groups connected with Skype. We had a moveable video camera that one person used to show the remote folks what we had created on the wall charts. The remote groups had breakouts and fed back ideas they had sketched on tablets, and some were presented on little videotaped presentations. Two interns manned the technology. It was truly one meeting, in spite of the different feeds and types of visualization, and we were able to improvise flexibly. I believe this way of working will be quite common in larger, distributed organizations, and shared visual languages will help support this being possible.

CASE FOR GRAPHIC COMPUTING

This is a representation of a little drawing Fred Lakin made in 1972 arguing that designing computers for graphics handles all the other languages, and that is why computers would go graphic. This was before graphical user interfaces.

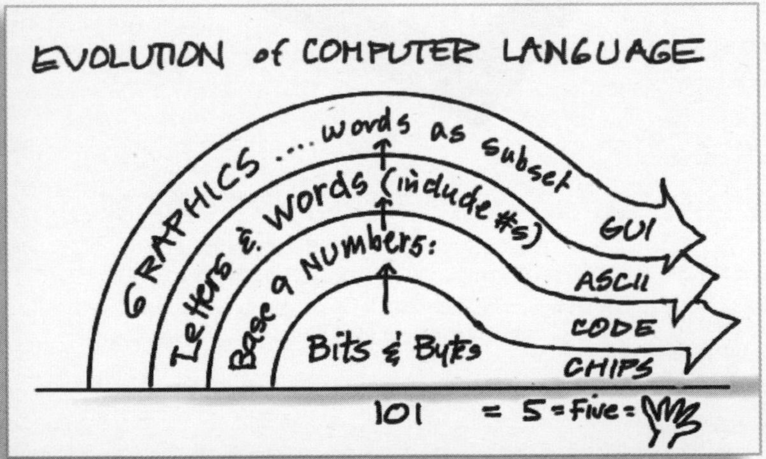

Object Oriented Design Tools

In the early 1970s when I was beginning to work visually, a farsighted artist-inventor from Stanford named Fred Lakin sketched out this drawing about why graphics would be so important in computing. Since bits and bytes can be represented by regular numbers, and numbers are another kind of letter, and letters are really a subset of graphic display, he believed that graphical user interfaces and object-based languages would be the way we would work with computers in the future. This is more or less happening as he predicted, although coding is still mostly language and numbers based. However, instructional design now takes place on programs that have drag and drop icons for different functions as you design. So do the blog templates, website templates, and social networking software. They all allow users to design their sites with drag and drop components and graphic menus of choices and layouts.

On the high end, building information modeling in architectural design is revolutionizing the profession. In simple terms, BIM, as it is called, looks a lot like the 3-D computer aided design systems, except that all the windows, doors, and other features that are being modeled also carry what is called "metadata" about their costs, insulation properties, energy use, materials, strength, and so on. If constructed carefully, the models of buildings can then produce estimates of cost, energy efficiency, and the like. The visual model is literally the calculator and the interface for the designer. This development is throwing engineers and architects together in the design process as never before, and opening the possibility for things like overseas production of mechanical drawings, and high-level modular design, a real leap forward in sustainable design.

All these tools assume that graphical interfaces are not only intuitive but inclusive of words and numbers which then run the binary codes upon which all computing is still based. I think the companies that understand the future of object orientation in design will have a distinct advantage in being able to use the new tools as they become available in other fields of work.

A leading example of using information graphics and maps as interfaces to larger collections of information is the use of "mouse over" graphics on websites. These are programs that pop up a second layer of information when you click on a certain part of the visual display. In some ways the "drill down" navigation systems designed for websites are demonstrating how this kind of visual linkage can be established. Doing this with conceptual maps that represent organizational futures or new processes is technically possible today.

Collaboration Software and Social Media

All during the 1990s I worked on the Groupware Users' Project with the Institute for the Future, a futures research organization in Palo Alto, California. We tracked the development of software aimed at supporting group work and collaboration. The seeds of these ideas have grown quite

LEADING BUSINESS TEAMS

This book published in the Addison Wesley OD series was one of the first to define the field of group oriented software, or "groupware" as it was called in the 1990s. I was one of the authors and helped design the visual frameworks that are used to describe the field. It is still full of very useful information (and graphics).

quickly in the 20 years since. The biggest impact on visual meetings is the development of web conference software that almost always allows for shared whiteboards, slide shows, any kind of visual documents, as well as chat, polling, questions, and teleconferencing. A network of graphic facilitators who work on tablets is beginning to grow, right along with virtual meetings. As I explained earlier, any of the programs that are available for a personal computer can be shared on a web conference, so that participants can see the screen of the host. This allows for remote scribing, design, and presentation annotation right now! Even Skype has screen sharing.

Another seed is the idea of virtual team rooms that exist as a single point of reference on the Internet. There are many versions available now, ranging from very detailed project management platforms, to social networking programs that have been adapted to team use. Most of these now allow for storage and retrieval of visual media and other documents. The annotation tools are still undeveloped, but are coming along. I believe in the future people will collaborate on drawings in visual wiki environments (these are sites where multiple people can enter information, the most well-known being Wikipedia). Early examples include Google maps and mash-ups that allow networks to visualize where members are located in a collaborative way. Adding metadata like this is technically possible now for vision maps and other visual material, and should become more widespread as organizational platforms become more sophisticated.

3-D and Virtual Environments

Ever since computers became common in organizations, people have imagined completely realistic virtual environments. The early versions were quite simplistic and crude, but compelling. Now the technology for 3-D is here. As I write, *Avatar,* a film produced in 3-D, became the largest grossing film ever made at that time, with *Alice in Wonderland* following hard on its heels with box office records. Commentators are heralding the arrival of 3-D as a new exciting genre for creative work. Second Life, World of Warcraft, and other virtual environments in the United States have literally millions of members in immersive, interactive 3-D environments. How this all develops is subject to a lot of variables, but there is no question that our visual technology is capable of very realistic representations, and that all of this can serve the creation of highly visual virtual environments where it is possible to have meetings!

In 2006 I took a look at Second Life, then just emerging as a possible virtual environment for large-scale collaboration. My catalyst was an invitation to come to a symposium of artists in SL sponsored by the New Media Consortium (NMC), a client that was supporting colleges and universities understanding how multimedia can support education. NMC was heavily involved in Second Life, creating labs for different schools, and helping them construct their virtual environments. I remember "flying" into that first symposium with my new avatar, and feeling very like I was in the space bar in *Star Wars*.

SUNSEED AT NMC SYMPOSIUM

Here is my avatar attending my first ever virtual reality symposium at the New Media Consortium campus in Second Life. Search NMC in Second Life to visit its extensive campus. Search for "The Grove" to find a wealth of visual material on our work.

But I felt this was indeed a foreshadowing of the future of visualization and set out to explore its capabilities. After creating a sim called Third Life, dedicated to exploring the relationship between our "real life" and virtual worlds, I built out another sim (which is what they call an "island" worth of virtual, simulated property) that mimics The Grove itself, replicating our headquarters in the Presidio of San Francisco, and creating a learning center and gallery space that in 3-D shows people what is possible with panoramic visualization, templates, recording, and all the visualization tools described in this book.

As a tool for meeting and collaborating I found that the interface is far too difficult to learn for regular people to come in and have a virtual meeting. However, companies such as IBM have found that with technically comfortable clients, they can bring people in and virtually walk through the computer system that they are building. Educators working with younger students are having all kinds of gatherings. The World Café network is experimenting with doing dialogue in Second Life. Organizations working with people who have developmental disabilities are finding an amazing creative platform.

I did discover that I could project Second Life on a screen in a conference room, and have a presentation platform that was extraordinarily flexible in showing people what is possible. I can zoom, pan, teleport, run slide presentations, and trigger animations all in the same environment. This is the kind of flexibility that one has in one's own library or studio with a visitor, where conversation can hop from topic to topic, with exhibits and examples appearing as needed from the stacks and shelves.

GROVE LEARNING CENTER IN SECOND LIFE

On a gallery level in the Second Life sim called "The Grove," there is a complete learning center with examples of all the kinds of graphics that can be used to support meetings. Here is the front entrance.

I have no doubt that as the computing power continues to increase, these kinds of 3-D visual interfaces will be widespread and common, and increasingly used in education. In leadership development many of our clients are already moving toward simulations as a much more engaging, experience-based way of building sophisticated skills in finance, decision making, and planning.

The Game Is Still between the Ears

No matter how whizzy technology gets, the interface with human beings is still through our senses and into our brains. Even in 3-D representations, humans are still only able to look at one view at a time, and then assemble the rounded out picture in our inner minds. Complex data visualizations in 3-D have turned out to be very difficult to use. It takes concentrated training to learn to interpret X-ray, magnetic resonance imagery (MRIs), BIM, and other sophisticated visualization. Because of this I believe that the basic building blocks of visual understanding, represented by the archetypes illustrated in the Group Graphics® Keyboard, will continue to be the "sentence structure" of visual language. My vision for this work is that the enormous focus on technology will turn toward a more integrative perspective—with a new focus on biology and the human interface—as we realize that people and how they work together and with nature is fundamental to sustainable systems.

GARDEN ROOM SIMULATION

The Grove's meeting room in real life is called the "Garden Room" and looks like this. Here a strategic visioning process is replicated at the Grove Global Network Center in Second Life. (Yes, that is me all dressed up.)

Daniel Pink argues in *A Whole New Brain* that right-brain, image, and creativity-based thinking will be increasingly advantageous in a world where more and more of the mechanical things can be done by machines. I don't believe that being rational and being intuitive and creative are opposites, or incompatible. I believe, like Jill Bolte Taylor, that humans come with magnificent capabilities and can develop choices and flexibility. But we are in a time that has hugely overemphasized the objective, rational, and mechanical in the developed world's concentration on engineering and reengineering the physical world to answer our "needs." Visual meetings open the doorway to balancing this situation. Without denying or undervaluing the precise and logical, visualization brings imagery, metaphor, and movement back to the process of meeting together.

As I watch a new generation of young people use multimedia and imagery as fluidly as they talk and text, I'm hopeful about where we are heading. I do believe that most everything that manifests materially moves through a stage of being represented in word and image by someone with an idea. Reclaiming our ability to draw and express ourselves visually will greatly increase the number of ideas we can share. Expanding the use and scope of visual meetings should broaden about ability to meet challenges using all of our faculties, and dream the dreams we will need in these fluid times.

RE-AMP ANNUAL MEETING

RE-AMP is a consortium of 120 non-government organizations and 15 foundations working to clean up global warming pollutants in the upper Midwest of the United States. Here Rick Reed, its original catalyst, orients everyone to the annual meeting using large Storymaps showing the year's plans and overall system that supports the network. RE-AMP's motto of "thinking systemically/acting collaboratively" has manifested in visual meetings since its beginning.

23. Resources & Networks

This book is not a research thesis, but a sharing of 38 years of working visually in a wide range of client settings and organizations. This resources section contains links with all the books and authors mentioned plus some others that have been influential over the years. It also contains links to websites and networks that are sources of additional information.

Organizations & Websites

Following are some of the sources online for furthering your understanding of visual meetings, facilitation, and organizational work with imagery.

- **The Grove Consultants International:** The Grove is a full-service organization development and publishing firm in the Presidio of San Francisco. It has been offering tools for visual meetings since 1977 when it was formed by me, the author of this book. We offer an extensive line of Graphic Guides® templates, Leader's Guides and books for personal visioning, facilitation, team performance, and visual planning for anyone needing effective group processes. The Grove regularly sponsors training in the Principles of Graphic Facilitation, Strategic Visioning, and Team Performance. We also carry all the supplies for visual meetings — watercolor Charters® markers, big paper, sticky notes, and white tape. (www.grove.com)
- **Arthur M. Young/Theory of Process:** Link to a comprehensive website about the work of inventor and cosmologist Arthur M. Young, whose books on the Theory of Process and the nature of thinking have been seminal in the work of The Grove. See (www.arthuryoung.com)
- **Autodesk:** This company leads in 2-D and 3-D design software for architecture,

THE GROVE

This is the home page for the website of my company, The Grove. It's the hub of a network of people and resources visualizing change. We bend over backward to share our ideas, hoping to transform the art of collaboration worldwide! Visit www.grove.com. There are articles, blogs, and links to most of what you would need to make your visual meetings work.

engineering, computer graphics, and animation. Its website is loaded with forums and information about the visualization tools professionals are using.
(usa.autodesk.com)

- ❏ **Center for Graphic Facilitation:** Peter Durand at Alphachimp created a blog focused entirely on graphic facilitation. It is full of wonderful links to all kinds of resources in the field.
(www.graphicfacilitation.com)

- ❏ **Cognitive Edge:** For those of you interested in the cutting edge of cognitive science, David Snowdon's network will get you to some of the best thinking in the field. Founded in 2005, Cognitive Edge is focused on developing new methods and tools to assist organizations with truly complex problems and opportunities.
(www.cognitive-edge.com)

- ❏ **Coro Centers for Public Affairs:** Coro was the seedbed for Group Graphics and, founded in 1948, is one of the pioneers of experience-based education for public service. It's in seven cities. Check it out if you are interested in an unparalleled approach to leadership development.
(www.coro.org)

- ❏ **Crowley & Company:** Deirdre Crowley worked at The Grove for seven years and went back to her East Coast roots to take on Washington, D.C. and Europe. She is a deep resource all by herself.
(www.crowleyandco.us)

- ❏ **DavidSibbet.com:** I keep a regular blog posting all kinds of things I discover about visual meetings and other areas of interest having to do with organizational development, cognition, personal development, and information design.
(www.davidsibbet.com)

- **DigitalRoam:** Dan Roam, author of the very successful *Back of the Napkin: How to Visually Problem Solve with Pictures,* has a website and blog loaded with great ideas. (www.digitalroam.com)

- **Institute for the Future:** The Institute for the Future (IFTF) is an independent nonprofit research group, spinning off from Rand corporation in 1970. It works with organizations of all kinds to help them make better, more informed decisions about the future, providing the foresight to create insights that lead to action. IFTF's work with The Grove during the 1990s led to their heavy involvement in mapping and other visualization strategies. (www.iftf.org)

- **Interaction Associates:** Interaction Associates wrote the book on group process, facilitation, and building collaborative cultures: *How to Make Meetings Work* by cofounders David Straus and Michael Doyle. They were my early teachers in facilitation, and Michael and I invented many graphic strategies that are still used today. Their strategy, leadership development, and facilitation training is first rate. (www.interactionassociates.com)

- **International Forum of Visual Practitioners:** In 1995 a small group of graphic recorders held a conference to share ideas and support each other. This organization has grown and is now a worldwide network of graphic recorders, facilitators, and designers interested in supporting visual meetings. Their website is full of examples of what everyone in the network is doing. (www.ifvp.org)

- **Isee Systems:** For getting systems diagramming tools developed by consultants associated with MIT, see www.iseesystems.com.

- **Make Your Mark:** When Christina Merkley couldn't get her green card renewed to keep working at The Grove, she went back to her native Canada and became a whirlwind source of training and information about graphic facilitation. Her website is great. (www.makemark.com)

- **Neuland:** The Grove partnered with Neuland to take out templates to the German market. They are makers of all kinds of meetings equipment, including large portable walls directly inspired by visual practitioners.. (www.neuland.biz)

- **Organization Development Network:** I learned about organization development through this network in the 1970s and continue to find its reach relevant to our times. The practice of OD is rooted in open systems thinking and treating organizations as living systems. (www.odnetwork.org)

- **Resonance:** Firehawk Hulen and Pele Rouge are dedicated to bringing forward Earth wisdom to our times. Firehawk is a gifted videographer and a wonderful example of the engaging power of imagery. (www.resonance.to/index.html)

- **Society for Organizational Learning:** SoL was formed in April of 1997 to continue the work of MIT's Center for Organizational Learning (1991–1997). Peter Senge, author of the *The Fifth Discipline: The Art and Practice of the Learning Organization* is the founding chairman of SoL. Visual thinking in the form of systems thinking is at the heart of this organization's approach and their network is a rich resource. (www. solonline.org)

- **TED:** This network exploring the intersections of technology, entertainment and design lives its motto, "Ideas Worth Spreading." It's one of the best examples of using integrating face-to-face conferences, video, and online media for communication. Its

18-minute presentations, the signature format of its annual conference, are always well designed and often breathtaking.
(www.ted.com)

- **Tom Wujec Blog:** Tom is an Autodesk Fellow with a long history in visual collaboration. His blog is packed with information about visualization, tools, TED, and many other subjects.
(www.tomwujec.com)

- **Tony Buzan:** Inventor of Mind Mapping, Buzan is a force all to himself. A prolific author and speaker, he has done as much as any one I know to popularize applications of visual thinking outside design.
(www.thinkbuzan.com/uk)

- **Visual Grammars for Visual Languages:** Fred Lakin has been exploring the underlying structures of visual language—like that used by graphic recorders—since the mid 1970s. His self-published books are loaded with stimulating information.
(www.visualgrammarsforvisuallanguages.com)

- **VizThink:** VizThink was initially conceived by Dave Gray, chairman of XPLANE. A longtime proponent of visual communication, Dave envisioned the creation of a global community of visual thinkers. In 2006 XPLANE expanded to Europe through a new partner, Rodolfo Carpintier of Digital Assets Deployment, a business incubator firm in Madrid, who funded Dave's vision as VizThink. It now has a robust social networking website. The organization sponsors conferences, papers, and online webinars for visual thinkers around the world.
(www.vizthink.com)

Bibliography

The following are print resources mentioned in this book, plus some additional helpful books.

Boulding, Kenneth. *The Image: Knowledge in Life & Society*. Minneapolis: University of Michigan, 1956.

Brookes, Mona. *Drawing for Older Children & Teens*. New York: Jeremy P. Tarcher/Putnam, 1991.

Buzan, Tony. *The Mind Map Book : Unlock Your Creativity, Boost Your Memory, Change Your Life*. New York: Pearson BBC Active, 2010.

Christensen, Clayton M. *The Innovator's Dilemma: When New Technologies Cause Great Firms to Fail*. Cambridge, MA: Harvard Business School Press, 1997.

Doyle, Michael. *How to Make Meetings Work*. New York: Penguin Putnam, Inc., 1976.

Durate, Nancy. *slide:ology: The Art and Science of Creating Great Presentations*. Sebastopol, CA: O'Reilly Media, Inc., 2008.

Friedhoff, Richard Mark and William Benzon. *Visualization: The Second Computer Revolution*. New York: Harry N. Abrams, Inc., 1989.

Frost, Seena B. *SoulCollage®: An Intuitive Collage Process for Individuals and Groups*. Santa Cruz. CA: Hanford Mead Publishers, Inc., 2001.

Gardner, Howard. *Frames of Mind: The Theory of Multiple Intelligences*. New York: Basic Books, Inc. Publishers, 1985.

Gleick, James. *Chaos: Making a New Science*. New York: The Penguin Group, 1987.

Gordon, William J.J. *Synectics, The Development of Creative Capacity*. New York: Harper, 1961.

Hoffman, Donald D.. *Visual Intelligence: How We Create What We See*. New York: W.W. Norton & Co., Inc., 1998.

Hollman, Peggy and Tom Devane and Steven Cady *The Change Handbook, Second Edition The Definitive Resource on Today's Best Methods for Engaging Whole Systems*. San Francisco: Berrett-Koehler Publishers, Inc., 2007.

Horn, Bob. *Visual Language: Global Communication for the 21st Century*. Bainbridge Island, WA: 1998.

Johansen, Bob. *Leaders Make the Future: Ten New Leadership Skills for an Uncertain World*. San Francisco: Berrett-Koehler Publishers, Inc., 2009.

_____. *Get There Early: Sensing the Future to Compete in the Present*. San Francisco: Berrett-Koehler Publishers, Inc., 2007.

Kleiner, Art. *The Age of Heretics: A History of the Radical Thinkers Who Reinvented Corporate Management.* San Francisco: Jossey-Bass, 2008.

Lakoff, George. *Don't Think of an Elephant!: Know Your Values and Frame the Debate—The Essential Guide for Progressives.* White River Junction, VT: Chelsea Green Publishing Company, 2004.

Lakoff, George and Mark Johnson. *Metaphors We Live By.* Chicago: The University of Chicago Press, 1980.

Margulies, Nancy. *Visual Thinking: Tools for Mapping Your Ideas.* Norwalk, CT: Crown House Publishing Company LLC, 2005.

McCloud, Scott. *Understanding Comics: The Invisible Art.* New York: Harper Collins Publishers, Inc., 1993.

McKim, Robert H. *Experiences in Visual Thinking.* Monterey, CA: Brooks/Cole Publishing,1980.

Morgan, Gareth. *Images of Organization.* Thousand Oaks, CA: Sage Publications, Inc., 1997

Nachmanovitch, Stephen. *Free Play: The Power of Improvisation in Life and the Arts.* New York: G.P. Putnam's Sons, 1990.

Osterwalder, Alexander and Yves Pigneur. *Business Model Generation. A Handbook for Visionaries, Game Changers, and Challengers.* Amsterdam: Self published (see www.businessmodelgeneration.com), 2010.

Pink, Daniel H. *A Whole New Mind: Why Right-Brainers Will Rule the Future.* New York: The Penguin Group, 2005.

Raymond, Larry. *Reinventing Communication: A Guide to Using Visual Language for Planning, Problem Solving, and Reengineering.* Milwaukee, WI: ASQC Quality Press, 1994.

Roam, Dan. *The Back of the Napkin: Solving Problems and Selling Ideas with Pictures.* New York: The Penguin Group, 2008.

Rowland, Regina. *Mapping the CoConstruction of Meaning: Interactive Graphic Facilitation And Collaborative Visual Mapping In Polycultural Small Group Environments.* Saarbrücken, Germany: LAP - Lambert Academic Publishing, 2009.

Rudebeck, Ulric. *Strategic Vision Work: Create an Organization that Works for You.* Stockholm: Urvision AB, 2008.

Schrage, Michael. *Serious Play: How the World's Best Companies Simulate to Innovate.* Cambridge, MA: Harvard Business School Press, 2000.

Senge, Peter. *The Fifth Discipline: The Art and Practice of the Learning Organization.* New York: Currency Doubleday, 1990.

See The Change Handbook, Second Edition for two chapters I wrote: #40 on Strategic Visioning: Taking Insight to Action and # 61 Visual Recording and Graphic Facilitation: Helping People See What They Mean with Nancy Margulies.

Senge, Peter, Art Kleiner, Charlotte Roberts, Rick Ross, Bryan Smith. *The Fifth Discipline Field Book: Strategies and Tools for Building a Learning Organization*. New York: Doubleday, 1994.

Sibbet, David. *Best Practices for Facilitation*. San Francisco: The Grove Consultants International, 2002.

_______. *Graphic Facilitation, Transforming Group Process with the Power of Visual Listening*. San Francisco: The Grove Consultants International, 2006.

_______. *Principles of Facilitation: The Purpose and Potential of Leading Group Process*. San Francisco: The Grove Consultants International, 2002.

_______. *Strategic Visioning Agenda Planning Kit*. San Francisco: The Grove Consultants International, 2009.

_______. *Team Leader Guide: Strategies and Practices for Achieving High Performance*. San Francisco: The Grove Consultants International, 2006.

_______. *Visual Intelligence: Using the Deep Patterns of Visual Language to Build Cognitive Skills* . Theory Into Practice journal, Volume 47, Number 2 —Digital Literacies in the Age of Sight and Sound. Ohio, Ohio State University, 2008.

Taylor, Jill Bolte. *My Stroke of Insight: A Brain Scientist's Personal Journey.* New York: Viking Penguin, 2008.

Tufte, Edward. *Visual Explanations: Images and Quantities, Evidence and Narrative*. Cheshire, CT: Graphics Press, 1997.

Waldrop, Michael. *Complexity, The Emerging Science at the Edge of Order and Chaos*. New York: Simon and Schuster, 1992.

Wenger, Etienne. *Communities of Practice: Learning, Meaning & Identity*. Cambridge, MA: Cambridge University Press, 1998

Woolsey, Christina Hooper and Scott Kim and Gayle Curtis. *VizAbility;Learn to Communicate Visually* (paperback & CD ROM). Florence, KY; Course Technology, 2004.

Wujec, Tom and Sandra Muscat. *Return on Imagination: Realizing the Power of Ideas*. New York: Penguin, 2003.

Young, Arthur M.. *Reflexive Universe*. San Francisco: Robert Briggs & Associates, 1974. Cambria, CA: Anados Foundation, 1999 Revised Edition.

_______. *The Geometry of Meaning*. New York: Delacorte Press/S. Lawrence, 1976.

Index

DAVID SIBBET is president and founder of The Grove Consultants International, a firm leading strategy, visioning, creativity, future-forces, leadership development, and large-scale system change processes worldwide since 1977. He was involved with the growth of Apple Computer in the 1980s, facilitated the change management team at National Semiconductor during its turnaround in 1990, and worked at HP and then Agilent Technologies for many years, leading strategic visioning sessions for groups and divisions, helping develop leadership programs, and designing Grove Storymaps® for special kickoffs and change projects. He and The Grove facilitated the community visioning processes and planning fairs connected with the conversion of the Presidio in San Francisco to a national park. As a founding director of Headlands Center for the Arts and tenant in the Thoreau Center for Sustainability he has long experience as a park partner.

In addition to corporate and government work, David has sustained a diverse involvement with foundations, nonprofits, schools, and professional associations. Over the years David has helped design and lead many board/staff retreats, strategy sessions, and cross-organizational projects working on social change.

David is the author and designer of many of The Grove's extensive line of process consulting tools and guides, including the Grove's Visual Planning Systems™, the Drexler/Sibbet/Forrester Team Performance System™, the Sibbet/LeSaget Sustainable Organization Model™, the Grove's Strategic Visioning Process™ and related graphic templates, and The Grove's Facilitation Series. In 2007 the Organizational Development Network awarded David and the Grove their Membership Award for creative contributions to the field of organization development.

David holds a master's degree in journalism from Northwestern University and a BA in English from Occidental College. He was awarded a Coro Fellowship in Public Affairs in 1965 to study metropolitan public affairs in Los Angeles. For eight years in the 1970s he was executive director and director of training for the Coro Foundation, designing experience-based education programs for young leaders. He began his own organizational consulting firm in 1977. David is a longtime affiliate with the Institute for the Future in Menlo Park, a member of the Global Business Network in San Francisco, a longtime member for both the Organizational Development Network and the International Association of Facilitators, and a member of Heartland Circle's Thought Leader Network. He is president of the Argonne Community Garden and currently on the board of Coro. David lives in San Francisco with his poet/teacher spouse, Susan.

For additional information, explore www.grove.com and www.davidsibbet.com.